Healthcare and the False Claims Act

2nd Edition

David B. Honig, et al.

Healthlaw Publishing LLC

Copyright 2019
Healthlaw Publishing LLC
9425 N. Meridian
Suite 201
Indianapolis, IN 46033
Website: healthlawpublishing.com
Email: publisher@healthlawpublishing.com
All rights reserved.
No part of this publication may be reproduced, stored in a retrieval system, or transmitted, in any form, or by any means, electronic, mechanical, photocopying, recording, scanning, or otherwise, without the express, written permission of the publisher.
Printed in the United States of America
ISBN-13: 978-0-9986018-1-6
Library of Congress Control Number: 2078906690

+

The publisher does not provide legal or other professional services. If legal advice or other expert services are required, please contact the appropriate licensed professional.

ABOUT THE CONTRIBUTORS

David B. Honig, Lead Author, is a Shareholder with Hall, Render, Killian, Heath & Lyman (Hall Render) and chair of Hall Render's Government Enforcement/FCA Task Force. He practices out of Hall Render's Washington DC and Indianapolis offices. He has represented hospitals, physician practices, long term care facilities, and other healthcare providers in government investigations and False Claims Act cases in more than a dozen states across the country. Mr. Honig is also an adjunct professor at the Robert H. McKinney School of Law: Indiana University.

Mr. Honig was the Chief of the Major Case Unit in Florida's Medicaid Fraud Control Unit (MFCU). He led the nation's first MFCU Major Case Unit, where he investigated civil and criminal healthcare fraud and prosecuted civil False Claims Act cases at the trial and appellate levels.

Since joining Hall Render, Mr. Honig has successfully defended healthcare providers in government investigations and in False Claims Act cases, brought both by the Government and by whistleblowers. He has represented healthcare providers in False Claims Act cases before state and federal courts, at the trial and appellate levels, and before the United States Supreme Court.

Mr. Honig is licensed to practice in Florida, Indiana, Illinois, and Washington D.C., and is admitted before the United States Supreme Court, the Second, Seventh, Eleventh, and D.C. Circuit Courts of Appeal, and many federal district courts, including the Northern and Southern Districts of Indiana, the Northern, Central, and Southern Districts of Illinois, the Northern, Middle, and Southern District of Florida, the Eastern and Western District of Michigan, and the D.C. District Court. He has also been admitted *pro hac vice* to practice before several other federal courts, including district courts in Arizona, Alabama, Tennessee, and Connecticut. He has been awarded membership in the Northern District of Illinois Trial Bar.

Mr. Honig has written extensively about the False Claims Act and his writing has been cited by several courts. He has lectured extensively on the False Claims Act, for both attorneys and healthcare providers.

Mr. Honig is an adjunct professor in negotiations at IU McKinney School of Law, and has been featured in national and international media for his knowledge in that area, including PBS, MSNBC, and BBC.

Mr. Honig received his law degree, with honors, from the University of Florida, and his B.A. degree from Washington University in St. Louis.

Drew B. Howk is a Shareholder in Hall Render's Indianapolis office and is a member of the firm's Health Care Litigation practice group, devoting his practice to defending clients against government and whistleblower actions alleged under the False Claims Act and representing healthcare and business clients in commercial litigation, including federal multi-district litigation and appeals.

In addition to his legal practice, Mr. Howk is also an adjunct professor at Richard M. Fairbanks School of Public Health at Indiana University – Purdue University Indianapolis, where he teaches an undergraduate course on the legal aspects of healthcare administration. Before joining Hall Render, Mr. Howk clerked with the Civil Division of the United States Attorney's Office for the Southern District of Illinois.

Mr. Howk was a *cum laude* graduate of Wabash College (A.B.) and Saint Louis University School of Law (J.D.), where he also earned a Certificate in Health Law.

Mr. Howk writes and speaks extensively about the False Claims Act, Work Product and the Attorney-Client Privilege, and eDiscovery.

Mr. Howk is a graduate of the Indiana State Bar Association Leadership Development Academy, a program that recognizes and develops the future leaders of the Indiana State Bar Association.

Mr. Howk is admitted to practice in Indiana, as well as before federal district courts in New Mexico and the Northern and Southern Districts of Indiana.

Laetitia Cheltenham is a licensed and nationally certified healthcare provider and health law attorney. She focuses her practice on advising hospitals, health systems, clinical laboratories and other healthcare providers on a broad range of strategic and operational issues, including managed care contracting; reimbursement; licensure and certification matters; clinical services and patient care issues; scope of practice; federal False Claims Act lawsuits and investigations; and regulatory and compliance matters.

Prior to law school, Ms. Cheltenham worked as a therapist, consultant and educator in both private and governmental healthcare settings. Her decade of experience as a provider inside healthcare organizations, such as medical centers, long-term care facilities and mental health agencies, informs her pragmatic and clinical perspectives on current health law issues.

Ms. Cheltenham earned her B.S. from East Carolina University in 1999, her M.S. from the University of North Carolina at Greensboro, her M.A. from the Catholic University of America in 2006, and her J.D. from the University of North Carolina in 2013.

Ritu Kaur Cooper, is a Shareholder in Hall Render's Washington, DC office and is a member of the firm's Health Counsel section. Ritu represents healthcare providers such as hospitals, health systems, laboratories, dialysis facilities, large physician practice groups, and medical device companies in False Claims Act litigation, regulatory and compliance matters with a particular focus on fraud and abuse and compliance as well as internal and government investigations. She served as General Counsel for Capital Clinical Integrated Network, a care coordination entity providing the DC Medicaid population with care coordination services. She currently serves as Interim Chief Compliance Officer for Beaver Dam Community Hospitals, Inc.

Ms. Cooper is licensed to practice in New Jersey, Pennsylvania, Missouri, and the District of Columbia. She is also admitted before the United States Supreme Court and the District Court of the District of New Jersey.

Ms. Cooper is an honors graduate from The George Washington University (B.A.), a *cum laude* graduate from Syracuse University (J.D.), and was awarded an LL.M. in Health Law by Saint Louis University.

Ms. Cooper served as the American Health Lawyers Association's Vice-Chair of Research and Website for the Hospitals and Health Systems Practice Group (HHS PG) for four years. She is now Vice-Chair of Strategic Planning and Special Projects for the HHS PG.

David A. French is a Shareholder in Hall Render's Troy, Michigan office and has been doing commercial and healthcare litigation for more than 25 years, from state trial courts to the United States Supreme Court, where he prepared the brief, presented the oral argument and prevailed in a 9-0 decision. His representative cases involving the False Claims Act include *United States ex rel. Swafford v. Borgess Medical Center*, in which he obtained summary judgment and prevailed on appeal before the United States Court of Appeals for the Sixth Circuit. He has also obtained dismissal, with no payment by his firm's clients, of other *qui tam* cases prior to reported decisions through successful negotiations with the United States Department of Justice and United States Attorney's Office.

Mr. French has been identified as one of the top litigators in the State of Michigan by the Detroit Legal News, Oakland County Legal News and Washtenaw County Legal News. He is a member of the State Bar of Michigan, the Washtenaw County Bar Association and the American Health Lawyers Association. Mr. French has written numerous articles and has lectured at several programs that focus on the healthcare industry.

Mr. French is admitted to practice in Michigan, as well as before the Eastern and Western U.S. District Courts in Michigan, the Fifth and Sixth Circuit Courts of Appeal, and the United States Supreme Court. He was awarded his B.A. with high distinction by the University of Michigan and his J.D. from Wayne State University Law School.

Alyssa C. James works in Hall Render's Indianapolis office and assists clients in numerous aspects of healthcare law. Her work involves counsel regarding hospital and physician contracting matters, hospital and health system relationships, regulatory and compliance issues, organization governance and hospital/physician alignment. She regularly counsels clients on a national basis regarding fraud and abuse matters, including analyses related to federal Stark, Anti-Kickback and Civil Monetary Penalties laws.

Ms. James is a graduate of Butler University (B.A.) and earned her law degree and Graduate Certificate in Health Law from Indiana University Robert H. McKinney School of Law (J.D.).

Ms. James has made several presentations in the area of fraud and abuse, including for the Healthcare Financial Management Association, World Congress and Indianapolis Bar Association.

Katherine A. Kuchan, R.N., J.D. is a nurse and Shareholder in Hall Render's Milwaukee office and provides legal counsel to hospital systems, individual hospitals, inpatient rehabilitation facilities, physician groups, skilled nursing facilities, laboratories and other licensed healthcare providers across the country regarding regulatory and compliance matters. She advises clients on federal False Claims Act lawsuits and investigations; internal and government investigations; fraud and abuse matters, including voluntary self-disclosures to appropriate government agencies; EMTALA; CLIA; and special regulatory problems involving survey and licensure. Ms. Kuchan counsels clients on the design, implementation and assessment of their compliance programs. She also assists clients with compliance and reporting under Corporate Integrity Agreements. Ms. Kuchan's experience as a Registered Nurse offers her clients the advantage and value of working with legal counsel who has practical, clinical knowledge and real life experience from working in the healthcare industry.

Ms. Kuchan attended Marquette University (B.S.), the University of Wisconsin-Madison (M.S.), and was a *magna cum laude* laureate at the Marquette University Law School. She is admitted to practice in Wisconsin.

Matthew J. Paradiso works in Hall Render's Detroit office and is a member of the firm's Health Care Litigation practice group. Mr. Paradiso's practice is focused on representing hospitals and health systems in commercial and healthcare related litigation. Mr. Paradiso is licensed to practice in Michigan.

Mr. Paradiso graduated *cum laude* from Wayne State University Law School and received his B.A. from the James Madison College at Michigan State University.

Jonathon A. Rabin is a Shareholder in Hall Render's Detroit office. He represents healthcare organizations and other employers in litigation and administrative proceedings. Mr. Rabin defends organizations in False Claims Act litigation, state and federal whistleblower actions and many other health-care related litigation disputes. In addition, he regularly represents employers in the defense of civil rights and employment disputes, including class and collective actions.

Mr. Rabin is a member of the State Bar of Michigan, the American Health Lawyers Association, the American Society for Healthcare Human Resources Administration, the Michigan Healthcare Human Resources Association and the Society for Human Resource Management.

Mr. Rabin attended Wayne State University in Detroit (B.A. and M.A.) and the Columbus School of Law at the Catholic University of America.

Matthew Schappa works in Hall Render's litigation practice group and concentrates his practice on defending clients against actions alleged under the False Claims Act. He also represents clients on a wide range of healthcare and business matters, including managed care and provider reimbursement issues. He earned his undergraduate degree from Ohio University in 2010 and his law degree from the University of Dayton School of Law in 2014. Matt was a two-time member of the National Moot Court team and participated in the New York National Moot Court Competition and the Indiana National Professional Responsibility Moot Court Competition for which he earned a membership to the Order of the Barristers.

Mr. Schappa graduated from Ohio University with a B.A. and earned his JD at the University of Dayton School of Law in 2014.

Gregg "Wally" Wallander has been practicing law as a healthcare attorney for 25 years. He represents a wide variety of clients, working with health systems, manufacturers, physician groups and ancillary providers.

Mr. Wallander's counsel is often sought out by clients facing challenges regarding highly technical matters involving anti-kickback, Stark Law, board governance, physician alignment models, managed care initiatives and value-based care strategies. Most frequently, he works with organizations on strategic planning and transactions in order to structure initiatives that are in furtherance of applicable fraud and abuse laws.

Active in his community, Mr. Wallander serves on the Board of Bishop Chatard High School and with Catholic Charities in Indianapolis. He enjoys spending time with his family as well as traveling, cooking, and running (in that order).

Gregg earned his B.S. in Finance from the Indiana University Kelley School of Business, and graduated *magna cum laude* from Indiana University Robert H. McKinney School of Law in 1993.

Dimitar P. Georgiev is a law clerk at Hall Render and law student at American University Washington College of Law where he is a member of the American University Law Review and the Moot Court Honors Society. Mr. Georgiev has extensive compliance and operations experience acquired though work experience as a global strategy and operations analyst at the Crumpton Group and private equity analyst at Fortress Investment Group. A native of Bulgaria, Mr. Georgiev graduated *magna cum laude* from St. Francis College (B.A.) and Georgetown University (M.A.).

Kathryn Costanza is a summer law clerk in Hall Render's Denver office and is a law student at the University of Colorado Law School graduating with the class of 2019. After receiving an undergraduate degree in Music Therapy, she practiced as a music therapist for five years before attending law school. Following her first year of law school, she interned in the Office of General Counsel for Region VIII of the Department of Health and Human Services in Denver, Colorado. During that time she had the opportunity to work on projects for the Centers for Medicare & Medicaid Services, the Office of Civil Rights, and Indian Health Services. During her second year of law school she also represented clients in divorce, asylum, and Social Security disability benefit proceedings in the University Civil Practice clinic. She plans to pursue a career in health law.

ACKNOWLEDGEMENTS

Healthcare and the False Claims Act, 2nd Edition was more than a year in the making, and many people contributed to the effort. Drew Howk was the Editor, pulling the work together into a consistent and cohesive product. Members of Hall Render's Government Enforcement/FCA Task Force assisted with editing and fact-checking, but more importantly, they did the work throughout the year, both writing and representing clients in False Claims Act investigations, that provided the experience and expertise to produce the book. Special thanks must go to superstar legal assistants Pam McFarland-Johnson and Jennifer Thieke, without whom I could not imagine trying to get anything done.

Any errors or omissions are mine alone as are any opinions set forth in *Healthcare and the False Claims Act, 2nd Edition.* These views do not reflect the opinion of any other lawyer at Hall, Render, Killian, Heath & Lyman.

David Honig, Lead Author

About the Book

Health Care and the False Claims Act, 2nd Edition was written to inform and educate healthcare providers and healthcare attorneys about recent significant events surrounding the False Claims Act (FCA), as well as to summarize the current status of the law.

The book opens with a short introduction and then a general discussion about the FCA. The next three chapters cover the most important events and trends in the past year:

> Chapter 3: The Government's changing priorities in FCA enforcement, including increased focus on individual liability for false claims, reduced emphasis on corporate liability, more critical review of *qui tam* lawsuits, and limitation of affirmative civil enforcement to statutory and regulatory violations.
>
> Chapter 4: A new trend in whistleblowing – malpractice attorneys using discovery in their clients' cases for their own benefit as whistleblowers.
>
> Chapter 5: The continuing development and application of "materiality" as set out in the Supreme Court's 2016 decision in *Universal Health Services v. United States ex rel. Escobar.*[1]

Following these updates, the book explores FCA filing, investigation, and litigation:

> Chapter 6: Analysis and application of the "public disclosure" and "original source" requirements for certain *qui tam* whistleblowers.
>
> Chapter 7: Analysis of the first stages of litigation including pleadings, discovery, and required showings;
>
> Chapter 8: Discussion of self-disclosure both to the OIG and CMS;
>
> Chapter 9: Discussion of the Stark Law and the Anti-Kickback Statute and how they often spark FCA lawsuits;

---

[1] 136 S. Ct. 1989 (2016).

Chapters 10: Analysis of changes to the treatment of FCA settlements in the 2017 tax law; and

Chapter 11: Discussion of attorneys' fees, both to whistleblowers and to prevailing defendants;

Chapter 12: New interpretation of the FCA's statute of limitations has changed the rules for old fraud claims;

Chapter 13: Impact of recent expansions to the FCA's retaliation provisions.

Chapter 14: Proposed changes to physician office billing that could significantly reduce the risk of *qui tam* lawsuits for evaluation and management billing.

In the appendices are the remarks by Leslie R. Caldwell, Assistant Attorney General, the *Yates Memo*, the *Granston Memo*, the *Brand Memo*, the OIG's Self-Disclsoure Protocol, and relevant portions of the reviewed cases.

TABLE OF CONTENTS

About the Contributors v
Acknowledgements xi
About the Book xiii
Table of Contents xv
1. Introduction 1
2. The False Claims Act 3
3. Government Enforcement and Priorities 7
4. A New Kind of Whistleblower 19
5. Escobar Update: False Certification and Materiality 23
6. Original Source, Public Disclosure, and the First-To-File Bar 31
8. Pleading and Discovery 39
9. Self-Disclosure 49
10. The Stark Law and the Anti-Kickback Statute 65
11. The New Tax Law and the FCA 71
12. Attorneys' Fees 73
13. The FCA Statute of Limitations 81
14. Retaliation 85
16. The FCA and Evaluation and Management Codes 93
17. Conclusion 97
Appendix A: Leslie R. Caldwell Remarks 99
Appendix B: The Yates Memo 105
Appendix C: The Granston Memo 112
Appendix D: The Brand Memo 118
Appendix E: Department of Justice Cooperation Credit Gudelines .. 120
Appendix F: OIG's Provider Self-Disclosure Protocol 125
Appendix G: Cases 141
Index 283

1. Introduction

By David Honig

In December 2017, the United States Department of Justice announced the recovery of more than $3.7 billion in False Claims Act (FCA) settlements and judgments, down $1 billion from 2016. The number came down again in 2018, to $2.8 billion. In both years, though, more than $2.5 billion came from the healthcare industry, suggesting a continued focus on healthcare in FCA litigation.

Only a small percentage of the recoveries came from jury verdicts. Most of the money recovered came from settlement agreements – usually without findings of wrongdoing – with doctors, hospitals, drug manufacturers, and others facing the enormous risks in FCA litigation.

In 2016, a crucial Supreme Court decision, *Escobar*,[2] was the most significant event of the year. There were no blockbuster Supreme Court FCA decisions in 2017 or 2018. Instead, courts focused on interpreting and applying *Escobar* and wrestling with the proper application of the FCA's statutory restrictions on lawsuits based on publicly disclosed information. But these years saw changes for the FCA on the political front, as a change in presidential administrations brought changes in focus and enforcement priorities. In 2019, the Supreme Court issued its decision in *Cochise Consultancy*,[3] its most significant decision since *Escobar*. The Court, in *Cochise*, expanded the application of the FCA's statute of limitations to give relators, as well as the Government, as long as ten years to file an FCA complaint.

The FCA will remain the Government's primary weapon in its fight against healthcare fraud for a long time. It is critical that anybody in the healthcare field remain up to date on the FCA and how it is being applied, to better understand how to avoid becoming the target of a whistleblower or the Government.

Healthcare and the False Claims Act, 2nd Edition summarizes the important laws, regulations, pronouncements, and cases of the past two years, to inform healthcare providers and healthcare attorneys on the state of this crucial statute in the healthcare industry.

---

[2] 136 S. Ct. 1989 (2016).
[3] Cochise Consultancy, Inc. *et al.* v. United States *ex rel.* Hunt, 139 S. Ct. 1507 (2019).

2. THE FALSE CLAIMS ACT

By David Honig

The first False Claims Act (FCA),[4] known as Lincoln's Law, was passed during the Civil War in response to fraudulent military procurement contracts. This statute incorporated the English concept of the *qui tam*[5] relator, a whistleblower who brings suit on behalf of Government in return for a percentage of any award.

The *qui tam* concept has a long history in English and Colonial law. The earliest record of a *qui tam* statute dates to King Wihtred of Kent, in 695 C.E.:

> if a freeman works during the forbidden time between sunset on Saturday evening and sunset on Sunday evening, he shall forfeit his healsfang,[6] and the man who informs against him shall have half the fine, and the profits arising from the labour.[7]

Qui tam laws were common in Colonial America as well. One example, the 1646 Bakers Law of Massachusetts, set the mandatory weights for bread at different prices and awarded an appointed *qui tam* relator one-third of the forfeiture set for each penalty.

Problems with avaricious whistleblowers appear to be almost as old as the statutes themselves. Edward Coke, in the 16th Century, described whistleblowers as "viperous vermin" who:

> endeavored to have eaten out the lives of the Church and Commonwealth: . . . who under the reverend mantle of law and justice, instituted for protection of the innocent and the good of the Commonwealth, did vex and depauperize the Subject, . . . for malice or private ends, and never for love of Justice.[8]

The Civil War version of the statute allowed civilian whistleblowers to bring fraud actions on behalf of the Government. The statute imposed civil penalties of

---

[4] Act of Mar. 2, 1863, ch. 67, 12 Stat. 696 (1863).
[5] "*Qui tam*" is short for "*qui tam pro domino rege quam pro sic ipso in hoc parte sequitur*" meaning "who as well for the king as for himself sues in this matter."
[6] Old English roughly translated to mean the payment of a fine.
[7] Attenborough, F.L. (Ed.), *The Laws of the Earliest Kings*, Cambridge University Press, Cambridge, UK (2015).
[8] Coke, Edward, *Third Part of the Institutes of the Laws of England, Sixth Edition*, W. Rawlins, London, England (1680).

$2,000 per claim, double damages, and costs. Whistleblowers were entitled to a bounty of half the penalty recovered plus costs.

The statute was amended in 1943 in response to parasitic *qui tam* lawsuits, actions based solely on public information that provided no unique information to the Government. The 1943 version of the statute required a whistleblower to bring the allegations to the Government's attention 60 days before filing a suit, barred actions based on information already known to the Government, and cut the whistleblower's share in half.[9]

As a result of the 1943 amendment, *qui tam* cases became rare. Whistleblowers were not pursuing fraud cases on behalf of the Government and the statute fell into relative disuse. In 1986, hoping to reinvigorate *qui tam* suits in the face of fraud in the defense industry, Congress rewrote the statute to create the modern FCA.[10] The statute increased the penalties and created a legal framework that incentivized whistleblowers. Penalties per claim increased to $5,000 – $10,000, damages trebled, and a whistleblower's share increased to as much as 30% of any reward. The statute of limitations increased to six years or 10 years in certain situations. The scienter standard was knowledge, without specific intent. Finally, the statute offered whistleblowers protection through a new cause of action against employers who retaliated against them for disclosing alleged fraud.

The Congressional overhaul achieved its goal and use of the FCA skyrocketed. In 1987, after only a year, whistleblowers filed 10% of the new FCA cases and total recovery was a mere $86 million. But by 1994, almost 500 new cases were filed—nearly half by whistleblowers—and for the first time total recovery under the FCA topped $1 billion. They hit the $2 billion mark in 2003, $3 billion in 2006,[11] and almost $6 billion in 2014.[12] Today, the FCA has become a big money recovery statute and the most important tool in the Government's fight against healthcare fraud.

For healthcare providers, the picture grew starker. In 1987, only 4% of new FCA cases involved healthcare. Total recoveries from healthcare providers ranged from $2 million to $14 million in the first few years after the 1986 amendments. But by 1997, 85% of the new healthcare FCA cases were initiated by

---

[9] 31 U.S.C. § 232(C) (1946).
[10] 31 U.S.C. § 3729 *et seq.* (1986).
[11] *Fraud Statistics Overview*, USDOJ (December 23, 2013), https://www.justice.gov/sites/default/files/civil/legacy/2013/12/26/C-FRAUDS_FCA_Statistics.pdf.
[12] *Justice Department Recovers Nearly $6 Billion from False Claims Act Cases in Fiscal Year 2014*, USDOJ (November 20, 2014), https://www.justice.gov/opa/pr/justice-department-recovers-nearly-6-billion-false-claims-act-cases-fiscal-year-2014.

whistleblowers, not the Government, and by 2016, healthcare providers often accounted for more than $2 billion in FCA recoveries per year.[13]

In 2009, the FCA was amended again, through the Fraud Enforcement and Recovery Act of 2009 (FERA).[14] FERA significantly amended the FCA, making it even easier for whistleblowers to sue Medicare and Medicaid providers and other government contractors. It also created a new type of false claim: improper retention of overpayments. The retained-overpayment theory was clarified a year later by the Patient Protection and Affordable Care Act of 2010 (ACA) and requires that an overpayment be reported and returned within 60 days of identification.[15]

Before FERA, there was a simple rule in FCA cases: they required factually false claims.[16] After FERA, a new type of FCA case exists—the retained—overpayment false claim. Once a government contractor knows of an overpayment, through actual knowledge, willful ignorance, or reckless disregard for the truth,[17] it must repay the money within 60 days. On the 61st day the retained overpayment becomes a false claim, even if the original error that led to the overpayment was perfectly innocent.

The amendments arrived as whistleblowing became big business. Whistleblower law firms popped up around the nation, advertising "Our lawyers have had unmatched success representing whistleblowers in qui tam lawsuits brought under the False Claims Act.,[18] and "Very few lawyers can legitimately claim real expertise in qui tam litigation. **We can.**"[19]

In 2016, the Centers for Medicare & Medicaid Services (CMS) issued its long-awaited Final Rule implementing the overpayment reporting and repayment provision of the ACA, bringing needed clarity, but also adding burdens to providers grappling with potential overpayment obligations.[20] The Final Rule

---

[13] *Justice Department Recovers Over $4.7 Billion From False Claims Act Cases in Fiscal Year 2016*, USDOJ (December 14, 2016), https://www.justice.gov/opa/pr/justice-department-recovers-over-47-billion-false-claims-act-cases-fiscal-year-2016.

[14] Public Law No. 111-21, the Fraud Enforcement and Recovery Act of 2009, May 20, 2009.

[15] Patient Protection and Affordable Care Act, 42 U.S.C. § 18001 (2010).

[16] United States *ex rel.* Aflatooni v. Kitsap Physicians Services, 163 F.3d 516 (9th Cir. 1999).

[17] 31 U.S.C. § 3729(b)(1)(A).

[18] Phillips & Cohen LLP, http://www.phillipsandcohen.com/ (last visited May 15, 2019).

[19] Warren Bensen Law Group, http://warrenbensonlaw.com/ (last visited May 15, 2019).

[20] 81 Fed. Reg. 7654-7684 (Feb. 12, 2016).

focuses on reasonable inquiry and includes discussion of what constitutes an identified overpayment.

The amendment and the Final Rule have turbocharged FCA litigation against healthcare providers. The submission of knowing false claims is no longer an essential element of an FCA case. Instead, a whistleblower needs only allege that she knew of billing errors, told her employer about them, and the employer failed to act. Providers risk severe sanctions absent an active and robust compliance program to investigate such allegations and, when necessary, timely refund identified overpayments.

The only statutory change relevant to the FCA in 2017 or 2018 came as part of the Tax Cuts and Jobs Act (TCJA)[21] enacted in December 2017. The TCJA limited tax deductions for certain payments under the FCA, and imposed new and strict rules on how FCA awards and settlements are defined and categorized for different treatment under the tax code.

---

[21] 26 U.S.C. § 162(f).

3. Government Enforcement and Priorities

By David Honig

A series of speeches and memos from the DOJ have signaled key changes in the Government's plans and priorities for fraud enforcement using the FCA. The DOJ, under Attorney General Jeff Sessions, revealed an even greater focus on individual liability and a reduced focus on corporate penalties. It was a new approach to *qui tam* lawsuits, demonstrating a willingness to dismiss frivolous actions rather than allowing whistleblowers to proceed on their own. The DOJ also hinted that, while it will continue to vigorously enforce violations of statutes and regulations under the FCA, it is less likely to use government agency guidelines and pronouncements as the basis for fraud litigation. Finally, the Department of Justice updated its Manual, adding guidelines for cooperation credit in civil FCA cases.

A.   Individual Liability.

The FCA is the Government's principal enforcement tool to combat fraud. FCA cases are brought either by the Government or by whistleblowers acting on behalf of the Government in exchange for a percentage of the final award. In the last few years the Government has increased its FCA focus on criminal actions and on individual liability. Since 2014, every FCA case brought by a whistleblower is first reviewed by the DOJ's criminal division, before the unsealing of any civil action. In 2015, Deputy Attorney General Sally Quillian Yates released *Individual Accountability for Corporate Wrongdoing*, more commonly known as the Yates Memo.[22] The Yates Memo ordered a focus on identifying individuals responsible for corporate FCA violations. The Caldwell Announcement and the Yates Memo established the DOJ's policies for FCA enforcement during the Obama administration.

In 2016, the provider community began to see the results of the Caldwell announcement and the Yates memo.

In September 2016, North American Health Care, Inc. (NAHC), settled allegations of billing for medically unnecessary rehabilitation therapy services for $28.5 million. But the settlements did not stop with NAHC. Its chairman of the board agreed to pay $1 million and one of its senior vice presidents agreed to pay $500,000 as part of the deal. The Government's own press release clearly stated that these settlements were not based on any finding of wrongdoing:

---

[22]   Yates, Sally, *Individual Accountability for Corporate Wrongdoing*, USDOJ (September 9, 2015), https://www.justice.gov/dag/file/769036/download.

> The claims resolved by the settlements are allegations only and there has been no determination of liability.[23]

September saw another big individual liability settlement, which came a year after Tuomey Healthcare's $72.4 million corporate FCA resolution. Tuomey's former CEO settled with the Government for $1 million, with a waiver by him of any claim against Tuomey for his loss. While the Government prevailed in its trial against Tuomey Healthcare, it never won a verdict against the CEO. Again the Government's press release made clear that the settlement was not founded upon any finding of actual wrongdoing:

> The claims resolved by the settlement with Cox are allegations only, and there has been no determination of his individual liability.[24]

Tuomey's former CEO voluntarily and permanently excluded himself from participation in Medicare and Medicaid.

But the Government's targeting of individuals was not limited to blockbuster settlements against large defendants. Smaller providers felt the newly implemented policies as well. In Jacksonville, Florida, the U.S. Attorney announced a settlement against owners of a compounding pharmacy, QMedRx, even before there was any finding of liability against the pharmacy.[25] Similarly, a Nashville pharmacy, Nashville Pharmacy Services, LLC, and its majority owner settled a whistleblower case alleging improper waiver of copays.[26]

---

[23] *North American Health Care Inc. to Pay $28.5 Million to Settle Claims for Medically Unnecessary Rehabilitation Therapy Services*, USDOJ (September 19, 2016), https://www.justice.gov/opa/pr/north-american-health-care-inc-pay-285-million-settle-claims-medically-unnecessary.

[24] *Former Chief Executive of South Carolina Hospital Pays $1 Million and Agrees to Exclusion to Settle Claims Related to Illegal Payments to Referring Physicians*, USDOJ (September 7, 2016), https://www.justice.gov/opa/pr/former-chief-executive-south-carolina-hospital-pays-1-million-and-agrees-exclusion-settle.

[25] *United States Settles False Claims Act Allegations Against Compound Pharmacy Owners For $7.75 Million 2016*, USDOJ (September 14, 2016), https://www.justice.gov/usao-mdfl/pr/united-states-settles-false-claims-act-allegations-against-compound-pharmacy-owners-775.

[26] *Nashville Pharmacy Services Settles False Claims Act Lawsuit*, USDOJ (January 5, 2016), https://www.justice.gov/usao-mdtn/pr/nashville-pharmacy-services-settles-false-claims-act-lawsuit.

B.   A New Administration.

In 2016, Donald J. Trump was elected President, and Jeff Sessions named his Attorney General. In 2017, then-nominee Sessions seemed to confirm continued application of the policies, saying at his confirmation hearing:

> Corporations are subject as an entity to fines and punishment for violating the law and so are the corporate officers. And sometimes, it seems to me … that the corporate officers who caused the problem should be subjected to more severe punishment than the stockholders of the company who didn't know anything about it.[27]

But, in response to a question about regulatory overreach, he said:

> But basically these agencies are oftentimes just set about their own agendas without asking for an opinion. And often they are narrow-minded or they're focused only on what they feel are the goals of their agency, and don't give sufficient respect to the rule of law and the propriety of what they're doing.
>
> In particular, did the Congress really intend this? Did this law really cover this? Or is it just something you want to accomplish and you're twisting the law to justify your actions? Those are the kind of things that we do need to guard against.[28]

These statements during the Attorney General's confirmation hearing foreshadowed the speeches and memos in 2017 and early 2018 signaling possible changes in the DOJ's direction for FCAct enforcement.

C.   Continued Emphasis on Individual Enforcement.

In a pair of speeches, in 2017, Acting Principal Deputy Assistant Attorney General Trevor N. McFadden emphasized the DOJ's continued emphasis on individual prosecutions, describing Attorney General Sessions's focus on "the importance of individual accountability for corporate misconduct."[29] Two days later, McFadden stated he intended to "dispel that myth" that the DOJ was no

---

[27] Hearing Transcript, Senate Judiciary Committee Hearing on the Nomination of Sen. Sessions to be Attorney General, Day 1, January 10, 2017, at 199.
[28] Id. at 106-107.
[29] Acting Principal Deputy Assistant Attorney General Trevor N. McFadden Speaks at Anti-Corruption, Export Controls & Sanctions 10th Compliance Summit, Justice News, USDOJ, April 18, 2017.

longer interested in white collar prosecutions.³⁰ He described criminal prosecutions against two Tenet Healthcare executives: "This settlement should send a clear signal and to hospitals and health-care companies around the country that they and their management will be held accountable for fraudulent misconduct."³¹

A week later, Attorney General Sessions, reiterated the DOJ's continued focus on individual responsibility:

> The Department of Justice will continue to emphasize the importance of holding individuals accountable for corporate misconduct. It is not merely companies, but specific individuals, who break the law.³²

In responding to questions, Sessions may have wandered slightly astray from the Yates Memo, saying it was "not always possible" to hold individuals accountable for misconduct, and that companies should not be punished for employees' isolated mistakes.³³

But 2017 saw the DOJ continue to pursue individuals, as well as corporations, for violating the FCA. In several cases, executives and corporations entered into settlement agreements together, sharing joint and several liability. In these cases, the executives were named in the settlement, but the amount was likely be paid by the companies. Examples include a $19.5 million settlement among Health Solutions, Inc., Olympia Therapy, Inc., Tridia Hospice Care, Inc., and their executives;³⁴ and a $1.6 million settlement among a hospital, its executives, and its physicians.³⁵ In other cases, the Government has reached separate agreements with executives, requiring them to pay their own portion of the settlement. An

---

[30] *Acting Principal Deputy Assistant Attorney General Trevor N. McFadden of the Justice Department's Criminal Division Speaks at ACI's 19th Annual Conference on Foreign Corrupt Practices Act, Justice News*, USDOJ, April 18, 2017.

[31] *Acting Principal Deputy Assistant Attorney General Trevor N. McFadden of the Justice Department's Criminal Division Speaks at ACI's 19th Annual Conference on Foreign Corrupt Practices Act*, Justice News, USDOJ, April 18, 2017.

[32] *Attorney General Jeff Sessions Delivers Remarks at Ethics and Compliance Initiative Annual Conference*, Justice News, USDOJ, April 24, 2017.

[33] *Sessions: Focus on violent crime doesn't mean lax enforcement for white-collar offenses*, Matt Zapotosky, Washington Post, April 24, 2017.

[34] *Three Companies and Their Executives Pay $19.5 Million to Resolve False Claims Act Allegations Pertaining to Rehabilitation Therapy and Hospice Services*, Department of Justice, Office of Public Affairs, July 17, 2017.

[35] *Oklahoma Hospital, Former Hospital Administrator, and Physicians Agree to Pay $1,618,750 to Settle Allegations of Submitting False Claims for Medical Services Provided to Medicare Patients*, Department of Justice, U.S. Attorney's Office, Western District of Oklahoma, April 11, 2017.

example is a Florida-based managed care service provider and its COO. The company agreed to pay approximately $31.7 million to settle an FCA suit, while the former COO agreed to pay $750,000 for his role in the case.[36] In 2018, Prime Healthcare Services and its CEO settled FCA allegations that the hospital admitted patients who only needed outpatient services. The company agreed to pay $61.75 million and the CEO agreed to pay $3.25 million to settle the matter.[37]

In late 2018, Deputy Attorney General Rod Rosenstein announced key changes to the DOJ's policies originally outlined in the Yates Memo. The core of the memo remained the same, but the strict mandates related to cooperation and settlement became guidelines, giving prosecutors flexibility, particularly in civil investigations.

The mandates of the Yates Memo were similarly softened in settlement and filing decisions. Previously, an individual could only be released as part of a corporate settlement in extraordinary circumstances, and such a release required approval by the appropriate Assistant Attorney General. Under the new guidelines, neither extraordinary circumstances nor approval were required. The Rosenstein announcement also eliminated, with no replacement, the requirement that Government attorneys consider several factors, including ability to pay when deciding whether to sue individuals for their role in corporate misconduct.

D.   Changing Priorities in the DOJ.

Two blockbuster memos in the first month of 2018 caught the attention of the FCA world. The first, and most discussed, was a leaked internal memo written by Michael D. Granston, Director of the DOJ's Fraud Section, Commercial Litigation Branch. It was a list of factors for Government attorneys to consider when evaluating the dismissal of frivolous FCA cases brought by whistleblowers. While the Government always had the authority to dismiss frivolous cases, it was rarely, if ever exercised. The few FCA cases dismissed over whistleblowers' objections raised national security questions, particularly in defense contracting cases.

E.   The Granston Memo.

The Granston Memo noted a massive increase in whistleblower cases, but no concomitant increase in Government interventions. Though it concluded that some of the new cases likely lacked merit, the Government would still call for the use of significant resources in monitoring, producing discovery, and otherwise

---

[36] *Medicare Advantage Organization and Former Chief Operating Officer to Pay $32.5 Million to Settle False Claims Act Allegations*, Department of Justice, Office of Public Affairs, May 30, 2017.

[37] *Prime Healthcare Services and CEO to Pay $65 Million to Settle False Claims Act Allegations*, Department of Justice, Office of Public Affairs, August 3, 2018.

participating. The memo noted that the Government had rarely used the dismissal authority in the past, but described it as "an important tool" to support the Governments "important gatekeeper role in protecting the False Claims Act."[38] It then listed factors for the Government to consider in dismissing *qui tam* lawsuits:

- Curbing Meritless *Qui tam*s. The DOJ should consider dismissing *qui tam* cases that are "factually lacking," either because the legal theory is wrong or the factual allegations are frivolous . Cases the Government does not immediately dismiss could be dismissed later if the whistleblower is unable to develope develop factual support.[39]

- Parasitic lawsuits. Before the passage of the Affordable Care Act, *qui tam* lawsuits that mirrored previously filed lawsuits or Government investigations were dismissed by the Court for lack of jurisdiction. Since the amendment, dismissal is only permitted with the permission of the Government. The Granston Memo supports dismissal of parasitic lawsuits that add no useful information.[40]

- Interference with Agency policies and programs. Dismissal is to be considered when litigation would interfere with Agency priorities.[41]

- Controlling litigation brought for the Government. Every *qui tam* case, even if prosecuted by a whistleblower, is brought on behalf of the Government, the real party in interest. When litigation might make bad precedent, interfere with other lawsuits or investigations, or otherwise conflict with the Government's overriding interests, dismissal can be considered.[42]

- Safeguarding national interests. *Qui tam* lawsuits that may implicate, or even lead to discovery with or about, intelligence agencies or defense contracts, should be dismissed if necessary to safeguard national interests.[43]

---

[38] Factors for Evaluating Dismissal Pursuant to 31 U.S.C. 3730(c)(2)(A), Michael D. Granston, January 10, 2018.
[39] *Id.* at 3-4.
[40] *Id.* at 4.
[41] *Id.* at 4-5.
[42] *Id.* at 5.
[43] *Id.* at 6.

- Preserving Government resources. *Qui tam* cases that will cost more to maintain, including monitoring and participation in discovery, than they are expected to gain, are ripe for dismissal.[44]

- Interference with the Government's efforts on the same matter. When a *qui tam* lawsuit interfers with the Government's own efforts, the Government should consider dismissal.[45]

The Granston Memo concluded by directing DOJ attorneys who are planning to recommend dismissal of a case to share their recommendation with the whistleblowers, as they "may choose to voluntarily dismiss their actions."[46]

While the Government does not acknowledge dismissals under the Granston Memo, there is a clear trend in whistleblower cases being dismissed at the same time they are unsealed.[47]

F.   The Brand Memo.

In 2018, Associate Attorney General Rachel Brand issued a memo entitled *Limiting Use of Agency Guidance Documents in Affirmative Civil Enforcement Cases*,[48] known in the industry as the "Brand Memo." The Brand Memo built upon a memo from Attorney General Sessions prohibiting the DOJ from issuing binding guidance outside the notice-and-comment rulemaking process. This followed the Trump Administration's preference for statutes and regulations over sub-regulatory rule-making. The Brand Memo noted that the principles in the Attorney General's memo are relevant beyond the DOJ, and should guide DOJ litigators "in determining the legal relevance of other agencies' guidance documents" in civil enforcement actions.[49] The memo made several affirmative statements of interest in FCA litigation:

- Guidance documents cannot create binding requirements that do not already exist by statute or regulation.

---

[44] *Id.* at 6-7.
[45] *Id.* at 7.
[46] *Id.* at 8.
[47] This suggests application of the Granston Memo evaluation. It will likely be years, though, before the Government admits its involvement in the dismissals. For now, government contractors and FCA attorneys will have to wrestle with an even more explosive but enigmatic memo.
[48] *Limiting Use of Agency Guidance Documents in Affirmative Civil Enforcement Cases*, Rachel L. Brand, January 25, 2018, https://www.justice.gov/file/1028756/download.
[49] *Id.* at 1.

- DOJ litigators may not use noncompliance with guidance documents as a basis for proving violations of applicable law.[50]

The memo went on to say:

> That a party fails to comply with agency guidance expanding upon statutory or regulatory requirements does not mean that the party violated those underlying legal requirements; agency guidance documents cannot create any additional legal obligations.[51]

The Brand Memo is of interest any government contractor, but is of particular import to healthcare providers. Many healthcare FCA cases are based on guidance in Medicare's Internet-only Manuals, or IOMs, which, according to Medicare:

> are a replica of the Agency's official record copy. They are CMS' program issuances, day-to-day operating instructions, policies, and procedures that are based on statutes, regulations, guidelines, models, and directives. The CMS program components, providers, contractors, Medicare Advantage organizations and state survey agencies use the IOMs to administer CMS programs.[52]

A review of recent appellate FCA cases demonstrates whistleblowers' reliance on Medicare's guidance documents. In *United States ex rel. Troxler v. Warren Clinic, Inc.*,[53] the case was based on Medicare's *Evaluation and Management Services Guide*, a document that identifies best practices for physician office coding. *United States ex rel. Petratos v. Genentech, Inc., et al.*[54] was based, in part, upon the Medicare Benefit Policy Manual's guidance that drugs need final approval from the FDA to be considered "reasonable and necessary."[55] *United States ex rel. Hartpence v. Kinetic Concepts, Inc.*[56] was based, in part, upon the Medicare Program Integrity Manual rule that durable medical equipment providers must obtain detailed written orders before dispensing supplies reimbursed by Medicare. All of these cases, and many more, would have fallen under the Brand Memo.

---

[50] *Id.* at 2.
[51] *Id.*
[52] Internet-Only Manuals (IOMs), Centers for Medicare & Medicaid Services, https://www.cms.gov/Regulations-and-Guidance/Guidance/Manuals/Internet-Only-Manuals-IOMs.html.
[53] 630 F.App'x 822 (10th Cir. 2015).
[54] 855 F.3d 481 (3d Cir. 2017).
[55] *Id.* at 487.
[56] 792 F.3d 1121 (9th Cir. 2015).

The Brand Memo specifically acknowledges its effect on federal healthcare FCA cases. In footnote 1, it defines "guidance document" as "any agency statement of general applicability and future effect … that is designed to advise parties outside the federal Executive Branch about legal rights and obligations."[57] The footnote goes on to say that the memo addresses "the Department's filing of civil lawsuits on behalf of the United States to recover government money lost to fraud or other misconduct or to impose penalties for violations of Federal health, safety, civil rights, or environmental laws."[58] And it adds, "this memorandum applies when the Department is enforcing the False Claims Act."[59]

G.   Cooperation Credit.

In 2015 the Yates Memo first discussed cooperation credit, generally a concept in criminal sentencing, to cooperation in civil FCA cases. Ms. Yates wrote, "to be eligible for any credit for cooperation, the company must identify all individual involved or responsible for the misconduct at issue, regardless of their position, status or seniority, and provide to the Departmnet all facts relating to that misconduct."[60] She went to say, "[t]his condition of cooperation applies equally to corporations seeking to cooperate in civil matters; a company under civil investigation must provide to the Department all relevant facts about individual misconduct in order to receive any consideration in the negotiation."[61]

In May 2019, the DOJ updated its Justice Manual to include guidance for awarding cooperation credit in civil FCA cases.[62] The guidance takes voluntary self-disclosure, identification of involved individuals, data preservation, investigation assistance, discipline, and remediation into consideration in awarding cooperation credit.

The new guidance is of utmost importance in FCA cases, for it is the first time the Department has affirmatively described the possible benefit to a potential FCA defendant in self-reporting to the DOJ – significant reduction in FCA fines and penalties – an advantage not offered by other forms of self-disclosure.

---

[57]   Limiting Use of Agency Guidance Documents in Affirmative Civil Enforcement Cases at fn. 1.
[58]   *Id.*
[59]   *Id.*
[60]   Yates, Sally, *Individual Accountability for Corporate Wrongdoing*, p. 3.
[61]   *Id.*
[62]   *Department of Justice Issues Guidance on False Claims Act Matters and Updates Justice Manual*, Department of Justice, Office of Public Affairs, May 19, 2019, https://www.justice.gov/opa/pr/department-justice-issues-guidance-false-claims-act-matters-and-updates-justice-manual.

The first, and most important, act which may allow for cooperation credit is "proactive, timely, and voluntary self-disclosure to the Department."[63] Additional credit would apply to entities that self-disclose additional misconduct discovered during an investigation into the entity's, or the Department's, original concerns.[64]

The second form of cooperation considered under the new guidance is cooperation with an ongoing government investigation. The guidance provides an illustrative list, though additional acts which assist an investigation will also be considered. The list includes identifying individuals responsible for the misconduct, preserving and disclosing relevant documents and providing them in native format to facilitate review, identifying individuals with knowledge about the misconduct, admitting liability or accepting responsibility, and assisting in recoverig losses for the misconduct.[65]

The Department will also look to remedial measures, including measures to address the root cause of the problem, improvement of a compliance program, discipline of those responsible, and anything else that demonstrates recognition of misconduct, acceptance of responsibility, and affirmative measures to prevent repetition of misconduct.[66]

It will also consider self-reporting to a relevant agency, public acknowledgement of the self-disclosure, and assistance in resolving any *qui tam* litigation with a relator, if relevant.[67]

The credit is discretionary with the Department and is generally exercised by reducing penalties or the damages multiple available under the FCA. The maximum credit available would be single damages plus lost interest, investigative costs, and relator share, if relevant.[68]

Under the new guidance, self-reporting to the Department of Justice offers something other self-reporting might not, including through the OIG's Self-Reporting Protocol – significant reduction of FCA fines and penalties. While the DOJ may take self-reporting to a relevant agency into consideration, it is but one factor considered. All the cooperation credit opportunities enumerated in the new guidance can be achieved only through self-disclosure to the Department itself. With this in mind, healthcare providers considering self-disclosure through the

---

[63] *Justice Manual*, § 4-4.112. May 19, 2019, https://www.justice.gov/jm/jm-4-4000-commercial-litigation#4-4.112.
[64] *Id.*
[65] *Id.*
[66] *Id.*
[67] *Id.*
[68] *Id.*

OIG Self-Disclosure Protocol may, instead, wish to consult with counsel about seeking credit through the new DOJ guidance, instead.

H.   Conclusion.

If the DOJ is to be bound by the Brand Memo, its own prosecution of FCA cases based on Medicare's manuals and other guidance should cease. This would be a radical departure in enforcement; it will take time to see if the memo is an aspirational statement of the goals of an administration that prefers statutes to regulations and guidance. The more interesting question is whether the Brand Memo will provide additional direction in applying the Granston Memo – will whistleblower cases based on guidance, rather than statute or regulation, be dismissed by the Government, over the objection of whistleblowers? Finally, the DOJ's new self-disclosure cooperation credit guidance offers the opportunity to reduce FCA risk and gives providers a new, and perhaps advantageous avenue to report discovered misconduct which could lead to liability under the Act.

4. A New Kind of Whistleblower

By David Honig

In 2010, as part of the Affordable Care Act, Congress amended the False Claims Act to exclude state law suits from the FCA's list of public disclosures that could bar parasitic whistleblowers. One unintended result was to invite medical malpractice plaintiff attorneys to use their clients' discovery to find cases to enrich themselves as whistleblowers. This new trend raises significant issues for healthcare providers required to participate in malpractice discovery but needing to protect themselves from FCA liability. It may also raise ethical questions related to the duty of plaintiff's attorneys to their clients rather than themselves.

A. Changes in the FCA Public Disclosure Bar.

Before 2010 the FCA's public disclosure bar read:

> No court shall have jurisdiction over an action under this section based upon the public disclosure of allegations or transactions in [i] a criminal, civil, or administrative hearing, [ii] in a congressional, administrative, or Government Accounting Office report, hearing, audit, or investigation, or [iii] from the news media, unless the action is brought by the Attorney General or the person bringing the action is an original source of the information.[69]

In 2010, that paragraph was amended to read:

> *The court shall dismiss an action or claim* under this section, *unless opposed by the Government*, if substantially the same allegations or transactions as alleged in the action or claim *were publicly disclosed*— (i) in a *Federal* criminal, civil, or administrative hearing in which the Government or its agent is a party; (ii) in a congressional, Government Accountability Office, or other *Federal* report, hearing, audit or investigation; or (iii) from the news media, unless the action is brought by the Attorney General or the person bringing the action is an original source of the information.[70]

The amendment included several major changes. First, the public disclosure element of the FCA was no longer a true jurisdictional bar. It did not deprive the court of jurisdiction – it merely called for the court to ask for the Government's approval to dismiss the case. Even the most parasitic of lawsuits can now proceed

---

[69] 31 U.S.C. §3730(e)(4)(1986).
[70] 31 U.S.C. §3730(e)(4)(2010) (with major changes in italics).

if the Government objects to dismissal. Second, it took away the confusing "based on" language that called for courts to determine what drove a whistleblower's filing decision, and replaced it with a simpler test, whether the same matters were already in the public sphere. But third, it removed state lawsuits, legislative actions, and investigations from the definition of "public disclosure."

B.   Early Efforts as Attorney-Relators are Barred.

Before 2010, FCA cases that closely tracked state lawsuits were barred – courts had to dismiss them for lack of jurisdiction. The application of the public disclosure bar to attorneys and other participants in litigation and investigations before 2010 is demonstrated in two cases, *United States ex rel. Hafter v. Spectrum Emergency Care, Inc.*[71] and *United States ex rel. Weddington v. Scott & White Memorial Hospital, et al.*[72]

In *Hafter*, a former emergency room physician worked with a medical malpractice attorney investigating claims on behalf of a client.[73] Hafter was later named as a fact witness in the malpractice case,[74] and eventually filed his own *qui tam* case as a whistleblower, based on the same allegations.[75] He argued he was an original source of the information in both lawsuits, and thus should be permitted to proceed as a whistleblower. He proffered an affidavit from the original malpractice attorney.[76] Tenth Circuit looked at the information in the affidavit and found that it generally described, information Hafter might have known, but it did not state with any particularity actual facts in support of the FCA lawsuit.[77] The court affirmed the trial court's dismissal for lack of jurisdiction.[78] The original state malpractice lawsuit created a jurisdictional bar to the new FCA action and dismissal was affirmed.

In *Weddington*, the whistleblower was an attorney representing a patient in a malpractice case. During cardiovascular surgery the surgeon removed a malfunctioning kidney. But the images of the kidneys were improperly displayed and the patient's only functioning kidney was removed. The patient died. The ensuing matter settled, but during a related suit it was revealed that Medicare was billed for the surgery.

---

[71]   190 F.3d 1156 (10th Cir. 1999).
[72]   202 F.3d 264 (5th Cir. 1999), *cert. denied* 120 S.Ct 1672, 529 U.S. 1067 (2000).
[73]   190 F.3d at 1158.
[74]   *Id.*
[75]   *Id.* at 1159.
[76]   *Id.* at 1162.
[77]   *Id.*
[78]   *Id.* at 1165.

After the malpractice case, Weddington filed an FCA suit as the whistleblower on the same facts. The trial court dismissed the case for lack of subject matter jurisdiction, finding that the malpractice claim and the public hearing constituted public disclosures, that Weddington was not an original source, and so the case was subject to the public disclosure bar. Weddington appealed and the Fifth Circuit affirmed the trial court's decision with a one word opinion: "Affirmed."[79] Weddington petitioned for *certiorari* with the Supreme Court and the petition was denied.

C.   The 2010 Amendment Invites Attorney-Relators.

With the 2010 amendment to the FCA, the rules changed. State lawsuits are no longer bars to whistleblowers. On its face the reasoning is sound – the federal government may not know of state lawsuits. But the effect was to invite attorneys to turn their clients' malpractice lawsuits into FCA cases for themselves. This raises ethical questions, as well as questions for healthcare providers defending against malpractice allegations.

Rule 1.8 of the American Bar Association's Model Rules of Professional Conduct states:

> A lawyer shall not acquire a proprietary interest in the cause of action or subject matter of litigation the lawyer is conducting for a client, except that the lawyer may:
>
> (1) acquire a lien authorized by law to secure the lawyer's fee or expenses; and
>
> (2) contract with a client for a reasonable contingent fee in a civil case.[80]

Rule 1.8 was addressed in a *qui tam* suit in *United States ex rel. Taxpayers Against Fraud and Walsh v. General Electric Co.*[81] Walsh retained Hall & Phillips to represent him as a whistleblower. Walsh was joined as relator by Taxpayers Against Fraud (TAF). The court noted that, while TAF had an executive director, a staff of five, and an independent board of directors, 95% of its expenses were legal fees to Hall & Phillips and it was founded by John R. Phillips, a partner of Hall & Phillips. On appeal of the legal fees the Sixth Circuit directed the trial court to "broaden [the] inquiry into the role that TAF played in this litigation," and "investigated whether Hall & Philip's relationship with TAF violated ethical cannons,"

---

[79]   202 F.3d at 264.
[80]   Rule 1.8(i), *Model Rules of Professional Conduct*, American Bar Association Center for Professional Responsibility, ABA 2018.
[81]   41 F.3d 1032 (6th Cir. 1994).

referencing Rule 1.8.[82] If TAF is just a front for Hall & Phillips, the court noted, "the ethical mandates of Rule 1.8(j)[83] have been implicated."[84]

It is unclear where the ethical lines are to be drawn between an attorney and a client when attorneys represent the client in a malpractice case but use information learned during that representation to enrich themselves as whistleblowers. Are they acquiring a "proprietary interest in … the subject matter of the litigation?" The question gets even more complicated when the attorney is representing the client and acting as a whistleblower simultaneously, a situation that can arise when attorneys files an FCA case under seal and continues to conduct discovery in the malpractice lawsuit. What is the attorney's duty to advise the client that discovery may be for their own benefit as a whistleblower? These issues will ultimately need to be addressed, for regular FCA practitioners have noted a recent trend of attorneys acting for themselves, as whistleblowers, at the same time they act for their clients, as malpractice counsel.

The new trend of medical malpractice attorneys developing FCA whistleblower cases while representing malpractice clients also creates significant new challenges and concerns for healthcare providers. Discovery in the malpractice case, even if it is directly relevant to that matter, might also provide a potential whistleblower with a wealth of information to develop an FCA case. It is possible that the purpose of the malpractice discovery is for an FCA case, using the malpractice case as a vehicle to gather information normally inaccessible before the filing and unsealing an FCA action.

Providers must now consider FCA risk while defending against malpractice lawsuits. This can be difficult as malpractice defense attorneys are often chosen by insurance companies, not the providers. Malpractice attorneys appropriately focus on defending the case before them, not the case that might be hiding behind a seal. Providers should ensure their malpractice counsel is well versed in FCA defense or consider retaining their own FCA counsel to shadow malpractice discovery. This would allow for a review of production for risk evaluation and, if necessary, to consider self-disclosure if errors are identified.

---

[82] *Id.* at 1044.
[83] Now Rule 1.8(i).
[84] *Id.*

5. ESCOBAR UPDATE: FALSE CERTIFICATION AND MATERIALITY

By Laetitia Cheltenham and Matthew Schappa

The Supreme Court's holding in *Escobar*[85] changed the game for FCA litigation. In that 2016 decision, the Court addressed the concepts of implied false certifications, scienter, and materiality.

In *Escobar*, the government argued that United Health Services' provided counselling services to patients even though the practitioners lacked proper licenses. The government argued that the submission of claims by United Health Services impliedly certified compliance with applicable statutes and regulations. United Health Services argued this theory could not apply unless one of the statues or regulations violated expressly indicated that reimbursement was conditioned upon such compliance.

The Court took a separate position and ruled that whistleblowers cannot rely on technical violations to skate past the FCA's materiality and knowledge requirements. Rather, the whistleblower must demonstrate that a defendant knowingly presented a false claim for payment and that the claims were material to the government's decision to pay. This holding clarified that the government's decision to pay claims is critical to determining materiality—not an arbitrary categorization.

The Court also addressed the importance of scienter in it decision, holding that liability under the FCA exists only when a defendant knowingly violates a requirement that the defendant knows is material to the government's payment decision.

This crucial and guiding decision from the Supreme Court has since been interpreted by several courts across the country—each addressing and applying *Escobar*'s materiality and scienter clarifications in its own way.

A. Materiality is Rigorous and Demanding.

In *United States ex rel. Kelly v. Serco, Inc.*, the Ninth Circuit was one of the first courts to reiterate the "rigorous" and "demanding" materiality standard in *Escobar*.[86] Kelly alleged that Serco flouted the Government's cost reporting guidelines. In particular, Serco, as a subcontractor for the Department of Defense, Navy Space and Naval Warfare Systems Command (SPAWAR), was required under

---

[85] 136 S. Ct. 1989 (2016).
[86] 846 F.3d 325 (9th Cir. 2017).

Statements of Work to provide project management and cost reports in a specific format known as the earned value management system (EVMS). Serco later informed SPAWAR that it could not accommodate the various task line-items required by EVMS, and instead Serco compiled the required time entries into spreadsheets and used them as monthly cost reports. SPAWAR agreed to accept these simplified cost reports and advised the Department of Homeland Security (DHS) of the change in Serco's cost tracking format.

The whistleblower, an analyst hired by Serco to evaluate Serco's performance on the SPAWAR contract, informed DHS that Serco's monthly cost reports did not conform to the Government's standards and were falsified to match the expected project budget.[87] Despite knowledge of Serco's noncompliance with EVMS, the Government continued to accept Serco's reports and pay Serco under the subcontract. The District Court granted summary judgment in favor of Serco.

On appeal, the Ninth Circuit applied *Escobar* and affirmed summary judgment for Serco. The Court held that the whistleblower failed to show that the alleged noncompliance was material to any Government payment decisions. The complaint failed the "rigorous" and "demanding" materiality standard in *Escobar* and this whistleblower's implied false certification claims failed.

Materiality's rigorous and demanding standard resurfaced throughout various FCA cases with a few additional twists and turns.

B. The FCA is not a "Trap" Set by the Government.

By clarifying the importance of materiality and scienter, *Escobar* established that the FCA is not a wide net that can be used to catch and penalize defendants for every minor mistake. Courts have applied the *Escobar* directions that an FCA plaintiff must show both materiality and scienter to reject the use of the FCA as a trap for the well-meaning but unwary healthcare provider. It may not accept all the benefits of good-faith services and then use disputed interpretations of the rules to come back for recoupment, fines, and penalties.

In an opinion loaded with linguistic hooks, a district court applied *Escobar*.[88] In *United States ex rel. Ruckh v. Salus Rehabilitation, LLC, et al.*, whistleblowers won a judgment against Defendants, who owned and operated 53 specialized nursing facilities. Whistleblowers case involved claims of upcoding and a failure to maintain patient care plans. After Defendants received a verdict against them for almost $350 million, they moved for judgment as a matter of law and requested a new trial. Defendants argued that whistleblower failed to offer evidence of

---

[87] The whistleblower filed this *qui tam* action after his position was eliminated by Serco supervisors that were unaware of the report to DHS.
[88] 304 F. Supp. 3d 1258 (M.D. Fla. 2018).

materiality as required by the United State Supreme Court's holding in *Escobar* and that whistleblower failed to prove that Defendants submitted claims for payment with knowledge that the Government would refuse to pay the claims had they known about the disputed practices.

The court granted Defendants' requests, finding that the state and federal governments either accepted or tolerated the practices in question. The court's order emphatically relied on *Escobar* for both materiality and knowledge, calling it "the unquestionably controlling and guiding authority on materiality and scienter under the False Claims Act," and offering up this quotable conclusion:

> *Escobar* rejects a system of government traps, zaps, and zingers that permits the Government to retain the benefit of a substantially conforming good or service but to recover the price entirely – multiplied by three – because of some immaterial contractual or regulatory noncompliance.

This rejection of the system of "traps, zaps, and zingers" is accomplished through *Escobar's* requirement of materiality and scienter. The FCA requires whistleblowers to prove both that a misrepresentation (or form of noncompliance) was material to the Government's payment decision and that a defendant knew at the moment the defendant sought payment that the misrepresentation was material to the Government's payment decision. A misrepresentation (or noncompliance) subjects a defendant to liability under the FCA only if it is knowingly "material to the other party's course of action."[89]

The Court held that the Government's continued payment, despite knowledge of some claimed defect, evidences a lack of materiality:

> the Government that continues to pay full fare for a product or service despite knowledge of some disputed practice, some noncompliance, or some other claimed defect, relentlessly works itself into a steadily tightening bind that at some point becomes disabling because the Government…must prove that had the Government known the facts the Government would have refused to pay.[90]

The court's skeptism continued, scorning the whitstleblower's attenuated attempt to link scattered events to a system-wide conspiracy:

> scattering of claims in a smattering of facilities is a wholly insufficient basis from which to infer the existence of a

---

[89] *Id.* at 1262.
[90] *Id.* at 1269.

massive, authorized, cohesive, concerted, enduring, top-down, corporate scheme to defraud the Government.

In another recent case applying *Escobar*, the Ninth Circuit Court of Appeals reiterated that an FCA complaint pleading materiality without scienter is futile. The Relator in *United States ex rel. McGrath v. Microsemi Corp.*,[91] alleged that its former employer (and the company that acquired employer) violated the FCA by submitting claims for payment for shipment of components protected by the International Traffic in Arms Regulation (ITAR), while failing to protect technical data from acquisition by foreign nationals. The district court dismissed the action and the whistleblower appealed.[92]

Applying *Escobar*, the Ninth Circuit affirmed the district court decision finding that the complaint failed to plead facts plausibly alleging that compliance with ITAR was material to the Government's payment decision.[93] The Ninth Circuit went on to state that:

> even assuming that the statement "ITAR controlled" on Microsemi's receipts constituted a false representation that Microsemi was in compliance with ITAR, the complaint cannot plead facts sufficient to support an inference that Microsemi knew it had failed to comply with ITAR at the time of the representation because Microsemi's good faith interpretation of the term "disclose" in 22 C.F.R. § 120.17 at that time was reasonable.[94]

In *United States ex rel. Badr v. Triple Canopy, Inc.*,[95] the Fourth Circuit too applied *Escobar*. The Government alleged that Triple Canopy knowingly employed security guards that had failed to satisfy the marksmanship requirement to serve on a United States airbase in Iraq. Despite the alleged lack of qualifications, the Government asserted that Triple Canopy submitted monthly invoices to the Government for payment.

Triple Canopy argued that it made no specific representation about the qualifications of the guards in its invoices and did not have to certify compliance

---

[91] 690 F. App'x 551 (9th Cir.), cert. denied sub nom. McGrath v. Microsemi Corp., 138 S. Ct. 407, 199 L. Ed. 2d 282 (2017).
[92] United States ex rel. McGrath v. Microsemi Corp., 140 F. Supp. 3d 885 (D. Ariz. 2015), aff'd, 690 F. App'x 551 (9th Cir. 2017).
[93] 690 F. App'x 551 (9th Cir.), cert. denied sub nom. McGrath v. Microsemi Corp., 138 S. Ct. 407.
[94] United States *ex rel.* McGrath v. Microsemi Corp., 690 F. App'x 551, 552 (9th Cir.), cert. denied sub nom. McGrath v. Microsemi Corp., 138 S. Ct. 407.
[95] United States v. Triple Canopy, Inc., 857 F.3d 174 (4th Cir.), cert. dismissed, 138 S. Ct. 370.

with the such requirements when submitting invoices for payment. Still, the Fourth Circuit, on remand, held that the Government had properly alleged that Triple Canopy, with the requisite scienter, made requests for payments under a contract and that the information withheld was material to such payments. The Fourth Circuit noted that knowingly withholding the fact that the security guards had failed to satisfy the marksmanship requirements fell within the type of "half-truths" discussed in *Escobar*. The court reiterated that common sense suggests that the Government's decision to pay a contractor for providing base security in an active combat zone would be influenced by the Government's knowledge that the guards lacked the ability to shoot properly.

C. Government Inaction after a Substantial Investigation Supports Dismissal Based on Materiality.

The Fifth Circuit applied *Escobar* to prohibit FCA claims if the Government pays a claim despite full knowledge of the allegedly fraudulent activity. In *Abbott v. BP Exploration & Production, Inc.*,[96] an employee and a consumer advocacy organization brought an FCA claim against BP alleging that BP made material misrepresentations to the Government about a floating oil production facility in the Gulf of Mexico.[97]

After the *qui tam* action was filed, the Department of the Interior began an investigation, reviewing BP's compliance with regulatory requirements. After a two-year investigation, the DOI concluded that "[the whistleblowers'] allegations about false submissions by BP to DOI are unfounded."[98] Thus, the district court granted summary judgment in favor of the Defendants.

On appeal, the Fifth Circuit upheld the district court, finding that:

> when the DOI decided to allow [BP] to continue drilling after a substantial investigation into Relator's allegations, that decision represents 'strong evidence' that the requirements in those regulations are not material.[99]

The Fifth Circuit applied *Escobar* by looking "to the effect on the likely or actual behavior of the recipient of the alleged misrepresentation."[100] While it is unlikely that many FCA actions will lead to an investigation requested by Congress, this holding may be used to support defendants in whistleblower actions where the alleged fraudulent claims have already been investigated by the Government.

---

[96] 851 F.3d 384 (5th Cir. 2017).
[97] *Id.*
[98] *Id.* at 386.
[99] *Id.* at 388.
[100] 136 S. Ct. 1989 (2016).

This may not apply when the Government continues to pay claims once the noncompliance, or alleged fraudulent activity, has been corrected. In *United States ex rel. Crampie v. Gilead Sciences, Inc.*, the Ninth Circuit reversed the dismissal of an FCA action, applying this theory.[101]

The *Crampie* action was brought by two former employees of Gilead Sciences who alleged that Defendant made false statements about its compliance with the FDA in its development of HIV pharmaceuticals. Before the filing of the action, Defendants remedied the false statements made to the FDA. The FDA was aware of the misrepresentations, yet continued to approve production of the HIV products.

On appeal, Relator argued that there are many reasons the FDA may choose not to withdraw a drug approval, unrelated to the concern that the Government paid out billions of dollars for nonconforming and adulterated drugs. Relator also argued that once the unapproved and contaminated drugs were no longer being used, the Government's decision to keep paying for compliant drugs does not have the same significance as if the Government continued to pay despite continued noncompliance. The Ninth Circuit reversed the district court's dismissal, holding that despite the arguments, the ultimate questions was what the Government knew and when—questioning its "actual knowledge."[102] Ultimately, the Ninth Circuit held that relators alleged more than a mere possibility that the Government would may refuse payment if it were aware of the violations and therefore sufficiently plead materiality.

D.   The FDA's Impact on Materiality.

One of the factors at issue in *Gilead Sciences, Inc.* was the Government's reliance on FDA approval for payment of claims.[103] In that case, the district court rejected relator's claims in part because the alleged fraud was directed at the FDA, not the payor agency. But the Ninth Circuit's reversal of that decision rested in part on its holding that "It is not the distinction between the agencies that matters, but rather the connection between the regulatory omissions and the claim for payment."[104]

In early 2018, the Second Circuit dealt with a similar situation. In *Coyne v. Amgen, Inc.*, the relator, a physician and former paid speaker for Amgen, alleged that the pharmaceutical company caused the Government to make unreasonable or unnecessary reimbursements for prescriptions for a kidney disease drug.[105] At the

---

[101] 862 F.3d 890 (9th Cir. 2017), *cert. denied* 139 S. Ct. 783 (2019).
[102] *Id.* at 906-07.
[103] *Id.* at 903.
[104] *Id.*
[105] 717 F.App'x 26 (2d Cir. 2018).

center of relator's allegations was that the packaging and marketing materials for the drug at issue included false information.

The Second Circuit upheld the district court's dismissal of the FCA action holding "it is not sufficient for a finding of materiality that the Government would have the option to decline to pay if it knew of the defendant's noncompliance—the complaint must present concrete allegations from which the court may draw the reasonable inference that the misrepresentations on [the drug's] packaging and marketing materials caused the Government to make the reimbursement decision."[106] The Court found that "any claims about quality of life improvements contained on the Clinical Experience portion of the label would be unlikely to impact CMS reimbursement. That is because FDA approval for Indications and Usage of a medication makes it presumptively 'reasonable and necessary' for the purposes of CMS reimbursements, and only the Indications and Usage section of the drug label relates to FDA approval."[107]

This holding, along with the Ninth Circuit's discussion of FDA approval and its relationship to FCA litigation draws an interesting conclusion: Misrepresentations that lead to FDA approval do not necessarily qualify as 'material' under *Escobar*. Rather, those misrepresentations must have directly caused the Government's reimbursement decision.

E. <u>Contingent Penalties are not Material Obligations under the FCA.</u>

In *United States ex rel. Schneider v. JPMorgan Chase Bank, Nat'l Ass'n*,[108] the D.C. Circuit reiterated that alleged fraud under the FCA must be material to an obligation to pay or transmit money or property to the Government. In the initial suit,[109] a whistleblower brought a *qui tam* action against mortgage loan servicer, JPMorgan Chase. The whistleblower alleged, in part, that Chase falsely claimed compliance with a settlement that it previously reached with the United States and state governments.[110] Under the settlement, Chase had to comply with certain servicing standards. A monitor was appointed to ensure that Chase complied with such standards. The whistleblower argued that the monitor's determination that Chase had complied with the servicing standards was incorrect because Chase falsely certified that compliance. As a result, the whistleblower's alleged damages

---

[106] *Id.* at *29.
[107] *Id.*
[108] 878 F.3d 309, 311 (D.C. Cir. 2017).
[109] United States *ex rel* Schneider v. J.P. Morgan Chase Bank, *N.A.*, 224 F. Supp. 3d 48, 51 (D.D.C. 2016), aff'd and remanded sub nom. United States *ex rel.* Schneider v. J.P. Morgan Chase Bank, Nat'l Ass'n., 878 F.3d 309 (D.C. Cir. 2017).
[110] The Circuit Court disagreed with the district court's exhaustion conclusion but affirmed its dismissal of the Settlement claims on a related basis. The circuit court did, however, agree with the district court's analysis of the HAMP claim.

were based on potential penalties for lender violations as set forth in the settlement.

The District Court for the District of Columbia granted Chase's motion to dismiss as to the settlement's claims because the whistleblower could not bring these claims without first exhausting the settlement's dispute resolution procedures. The D.C. Circuit affirmed the district court's decision.[111]

Although the Circuit Court rejected the district court's reasoning as to the settlement claims, it affirmed the Court's decision because potential exposure to penalties for alleged noncompliance with the settlement's servicing standards is not a material obligation under the FCA. According to the D.C. Circuit Court, such an obligation arises when there is "an established duty, whether or not fixed, arising from an express or implied contractual…or similar relationship."[112] The court noted that the settlement contained a series of steps before Chase could be assessed any penalties, including a citation from the monitor, failure to cure, failure of informal dispute resolution, the filing of a suit in the district court and the district court judge exercising his or her enforcement discretion to award monetary penalties. In its decision, the court re-affirmed its position that "contingent exposure to penalties which may or may not ultimately materialize does not qualify as a material 'obligation' under the FCA."[113]

---

[111] The Circuit Court disagreed with the district court's exhaustion conclusion but affirmed its dismissal of the Settlement claims on a related basis. The circuit court did, however, agree with the district court's analysis of the HAMP claim.
[112] 878 F.3d at 314-315.
[113] *Id.* at 315.

6. ORIGINAL SOURCE, PUBLIC DISCLOSURE, AND THE FIRST-TO-FILE BAR

By David B. Honig

The FCA allows whistleblowers to bring fraud cases on behalf of the Government. Over time, the statute evolved to prevent parasitic lawsuits brought by whistleblowers but based on information already known to the Government. These cases do not assist the Government by bringing fraud to its attention but deprive the Government of a slice of the damages it suffered. In the last several years, Congress again amended the FCA to prevent parasitic lawsuits while encouraging people with information about fraud on the Government to come forward. Only now are appellate courts beginning to consider the amendments' impacts. Courts continue to wrestle with both versions of the statute. They apply the older statute to cases filed before 2010 and need to defining the meaning of the new amendments in more recent cases.

Because the FCA repeated amendments for this purpose, it is valuable to discuss a brief history of the FCA, the practices of whistleblowers, and the amendments over the years.

A.   Parasitic Lawsuits under the Early FCA.

The FCA was enacted during the Civil War in response to fraud in sales to the Union Army. The FCA remained in its original form into the Second World War. During WWII, the DOJ and the FBI were investigating, and criminally prosecuting, a new generation of defense contractors exploiting the enormous American war machine. Would-be whistleblowers started hanging out at the federal courthouses waiting for indictments to be filed. As soon as the Government filed an indictment, whistleblowers filed their own FCA cases against the named defendants with no new information.

In 1943, the Supreme Court decided *United States ex rel. Marcus v. Hess, et al.*[114] The defendants had already been indicted, found guilty, and fined $54,000. Both the defendants and the Government, in an *amicus* brief, asserted that the whistleblower, Marcus, got all of his information from the Government's indictment. They argued that Marcus should not be permitted to bring the action as a whistleblower, as he contributed nothing to the investigation. The Government also argued that the litigation of criminal cases and connected civil

---

[114] 317 U.S. 537 (1943).

cases should be brought by the DOJ and the Attorney General, not whistleblowers.

The Court rejected the Government's position because of the plain language of the FCA: "[s]uits may be brought and carried on by any person," without limitation.[115] More important, the Court noted that policy changes are the province of Congress:

> The Government presses upon us strong arguments of policy against the statutory plan, but the entire force of these considerations is directed solely at what the Government thinks Congress should have done rather than at what it did . . . But the trouble with these arguments is that they are addressed to the wrong forum. Conditions may have changed, but the statute has not.[116]

The Attorney General responded to the *Marcus* decision by lobbying Congress to amend the FCA to bar parasitic lawsuits. Congress amended the FCA to cut the whistleblower's share in half and to add a first–to–file bar:

> The court shall have no jurisdiction to proceed with any such suit brought under clause (B) or pending suit brought under section 3491 of the Revised Statutes whenever it shall be made to appear that such suit was based upon evidence or information in the possession of the United States, or any agency, officer or employee thereof, at the time such suit was brought.[117]

The new language ended the use of the FCA by whistleblowers. Practically every case involving false claims submitted to the Government would involve some evidence of information in the possession of at least one government employee.

B. The Public Disclosure Bar in the 1986 FCA.

In 1986, the statute was completely rewritten. The revised statute included a new *qui tam* provision intended to encourage whistleblowers while preventing parasitic lawsuits. The maximum recovery increased to 30%, the fine increased to a maximum of $10,000, and penalties tripled. More important, the "any prior government knowledge" language was replaced with a jurisdictional bar on lawsuits brought based on a prior public disclosure in the media or a government record. The new statute also included a "first-to-file bar," prohibiting actions "based upon allegations or transactions which are the subject of a civil suit or an

---

[115] *Id.* at 546.
[116] *Id.* at 546-547.
[117] 31 U.S.C. § 232(c) (1946).

administrative civil monetary penalty proceeding in which the Government is already a party."[118]

The changes worked and within a few years, hundreds, then thousands, of whistleblower lawsuits were filed, leading to the recovery of billions of dollars.

In 2010, in the ACA, the FCA's original-source provisions were extensively rewritten. Congress removed the jurisdictional bar and replaced it with a requirement that courts dismiss suits "unless opposed by the Government."[119] The amendment redefined "original source" to include only an individual with materially new and independent information:

> who has knowledge that is independent of and materially adds to the publicly disclosed allegations or transactions, and who has voluntarily provided the information to the Government before filing an action under this section.[120]

Finally, Congress limited public disclosures to include only those made in Federal hearings, reports, audits, investigations, or the news media. Information publically disclosed at the state level no longer bars whistleblowers.

Cases interpreting and applying the amended statute have started to work their way through the courts. In 2017, nine different Circuit Courts considered the amended statute in more than a dozen different cases, laying the groundwork for the FCA's amended application of the first–to–file, public disclosure, and original source language.

In *United States ex rel. Ambrosecchia v. Paddock Labs., LLC*,[121] the relator argued that, because the statute's public disclosure language no longer created a jurisdictional bar, it could not be the basis for a motion to dismiss. She argued that public disclosure was a question of fact that could only be resolved at summary judgment or trial.[122] The court rejected the argument, noting that the motion to dismiss was brought based on Rule 12(b)(6), not 12(b)(1),[123] arguing that the complaint failed

---

[118] 31 U.S.C. § 3730(e)(4) (1986).
[119] 31 U.S.C. § 3730(e)(4)(A) (2010).
[120] 31 U.S.C. § 3730(e)(4)(B) (2010).
[121] 855 F.3d 949 (8th Cir. 2017).
[122] *Id.* at 953.
[123] Fed. R. Civ. P. 12: Defenses and Objections: When and How Presented; Motion for Judgment on the Pleadings; Consolidating Motions; Waiving Defenses; Pretrial Hearing:
(b) How to Present Defenses. Every defense to a claim for relief in any pleading must be asserted in the responsive pleading if one is required. But a party may assert the following defenses by motion:
(1) lack of subject-matter jurisdiction; . . . .

to state a claim, not challenging jurisdiction. The court went on to find that Ambrosecchia was not an original source. While she provided her information to the Government before filing her complaint, she did so after federal reports that qualified as public disclosures were published. The complaint provided no facts to demonstrate knowledge that materially added to the Government's knowledge.[124]

Amphastar Pharmaceuticals Inc. v. Aventis Pharma SA,[125] was a case filed before the 2010 amendment to the FCA. For that reason, it included a complete jurisdictional bar to claims already publicly disclosed unless the whistleblower was an original source. An original source needed to have both direct and independent knowledge of the issues in the lawsuit. *Amphastar* started out as a patent dispute between two drug manufacturers and ended with an FCA case, based on an error in the original patent application. The trial court, after a hearing on the public disclosure and original source questions, determined that the error was publicly disclosed before the filing of the lawsuit,[126] and that the whistleblower–manufacturer's CEO was not credible and the whistleblower–manufacturer did not independently discover the error.[127] The case was dismissed. The whistleblower argued on appeal that allegations of fraud had never been made in a publicly disclosed document. The court rejected the argument, observing that the underlying misrepresentations were public, and "'an allegation need not include an express reference to the False Claims Act for the public disclosure bar to apply.'"[128]

United States ex rel. Armes v. Garman[129] straddled both versions of the FCA's public disclosure bar, as it alleged fraudulent claims submitted both before and after the 2010 amendment. Armes filed his *qui tam* action in Tennessee, closely, but not perfectly, tracking allegations in a whistleblower case previously filed and then pending in Indiana. The trial court granted the defendants' motion to dismiss based on the prior public disclosure. It also refused Armes's motion to amend his complaint, filed long after his response was due and just days before argument on the motion, as both untimely and futile.

On appeal, the Sixth Circuit acknowledged that Armes added details absent from the Indiana case, but ruled it could still be based on the prior public disclosure, even if there is not:

---

(6) failure to state a claim upon which relief can be granted.

[124] *Id.* at 955.
[125] 856 F.3d 696 (9th Cir. 2017).
[126] *Id.* at 702.
[127] *Id.*
[128] *Id.* at 704. (quoting United States v. Alcan Elec. And Engineering, Inc., 197 F.3d 1014, 1019 (9th Cir. 1999)).
[129] 719 F.App'x 459 (6th Cir. 2017).

> a complete identity 'even as to time, place, and manner' between the publicly disclosed allegations or transactions and the later *qui tam* complaint.[130]

It also found that Armes's additional detail did not make him an original source under either version of the statute, because those details were not so significant that they would "affect a person's decision-making."[131]

The Sixth Circuit also affirmed the trial court's refusal to permit refiling for undue delay.

C. <u>The Public Disclosure Bar under the 2010 Amendment.</u>

The Seventh Circuit considered both public disclosure and original source questions in a case that straddled both recent versions of the FCA.[132] Universal Health Services of Hartgrove, Inc., was a psychiatric hospital.[133] It was mostly for children.[134] Hartgrove was licensed for 150 beds, including 136 beds for acute mental illness patients[135] but maintained 152 beds with newly admitted patients sometimes placed on roll-out cots in a "dayroom" rather than a patient room.[136]

In 2009 the Illinois Department of Public Health and CMS issued letters and an audit report describing Hartgrove's number and use of beds.[137] These reports did not include specific allegations of fraud.

Two years later Bellevue, a nursing counselor, filed a whistleblower lawsuit against Hartgrove, alleging Medicaid billing fraud linked to the use of more patient beds than permitted under its license.[138] Hartgrove moved to dismiss, both for failure to state a claim because, at the time, the Seventh Circuit did not recognize implied false certification as a basis for an FCA suit, and for lack of subject matter jurisdiction because the underlying facts had already been publicly disclosed and

---

[130] *Id.*, (quoting United States *ex rel.* Poteet v. Medtronic, Inc., 522 F.3d 503, 511 (6th Cir. 2009)).

[131] *Id.*, (quoting United States *ex rel.* Advocates for Basic Legal Equal., Inc., 816 F.3d 428, 432 (6th Cir. 2016)).

[132] Bellevue v. Universal Health Services of Hartgrove, Inc., 867 F.3d 712 (7th Cir. 2017).

[133] *Id.* at 715.

[134] *Id.*

[135] *Id.*

[136] *Id.*

[137] *Id.* at 718.

[138] *Id.* at 715.

Bellevue was not an original source.[139] The trial court dismissed for the former reason but rejected the latter one.[140]

On appeal, the Seventh Circuit reviewed the application of the public disclosure bar. Because the case alleged false claims before and after 2010, the court had to consider both iterations of the statute.[141]

First, the court noted that it had not yet decided whether the post-2010 version of the public disclosure bar was jurisdictional.[142] But because the claims straddled both versions of the FCA, it analyzed only the pre-2010 jurisdictional bar.

The court applied the three-step test for application of the public disclosure bar:

1. whether the allegations had been publicly disclosed;

2. whether the lawsuit was based on the publicly disclosed allegations; and

3. whether the whistleblower was an original source.[143]

Bellevue argued that, while the letters and audit report did state Hartgrove was over census, they did not state Hartgrove made a knowing misrepresentation of fact, an essential element in a fraud case.[144] But the court found that the reports contained enough facts to infer "that the defendant knowingly—as opposed to negligently—submitted a false set of facts to the Government."[145] The court found this because the number of beds used versus the number of beds licensed was an issue of fact that did not require any qualitative judgments such as standard of care.[146]

The court also held that Bellevue's allegations were substantially similar to the publicly disclosed allegations.[147] Bellevue argued that, even if the allegations for acts before the letters and audited were substantially similar, the allegations that post-dated those public disclosures should survive, as they covered a different

---

[139] *Id.* at 715-716.
[140] *Id.* at 716.
[141] *Id.* at 717.
[142] *Id.*
[143] *Id.* at 718. (quoting *Causes of Action*, 815 F.3d at 274).
[144] *Id.* at 718.
[145] *Id.* at 718-719. (quoting *Causes of Action*, 815 F.3d at 279).
[146] *Id.* at 719, (comparing Absher v. Momence Meadows Nursing Ctr., Inc., 764 F.3d 699, 708-709 (7th Cir. 2014)).
[147] *Id.* at 719.

period.[148] The court rejected the argument because, while the allegations covered different dates, they did not describe different conduct.[149]

Finally, the court held that Bellevue was not an original source as defined by the statute. While he may have had independent knowledge because of his employment at Hartgrove, he did not "materially add" to the public disclosure.[150]

The final finding is of the most interest. The court held that the test for whether the whistleblower's allegations are "substantially similar" is the same as the test for whether the whistleblower's information "materially adds" to the public disclosure. This makes the third step in the three-step test redundant, leaving only a two-step analysis for applying the public disclosure bar in the Seventh Circuit. Future cases will tell whether this is because of the facts in this case or if it states a new and more condensed test for the FCA's public disclosure bar.

The Second Circuit addressed whether the post-2010 public disclosure language created a jurisdictional bar.[151] The court noted that the amended language no longer included specific "jurisdiction" language, while other subsections of the statute still included explicit jurisdictional bars.[152] The court joined "the D.C. Circuit in holding that the FCA's first-to-file rule bears only on whether a *qui tam* plaintiffs has properly stated a claim,"[153] and so district courts retain subject matter jurisdiction on such claims.[154]

One relator tried, without success, to save his FCA case from dismissal by consolidating it with an earlier filed *qui tam* complaint. In 2009, Christine Ribik filed a whistleblower suit against Manor Care.[155] Two years later, Patrick Carson filed his own whistleblower suit against Manor Care, making similar accusations.[156] The two cases were consolidated in 2012 and the Government intervened in 2014.[157]

---

[148] *Id.* at 720.
[149] *Id.*
[150] *Id.* at 721.
[151] United States *ex rel.* Hayes v. Allstate Insurance Co., et al., 853 F.3d 80 (2d Cir. 2017).
[152] *See, e.g.,* 31 U.S.C. § 3730(e)(1) ("No court shall have jurisdiction over an action brought by a former or present member of the armed forces ... against a member of the armed forces arising out of such person's service in the armed forces.")
[153] *Hayes*, 853 F.3d at 86.
[154] *Id.* (cleaned up).
[155] United States *ex rel.* Carson v. Manor Care, Inc., et al., 851 F.3d 293, 300 (4th Cir. 2017).
[156] *Id.*
[157] *Id.* at 301.

Manor Care moved to dismiss Caron's claim, alleging it was barred by the first-to-file rule.[158] Carson argued his complaint should not be dismissed, as it had been consolidated with Ribik's earlier action.[159] The court swatted down Carson's position:

> While a novel argument, it has no merit. The FCA does not make an exception to the first-to-file rule for consolidated complaints. The first-to-file rule is "an absolute, unambiguous exception-free rule."[160] The statute is clear: "[w]hen a person brings an action under this subsection, *no person other than the Government* may intervene or bring a related action based on the facts underlying the pending action."[161] The statute does *not* read that "no person other than the Government may intervene or bring a related action based on the facts underlying the pending action *unless that person's case is consolidated with the earlier-filed case.*"[162]

In *United States ex rel. Lager v. CSL Behring, LLC, et al.*[163] the whistleblower alleged that his former employer reported an inflated Average Wholesale Price (AWP) for its drugs, causing increased profits for physicians, and thus overutilization and overpayment by Government payers. The trial court dismissed the claims, finding that industry-wide over-reporting of AWPs had been publicly disclosed through prior FCA lawsuits, media reports, and government investigations. On appeal, the whistleblower argued that the prior disclosures had not specifically identified the defendants and had not described the same allegations or transactions in his complaint. The Eighth Circuit found that the public disclosures, taken together, provided enough information for the Government to identify both the scheme and the defendants, and so affirmed the dismissal.

The public–disclosure bar and the first–to–file bar were significantly altered by the FCA's 2010 amendments. The public–disclosure bar no longer strips a court's jurisdiction to hear an FCA case, and the test of whether a whistleblower is an original source is, in most courts, a lower hurdle to leap. Appellate courts are only now dealing with a large volume of cases interpreted under the new version of the statute, and the law will continue to evolve over the next several years.

---

[158] *Id.*
[159] *Id.* at 305.
[160] *Carter*, 710 F.3d at 181.
[161] 31 U.S.C. § 3730(b)(5) (emphasis added).
[162] *Carson*, 851 F.3d at 305.
[163] 855 F.3d 935 (8th Cir. 2017).

8. PLEADING AND DISCOVERY

By David French and Matt Paradiso

The FCA targets fraud and thus, under the federal pleading standards, requires whistleblowers to detail their claims with particularity.[164]

For most civil complaints, Rule 8 requires *notice pleading*:

> A pleading that states a claim for relief must contain: . . . a short and plain statement of the claim, showing that the pleader is entitled to relief.[165]

Under Rule 8, a complaint need only set forth facts sufficient to notify defendants of the claims they must defend against. But FCA actions are fraud claims, and are thus subject to the heightened pleading standards under Rule 9(b):

> [A] party must state with particularity the circumstances constituting fraud or mistake. Malice, intent, knowledge, and other conditions of a person's mind may be alleged generally.[166]

Satisfaction of Rule 9(b) is a common hurdle in FCA cases, particularly those brought by whistleblowers hoping to ferret out a broader lawsuit during discovery. Rule 9(b)'s heightened pleading standards afford the opportunity for early review and challenge to the complaint through a motion to dismiss. As a result, a great deal of caselaw every year concerns the FCA's pleading requirements. Unfortunately, because every case is fact-specific, new decisions can confuse rather than clarify. In 2016, the Eleventh Circuit went out of its way to clear up confusion caused by a decade of inconsistent decisions. Other courts joined the Eleventh Circuit, reiterating the requirement that FCA complaints must state the "who, what, when, where, and how"[167] of any alleged fraud.

Rule 9(b)'s requirement requires a party to allege the "who, what, when, where, and how of the fraud."[168] Thus an FCA complaint must identify

- what false claim was submitted to the Government;
- when it was submitted;
- who submitted the claim; and

---

[164] Vermont Agency of Natural Resources v. Stevens, 529 U.S. 765, 781 (2000).
[165] Fed. R. Civ. P. 8(a)(1).
[166] Fed. R. Civ. P. 9(b).
[167] United States *ex rel.* Ge v. Takeda Pharm. *Co.*, 737 F.3d 116, 123 (1st Cir. 2013).
[168] *Takeda*, 737 F.3d at 123.

- how the claim was false.

Despite this requirement, the various Circuit Courts have enunciated different tests for pleadings to satisfy the "particularity" requirement.[169] The Fourth, Sixth, Eighth, and Eleventh Circuits are clear that plaintiffs must allege specific examples "of the alleged fraudulent conduct, specifying the time, place, and content of the acts and the identity of the actors."[170] But the First, Fifth, and Ninth Circuits have required that a plaintiff satisfy Rule 9(b) by alleging "particular details of a scheme to submit false claims paired with reliable indicia that lead to a strong inference that claims were actually submitted." Recently, several cases were decided which highlight the split in authority.

The Supreme Court has not yet resolved the split and has rejected several petitions to address it. The following recent cases demonstrate how various courts have addressed the FCA pleading requirements.

A. Rule 9(b) Requires Specific Claims to be Identified.

In *United States ex rel. Ibanez v. Bristol-Myers Squibb Co.*,[171] whistleblowers alleged that defendants engaged in an improper kickback scheme to promote an antipsychotic drug thus causing false claims to the Government.[172] In holding that the whistleblowers failed to meet the pleading standards of Rule 9(b), the court highlighted that

> where a relator alleges a complex and far reaching scheme…it is insufficient to simply plead the scheme, she must also identify a representative false claim that was actually submitted.[173]

The court also acknowledged a "personal knowledge" exception to the Sixth Circuit's general rule. Under the exception, a claim may survive if "it includes allegations showing 'specific personal knowledge' supporting a 'strong inference that a [false] claim was submitted.'"[174] But the court emphasized that the exception applies in limited circumstances—such as where the whistleblower reviewed the allegedly false claims as part of their job.[175] Since the whistleblower did not allege this type of personal knowledge, Rule 9(b) required that they "adequately allege the entire chain—from start to finish—to fairly show

---

[169] Foglia v. Renal Ventures Mgmt., *LLC*, 754 F.3d 153, 155 (3d Cir. 2014).
[170] *Id.* at 155-56.
[171] 874 F.3d 905 (6th Cir. 2017).
[172] *Ibanez*, 874 F.3d at 912.
[173] *Id.* at 914.
[174] *Id.* at 915.
[175] *Id.* at 915-16.

defendants caused false claims to be filed."[176] Although the whistloblowers alleged knowledge of a complex scheme, they did not provide a specific claim that submitted to the Government for payment, and thus failed to adequately plead a FCA violation.[177]

In *United States ex rel. Hirt v. Walgreen Company*,[178] a pharmacy owner filed a whisltblower claim against Walgreen Company (Walgreens), alleging that Walgreens improperly distributed kickbacks (in the form of $25 gift cards) to Medicare and Medicaid recipients when they transferred their prescriptions to Walgreens and that Walgreens induced false or fraudulent claims to the Government.[179] The district court dismissed the claim, holding that the whistleblower failed to state his claims with sufficient particularity under Rule 9(b).[180]

On appeal, the Sixth Circuit affirmed the district court's ruling. The court held that the complaint did not meet the Rule 9(b) heightened pleading standard because it

- did not state the names or initials of any of the customers allegedly lured to change pharmacies;

- did not state the dates on which the customers filled prescriptions at Walgreens; and

- did not state the dates in which Walgreens filed the reimbursement claims with the Government.[181]

The court also noted that the Sixth Circuit "raised the possibility" of:

> relaxing the requirement that a plaintiff identify at least one false claim with particularity if that plaintiff, through no fault of his own, cannot allege the specifics of actual false claims that in all likelihood exist.[182]

Even so, the court clarified that the Sixth Circuit never resolved this point, noting that it lacks the authority to "relax" the pleading standard under Rule 9(b). Rather, the court highlighted that the particularity requirement may be met where a

---

[176] *Id.* at 915.
[177] *Id.* at 916.
[178] 846 F.3d 879 (6th Cir. 2017).
[179] *Hirt*, 846 F.3d at 880-81.
[180] *Id.* at 880.
[181] *Id.* at 881.
[182] *Id.*

whistleblower has "sufficient personal knowledge of the defendant's claims submission and billing practices."[183]

B. <u>Rule 9(b) Requires Allegations that Strongly Suggest Fraudulent Billing Claims Must Have Been Filed.</u>

In *United States ex rel. Colquitt v. Abbott Laboratories*,[184] the whistleblower was a former employee of a company acquired by defendant Abbott, who sold stents to doctors.[185] The whistleblower filed an action against the company alleging FCA violations as part of Abbott's alleged practice of selling biliary stents for off-label use to doctors performing vascular procedures.[186] The alleged scheme provided "significant volume discounts and rebates to hospitals that could not be attained based solely on biliary use, but required substantial vascular use of the stents in order to receive the discount or rebate."[187] The whistleblower alleged that the scheme violated the Anti-Kickback Statute, rendering the companies' claims certifying compliance with the AKS false.[188]

The district court granted Abbott's motion to dismiss the AKS allegations because whistleblower had failed to satisfy Rule 9(b)'s heightened pleading standard.[189] The district court found that the complaint failed to describe "any details of the actual claims made by the physicians or hospitals that allegedly received kickbacks."[190] The court reasoned that

> although [whistleblower] had identified some specific hospitals and doctors that allegedly received kickbacks, he did not plead that any of these hospitals or doctors signed up to be Medicare providers or submitted certified claims for reimbursement for procedures using Abbott's stents.[191]

On appeal, the Fifth Circuit affirmed but noted that the district court's reasoning may have been "too rigid" an application of Rule 9(b).[192] The Fifth Circuit relied on its prior holding in *United States ex rel. Grubbs v. Kanneganti*[193] in which it "sounded a note of caution about its application in *qui tam* suits" and that "the time, place, contents, and identity standard is not a straightjacket for Rule 9(b)"

---

[183] *Id.*
[184] 858 F.3d 365 (5th Cir. 2017).
[185] *Id.* at 369-370.
[186] *Id.* at 370.
[187] *Id.* at 372.
[188] *Id.* at 370.
[189] *Id.* at 371.
[190] *Id.*
[191] *Id.*
[192] *Id.*
[193] 565 F.3d 180 (5th Cir. 2009).

but is rather "context specific and flexible."¹⁹⁴ The court explained that under the *Grubbs* standard,

> a relator's complaint, if it cannot allege the details of an actually submitted false claim, may nevertheless survive by alleging particular details of a scheme to submit false claims paired with reliable indicia that lead to a strong inference that claims were actually submitted.¹⁹⁵

The Fifth Circuit ruled that whistleblower failed to meet the first part of the *Grubbs* standard.¹⁹⁶ The court found that the whistleblower established a strong inference that false claims were submitted, however, he failed to allege the details of the scheme with sufficient particularity.¹⁹⁷ The court reasoned that the whistleblower devoted "a single, vague paragraph to the alleged kickback scheme" and "never link[ed] the alleged carrots to the purchase and use of the stents at either of the hospitals."¹⁹⁸

While a vague paragraph is insufficient, the First Circuit, applying its more flexible approach to Rule 9(b), found that fraud could be pleaded with sufficient particularity with the use of statistics to buttress indicia of fraud. In *United States ex rel. Nargol v. DePuy Orthopaedics, Inc.*,¹⁹⁹ physician whistleblowers alleged that DePuy misled the FDA in government approval for Pinnacle metal-on-metal hip replacement devices and that the devices were manufactured well below specifications, leading to the submission of false claims for inferior devices.²⁰⁰ The district court dismissed for failure to plead with particularity, as no specific claims were identified and the complaint lacked sufficient factual and statistical evidence to support an inference of fraud.²⁰¹

On appeal, the First Circuit affirmed the district court's dismissal based on defective design, finding that the allegations could not be material given the FDA's continued approval of the device after the whistleblowers' allegations were made known to the Agency.²⁰²

But the court reversed dismissal of the whistleblowers' claim alleging the devices provided did not meet FDA specifications, causing third-party false claims by the

---

¹⁹⁴ *Colquitt*, 858 F.3d at 372.
¹⁹⁵ *Id.*
¹⁹⁶ *Id.*
¹⁹⁷ *Id.*
¹⁹⁸ *Id.*
¹⁹⁹ 865 F.3d 29 (1st Cir. 2017).
²⁰⁰ *Nargol*, 865 F.3d at 32.
²⁰¹ *Id.* at 34.
²⁰² *Id.* at 34-36.

doctors performing the surgeries.[203] The court noted that the First Circuit applies a "more flexible" standard for indirect false claims where third parties are induced to file false claims with the Government.[204] The "flexible" approach may be satisfied where factual or statistical evidence to strengthen the inference of fraud is paired with "reliable indicia" that false claims were submitted.[205] The court found that the Complaint alleged a sufficient basis in fact through the statistical analysis, which showed that more than 50% of the devices were defective, there was no reason to believe physicians (who could not see the defects) would not bill for the devices, hip replacement surgery is most often insured, and thousands of devices were sold, making it likely some were paid for by government programs.[206]

The court also affirmed dismissal alleging DePuy directly submitted false claims to the Government, as it identified no direct claims, and the more flexible "reasonable indicia" standard does not apply to direct claims.

The Ninth Circuit also holds relators to a lower Rule 9(b) standard. In *United States ex rel. Vatan v. QTC Medical Services, Inc.*,[207] the court reversed a trial court's dismissal for failure to plead fraud with particularity. The trial court dismissed the complaint because the whistleblower did not plead the specific terms of the underlying contract that he alleged was violated in defendants' fraud.[208] The Ninth Circuit held it sufficient for the whistleblower to plead the contents "pursuant to information and belief,"[209] where "the relevant information is within the defendant's exclusive possession and control."[210]

C.   Rule 9(b) Requires Materiality to be Pleaded with Particularity.

In *Grabcheski v. Am. Int'l Grp., Inc.*,[211] a whistleblower brought an FCA claim alleging that AIG's subsidiaries were conducting a domestic insurance business and that AIG, in its debt-reduction agreements with the Federal Reserve Bank of New York, knowingly misrepresented that these subsidiaries were licensed to conduct such business.[212]

The Second Circuit affirmed the district court's finding that whistleblower failed to adequately allege an FCA claim because the whistleblower failed to plead

---

[203] *Id.* at 37-41.
[204] *Id.* at 39.
[205] *Id.*
[206] *Id.* at 40-41.
[207] 721 F.App'x 662 (9th Cir. 2018).
[208] *Id.* at 663.
[209] *Id.*
[210] *Id.*
[211] 687 F. App'x 84 (2d Cir. 2017).
[212] *Grabcheski*, 687 F. App'x at 86.

materiality with the requisite particularity under Rule 9(b).[213] Materiality requires particular facts showing that the false statements altered the likely or actual behavior of the recipient of the alleged misrepresentation.[214] Because the whistleblower failed to adequately allege that the debt-reduction agreements would have been different without the alleged misrepresentation, the whistleblower failed to state a FCA claim.[215]

Courts may look at the specific claims identified in support of Rule 9(b) and compare them to a whistleblower's allegations. In *United States ex rel. Roycroft v. Geo Group, Inc., et al.*,[216] the whistleblower offered a laundry list of alleged frauds and attached seven representative claims.[217] But he did not specify what was false in each of the claims.[218] Had the whistleblower identified what was false about each claim, rather than alleging the claims supported his allegations of "many allegations of treatment, staff, and licensing requirements,"[219] his complaint would have survived a 9(b) challenge.

D. <u>FCA Claims Based on Mere Speculation will be Dismissed.</u>

In *United States ex. rel Hanlon v. Columbine Management Services, Inc.*,[220] employees of a nursing home, who competed with defendants for healthcare business, filed a whistleblower action alleging that defendants formed a joint venture to operate a nursing home and to coordinate healthcare referrals to benefit the joint venture at the expense of other healthcare facilities and the federal government.[221] Whistleblowers alleged that defendants' actions violated the AKS, FCA, and state law.[222] The district court granted defendants' motion to dismiss holding that the complaint failed to specify the laws that the whistleblowers believed the defendants had violated or the conduct which was allegedly illegal.[223]

On appeal, the Tenth Circuit affirmed the district court's dismissal. The court found that whistleblowers' first claim did not put defendants on notice that they were pursuing FCA claims because the complaint mentioned only AKS, and not FCA, in the claim for relief.[224] By failing to mention the FCA as part of the AKS claim, the whistleblowers failed meet the basic pleading requirements under Rule

---

[213] *Id.* at 87.
[214] *Id.*
[215] *Id.*
[216] 2018 WL 266782 (6th Cir. January 3, 2018).
[217] *Id.* at *2.
[218] *Id.* at *3.
[219] *Id.*
[220] 676 F.App'x 787 (10th Cir. 2017).
[221] *Hanlon*, 676 F.App'x at 788.
[222] *Id.*
[223] *Id.* at 789.
[224] *Id.* at 790.

8.[225] As to their FCA claim, the court found that whistleblowers' allegations were speculative because they failed to point to a single claim to support their false certification theory.[226]

In *United States ex. rel. Takemoto v. Nationwide Mutual Insurance Company*,[227] a physician who owned a Medicare Secondary Payer compliance company alleged that various insurance industry participants, self-insured corporations, and third-party administrators violated the FCA by violating repayment obligations under the Medicare Secondary Payer Act.[228] The district court dismissed the whistleblower's complaint for grouping defendants together and failing to plead essential elements of his FCA claims.[229]

On appeal, the Second Circuit affirmed, holding that the whistlblower failed to meet the basic pleading requirements of Rule 8(a).[230] The court held that the facts alleged were merely speculative and could not sustain a plausible inference of an obligation on the part of the defendant.[231]

E. <u>Post-dismissal Amendment may be Denied.</u>

In most cases, when a complaint is dismissed for failure to plead properly as required, the whistleblower is given leave to file an amended complaint. This is based on Rule 15(a), which states a court "should freely give leave [to amend] when justice so requires."[232] Even so, amendments need not be allowed if:

1. there has been undue delay, bad faith, dilatory motive, or repeated failure to cure deficiencies in previous amendments;

2. allowing amendment would cause undue prejudice to the defendant; or

3. amendment would be futile.[233]

In *United States ex rel. Chase v. HPC Healthcare, Inc.*,[234] the court considered what to do after dismissing a complaint which had been repeatedly amended before the

---

[225] *Id.*
[226] *Id.* at 791.
[227] 674 F.App'x 92 (2d Cir. 2017).
[228] *Takemoto*, 674 F.App'x at 94.
[229] *Id.*
[230] *Id.* at 95.
[231] *Id.*
[232] Fed. R. Civ. P. 15(a)(2).
[233] Corsello v. Lincare, Inc., 428 F.3d 1008, 1014 (11th Cir. 2005).
[234] 2018 WL 526039 (11th Cir. Jan. 24, 2018).

court ruled on the motion to dismiss.[235] The whistlblower argued that she should be allowed to file an amended complaint after dismissal, as it was the first time her complaint "was subjected to adversarial testing."[236] In her response to the motion to dismiss, the whistleblower asked permission to amend if the court granted the motion. But she did not "set forth the substance of the proposed amendment or attach a copy of the proposed amendment."[237] The Eleventh Circuit affirmed, concluding "the District Court did not abuse its discretion in dismissing the complaint with prejudice."[238]

Chase raises the bar for whistleblowers, suggesting that, in responding to a motion to dismiss they must not only answer the argument – they must also attach a proposed amended complaint or describe, in detail, how they would amend a complaint.

---

[235] *Id.* at *2.
[236] *Id.* at *6.
[237] *Id.* (quoting *Long v. Satz*, 181 F.3d 1275, 1279-1280 (11th Cir. 1999)).
[238] *Id.* at *6.

9. SELF-DISCLOSURE

By Katherine Kuchan and Gregg Wallander

OIG Self-Disclosure Protocol

The Office of Inspector General (OIG) of the U.S. Department of Health and Human Services (HHS) encourages providers, contractors, and grantees to report self-discovered instances of noncompliance in various HHS programs. All healthcare providers, suppliers, and other entities and individuals subject to civil monetary penalties (CMPs), may use the OIG's Provider Self-Disclosure Protocol (SDP) to identify, disclose, and resolve instances of potential fraud involving federal healthcare programs.

Disclosures under the SDP may help mitigate a provider's exposure because disclosure typically reflects a robust and effective compliance program. Thus, there is a presumption against requiring a corporate integrity agreement when disclosing the conduct, as well as generally lower damage payment amounts. The OIG's SDP should not be confused with the Centers for Medicare & Medicaid Services (CMS) self-disclosure process or disclosures to the DOJ. CMS's process is limited to potential violations of the physician-self referral statute and the Stark Law.

This first half of this chapter focuses on the SDP's development, OIG's current SDP procedure and practical aspects of the process, benefits and limitations of using the SDP, significant statistics and examples, as well as tips for providers using the SDP process.

A.   History of the Self Disclosure Protocol.

OIG published the original SDP in 1998 as a notice in the Federal Register, outlining a voluntary process for providers to identify, disclose, and resolve instances of potential fraud involving federal healthcare programs.[239] Prior to the SDP, OIG worked informally with providers that came forward or cooperated with OIG when instances of fraud or abuse arose. Over time the OIG, along with the DOJ and various United States Attorneys' Offices, gained valuable insights into the variables influencing a provider's decision to self disclose to the Government. The original SDP guidance in the Federal Register demonstrated OIG's crystalizing views on the appropriate elements of a disclosure, including commitment of the provider to engage in specific self-evaluative steps relating to the disclosed matter. The original SDP also outlined the expectations for a voluntary submission that included basic information, details on the provider's

---

[239] Office of Inspector Gen., Publication of the OIG's Provider Self-Disclosure Protocol, 63 Fed. Reg. 58,399-58,402 (Oct. 30, 1998), https://www.gpo.gov/fdsys/pkg/FR-1998-10-30/pdf/98-29064.pdf.

internal investigation and assessment, as well as a full examination of the extent of the improper or illegal practices. But the OIG also took an interest in understanding how a provider learned of an incident and what steps a provider took to prevent future instances of noncompliance.

The original SDP focused on potential violations of the federal AKS that trigger CMPs and the employment of, or contracting with, excluded persons. The original SDP provided guidance on how to:

1. investigate the conduct;

2. quantify damages; and

3. report the conduct to the OIG to resolve a Provider's potential exposure under applicable federal laws.

Submissions through the SDP were initially low; but as healthcare enforcement expanded, providers increasingly relied on the SDP as a critical tool to mitigate risk by voluntarily disclosing wrongdoing before becoming a target of a government investigation.

Since the 1998 release of the original SDP, OIG has issued three Open Letters updating the SDP. These Open Letters issued in 2006, 2008, and 2009[240] sought suggestions from providers about improvements to the SDP. OIG also solicited comments from the public in 2012. The Open Letters made smaller pronouncements, such as the 2008 Open Letter which reaffirmed the presumption against requiring corporate integrity agreements when resolving disclosed conduct and the 2009 Open Letter which clarified that the SDP was not appropriate for pure Stark Law matters or AKS matters involving less than $50,000. In 2013, OIG issued an updated SDP incorporating several changes to improve the SDP process.[241] This revised SDP superseded and replaced the 1998 Federal Register Notice and subsequent Open Letters.

OIG's improvements changed and clarified the SDP through several important ways. Namely, OIG:

---

[240] Office of Inspector Gen., Dep't of Health & Human Servs., *An Open Letter to Health Care Providers* (Apr. 24, 2006), (Apr. 15, 2008) and (Mar, 24, 2009).

[241] *Updated – Provide Self-Disclosure Protocol*, Office of the Inspector Gen., Dep't of Health & Human Servs., (April 17, 2013), https://oig.hhs.gov/compliance/self-disclosure-info/files/Provider-Self-Disclosure-Protocol.pdf.

a. affirmed that providers should make submissions with a good faith willingness to resolve liability within the CMP law's six-year statute of limitations;

b. announced that providers can make submissions to the OIG through its website;

c. removed certain detailed reporting requirements;

d. recognized the application of different methods to calculate damages that had been used by providers and OIG for many years, depending on the type of conduct disclosed;

e. agreed to suspend overpayment reporting and repayment obligations under the 60-day refund requirement pending settlement, withdrawal, or removal from SDP;

f. clarified that it would coordinate with DOJ to resolve any false claims liability; and

g. articulated that pharmaceutical and medical device manufacturers may use the SDP.

OIG also expanded on various areas of noncompliance with more detail than in its prior statements. The topics of these expanded discussions include false billing, disclosures involving excluded persons, and combined AKS and Stark Law issues.

1. False Billing/Submission of Improper Claims

Providers are expected to conduct a review to estimate the total financial impact to government healthcare programs. Depending on the volume of claims, the damage estimate should consider all affected claims or a statistically valid sample of claims that may be extrapolated to the universe of affected claims. Providers should know that the SDP also prohibits the netting of underpayments and overpayments in samples in the total financial affect analysis. Providers that choose to calculate the financial impact through a statistically valid sample must use a sample of at least 100 claims and use the mean point estimate to calculate the financial impact. When a probe sample is used, those claims may be in the 100 claim sample if statistically appropriate. To avoid large sample sizes, OIG does not require a minimum precision level for review of the claims. As a result, providers have some latitude to select the sample size as long as it contains at least 100 claims.

2. Excluded Persons

The revised SDP also offers more detailed guidance to providers for disclosures involving excluded persons. In such cases, the disclosing provider must include specific information relating to the excluded person's hiring and employment along with the disclosing Provider's policies for screening persons against OIG's List of Excluded Individuals and Entities (LEIE). Before disclosure of employment of or contract with an excluded individual or entity, the provider making the SDP submission must screen all of its current employees and contractors against the LEIE. Calculating damages is fact specific and dependent on whether the excluded person was a direct provider, such as a physician or a pharmacist, and whether the items or services furnished, ordered, or prescribed by that person were separately billed to federal healthcare programs, or conversely, not billed separately. (e.g., items or services furnished by nurses or other administrative personnel).

3.   AKS and Stark Law Issues

The OIG also provided additional details about its handling of AKS and Stark Law issues. OIG stated that it would continue accepting disclosures about AKS and Stark Law violations, but reaffirmed that the SDP is unavailable for Stark Law—only disclosures. In reaffirming its general approach for resolving potential AKS violations, OIG emphasized applying a multiplier to the remuneration conferred by the disclosing provider versus calculating damages based on the amount of reimbursement received. Underscoring remuneration-based methodology for disclosures follows OIG's actions to encourage disclosures of potential AKS and Stark Law violations. OIG also expressed a push for transparency and limiting the damages related to potential violations revealed through SDP submissions. OIG outlined the minimum settlement amount of $10,000 for disclosures not involving the AKS while reaffirming that AKS-related submissions remained subject to a $50,000 minimum settlement.

Comparatively, the FCA may lead to fines of up to triple program's loss in addition to more than $22,000 per claim filed, based on the inflation-adjusted rate for 2019.[242] That a claim results from an AKS or Stark Law violation may result in bootstrap liability under the civil FCA as well as the AKS or Stark Law if it is found to be false or fraudulent. AKS and Stark Law penalties are also high, with AKS CMPs of up to three times per kickback and $50,000 per violation while Stark Law violations could lead to fines of $15,000 for knowing violations and fines of $100,000 for each arrangement willfully circumventing the law. Because of the significant monetary penalties and other penalties that may come with

---

[242] Previously under the Updated Self-Disclosure Protocol, claims under the FCA could lead to fines of up to three times a program's loss in addition to $11,000 per claim filed. For claims made after November 2, 2015, DOJ issued updates adjusted for inflation in its regulations. Dep't of Justice, Civil Monetary Penalties Inflation Adjustment, 83 Fed. Reg. 3,944-3,948 (Jan. 29, 2018), https://www.gpo.gov/fdsys/pkg/FR-2018-01-29/pdf/2018-01464.pdf.

violations of the fraud and abuse laws, OIG's SDP offers an attractive alternative for Providers willing to self-disclose violations rather than face a potential government-initiated investigation and formal litigation.

B.   Who May Use the SDP?

All providers subject to CMPs may use the SDP process, and OIG expects Providers using the SDP to disclose, with good–faith willingness, within the CMP law's six-year statute of limitations as described in the Social Security Act.[243] Proactive steps by providers to disclose and resolve issues reflect good–faith intentions. Note that the SDP may not be used for errors or mistakes with no potential violation of CMP laws, disclosures solely involving Stark Law liability, or to request an OIG Advisory Opinion about whether a violation occurred. Those using the SDP should ensure that corrective action has been taken to resolve the conduct leading to the potential violation before the disclosure. As for improper kickback arrangements, the disclosing provider must take corrective action and end the arrangement within 90 days of the SDP submission. In all cases, the provider should investigate and evaluate overpayment, noncompliant activity, or misconduct and address issues diligently and thoroughly.

C.   What Requirements Must SDP Disclosures Fulfill?

Disclosures may be submitted online or by mail, and should contain substantive information provided to OIG by a good–faith effort to bring the matter to OIG's attention for resolution. OIG stresses cooperation and coordination between providers and government entities. Any effective disclosure by a provider should include a report to the OIG on the findings of an internal investigation, or a certification that an internal investigation will be completed within 90 days of submission. Additionally, the submission must include

  a. The name and contact information of the disclosing provider;

  b. The name and contact information of any affected corporate divisions, departments or branches of the disclosing provider;

  c. The name and contact information of the disclosing provider's designated representative;

  d. A statement of the details of the conduct (e.g., the types of claims, the period, the implicated persons or entities, the transactions or events giving rise to the matter);

---

[243] 42 U.S.C. §1320a-7a(c)(1).

e. A statement of the laws potentially violated by the conduct;

f. A statement of the federal healthcare programs affected by the conduct;

g. An estimate of the damages caused by the conduct;

h. A description of the disclosing provider's corrective action upon discovery of the conduct;

i. A statement of whether the disclosing provider has knowledge that the matter is under current investigation by a government agency, contractor, or other inquiry related to a federal healthcare program;

j. The name of an individual authorized to enter into a settlement agreement on behalf of the disclosing provider; and

k. A certification by the disclosing provider or authorized representative stating that the submission was made truthfully and in good faith.

As noted above, there are additional requirements in the SDP for conduct involving:

A. false billing, the submission of improper claims to federal healthcare programs;

B. excluded persons, arrangements involving those appear on OIG's LEIE; and

C. both the AKS and Stark Law.

The provider making a disclosure must be prepared to repay any overpayments received as well as a CMP settlement for the damages for the disclosed conduct. Generally OIG assesses a multiplier of 1.5 times the single damages. But the calculation is subject to the OIG's discretion and OIG may also determine that no potential fraud liability exists for conduct disclosed under the SDP in which case the matter would be referred to the appropriate payor for acceptance of the overpayment and no CMP release will be provided. In cases of AKS submissions under the SDP, OIG generally requires a minimum settlement amount of $50,000. For all other matters under the SDP, OIG typically requires a minimum $10,000 settlement amount.

If the provider cannot pay the settlement amount, OIG will complete a financial hardship analysis requiring extensive financial information along with a certification of truthfulness about the financial disclosures. These providers should mention their inability to pay as early as possible in the SDP submission process and include an assessment of what amount they believe they can pay. OIG provides summaries of the information about self-disclosure settlements with providers made under the SDP on its website.[244]

D.   What are the Benefits of the SDP?

Several benefits of the SDP may motivate providers to take advantage of the process. Prompt disclosure through the SDP may reduce the likelihood of an external investigation or other civil and criminal liabilities. Absent extraordinary circumstances, a key benefit and consideration of disclosing through the SDP includes a presumption against requiring a corporate integrity agreement. Self-disclosure also may suspend providers' obligation to return overpayments within the 60-day period. Moreover, proactive conduct and a diligent response reflected in providers' use of the SDP process may lead to an expedited disposition and resolution that saves providers valuable time and resources defending known compliance issues. Aside from quicker timelines, the SDP process may result in lower damages with payments of 1.5 times the amount improperly paid rather than potential treble damages plus a per claim penalty.

Additionally, given the focus on corporate compliance and individual accountability, the SDP allows providers greater privacy and control over publicity and the resulting narrative surrounding the potentially fraudulent conduct. This could blunt the effect of prospective whistleblowers, parties who may file lawsuits, and those wishing to call a provider's reputation into question. Despite the benefits of using the SDP, there are also certain limitations that providers should consider when weighing the pros and cons of self-disclosure.

E.   What are the Limitations of the SDP?

Although there are many advantages to using the SDP, there are certain limitations to the process as well. Some of these limitations include the potential for increased government scrutiny that will no doubt occur through the SDP process. There is an expectation of cooperation, and a self-disclosure through the SDP is not a rubber stamp resolution. A provider will likely receive questions following OIG's review of the detailed submission. There may be questions about the provider's investigation, corrective actions, disciplinary actions, as well as sampling methodology and extrapolation. A provider is expected to cooperate with requests for information. In some cases, these requests could uncover deficiencies in the provider's investigative process or uncover other potential

---

[244]   *Provider Self-Disclosure Settlements*, Office of the Inspector Gen. Dep't of Health & Human Servs., https://oig.hhs.gov/fraud/enforcement/cmp/psds.asp (2018).

issues that may need to be disclosed. The provider must also certify to the potentially fraudulent conduct and cannot use a defense of mistake. The SDP requires that providers acknowledge the potential violation of law to benefit from the SDP. Likewise, a provider using the SDP cannot simultaneously submit a disclosure while seeking an Advisory Opinion in hopes that the conduct would not be considered a potential violation. Finally, providers must understand that each matter is reviewed and evaluated on its own merit which means that results cannot be guaranteed. These are not reasons to avoid using the SDP, but they are realities providers should be aware of to make sure that they enter into the SDP with a full understanding of the process.

Perhaps most important, while the SDP will lead to a public disclosure which can foreclose a whistleblower who has not yet filed a lawsuit, and while the Government has not shown a desire to prosecute entities which voluntarily self-disclose, the SDP does not legally immunize an entity from an FCA action.

F. Significant Statistics and Examples Involving the SDP.

The number of providers using the SDP process has expanded over the years. In 1998, only about 20 Providers made submissions using the SDP process.[245] This number increased as the SDP process played a more crucial role for providers interested in evidencing a commitment to corporate compliance. Among SDP settlements that OIG has published information about on its website, about 61 SDP settlements were reached in 2016 and 50 in 2017.[246]

Aside from its website, OIG also reports the results of SDP disclosure settlements to Congress in its semiannual report. During the semiannual reporting period from April 2017 to September 2017, Providers submitting to the SDP process led to more than $12,600,000 in HHS receivables through settlements. In 2015, the same reporting period saw the SDP process result in over $46,800,000 in receivables to HHS.

    a.   The SDP process generally takes about a year to resolve. To aid expediency, OIG streamlined its internal processes to reduce the average time a case is pending with OIG from the time it is accepted into the SDP. Still, providers should prepare themselves for a commitment that may potentially involve tangential issues that require significant efforts and time. In 2017, a group of affiliated home health providers in Tennessee entered into an FCA settlement agreement with

---

[245] Gov't Accountability Office Report to Congr. Requesters, *Medicare: Early Evidence of Compliance Program Effectiveness is Inconclusive*, 16-17 (Apr. 1999), available at http://www.gao.gov/archive/1999/he99059.pdf.

[246] *Provider Self-Disclosure Settlements*, Office of the Inspector Gen. Dep't of Health & Human Servs., https://oig.hhs.gov/fraud/enforcement/cmp/psds.asp (2018).

the DOJ and OIG after a self-disclosure process.[247] Although the voluntary disclosure was made in November 2010 after the potential violations were identified during an internal audit, supplements and a resolution took nearly seven years. The settlement of about $1,800,000 resolved self-disclosed, potential violations of the Stark Law, the AKS, and a failure to meet certain Medicare coverage and payment requirements for home health services. While most SDP processes do not require such a long period, the risk should be a factor for Providers contemplating use of the SDP to consider.

b. The SDP process may involve minor or large damages amounts. Although unusual because the case did not even meet the $10,000 minimum threshold, Health Management Services, Inc. agreed to pay $6,545.61 after it made a SDP submission disclosing that two individuals altered the continual positive airway pressure downloads for patients to obtain Federal healthcare program reimbursement.[248] On the other hand, Northwell Health Inc. agreed to pay $12,736,087 for a self-disclosure settlement over claims submitted that Northwell Health Inc. knew or should have known did not meet the Medicare Local Coverage Determination because of inadequate documentation.[249] This wide range in settlement amounts reflect both the flexibility of the SDP as a tool for providers, and the incentives to use the SDP process that may draw many providers.

c. The SDP process may be used by providers that include suppliers and vendors, not just hospitals or other more conventional "healthcare providers." For example, Theratech, Inc. self-disclosed to OIG that it submitted claims to Medicare for transcutaneous electrical nerve stimulators units and supplies without adequate documentation such as detailed physician orders and clinical documentation from patients' medical records to support

---

[247] *East Tennessee-Based Home Health Providers Agree To Pay U.S. $1.8 Million To Settle False Claims Act Liability*, U.S. Attorney's Office, E. Dist. of Tenn., Sept. 5, 2017, https://www.justice.gov/usao-edtn/pr/east-tennessee-based-home-health-providers-agree-pay-us-18-million-settle-false-claims.

[248] *Provider Self-Disclosure Settlements*, Office of the Inspector Gen. Dep't of Health & Human Servs., https://oig.hhs.gov/fraud/enforcement/cmp/psds.asp (2018).

[249] *Id.*

medical necessity and coverage.[250] Theratech agreed to pay $6,646,911 to resolve its CMP liability. Providers should keep in mind that many entities may use the SDP process.

G. Tips for Success.

To provide assistance with its SDP process, OIG issued guidance for users of the SDP through internet resources. The *Tips for Success in the OIG Self-Disclosure Protocol* guidance offers advice,[251] stating that providers:

a. should be careful not to self-disclose prematurely, it is necessary to complete an investigation and damages audit or commit to completing one within three months after acceptance;

b. need to know that full cooperation is essential;

c. need to follow all requirements in the SDP and other OIG-issued guidance;

d. must give complete descriptions of the conduct and investigation, including:

   1. What happened?
   2. What is the period?
   3. Why did it happen?
   4. Why is there potential legal liability for the conduct?
   5. Who was involved?
   6. How was the conduct discovered?
   7. What corrective actions have been taken?

e. should identify and specifically point out the fraud laws at issue;

f. should follow the sampling requirements in the SDP;

g. need to note that Stark Law-only conduct without an AKS claim is ineligible for the SDP (i.e., CMS's self-disclosure process addresses Stark-only claims); and

---

[250] *Id.*

[251] *Tips for Success in the OIG Self-Disclosure Protocol,* Office of the Inspector Gen. Dep't of Health & Human Servs., https://oig.hhs.gov/compliance/provider-compliance-training/files/HandoutSDPTips508.pdf.

h. should expect that a disclosure's settlement agreement will result in an amount that is a multiplier of damages, and simple overpayments are not appropriate for the SDP.

H. Conclusion

In a climate of increased government enforcement, it is critical for providers to understand how to respond when significant compliance issues arise. Those steps, often with help from counsel, will include considering various options and strategies for resolving the matter, including self-disclosure. The SDP offers providers an avenue and opportunity to self-report potential fraud involving federal healthcare programs. OIG designed the SDP process, modifying and improving upon it over the years to develop the tool in ways that encourage providers to self-disclose potential violations. While there are benefits to the SDP, there are also drawbacks that providers should consider when deciding whether to use the SDP.

For providers who may be unaware of or unfamiliar with the SDP process, it is especially important to approach self-disclosure with thorough deliberation to avoid errors or poor quality submissions to OIG. When done properly, a submission gives the provider an opportunity to describe for OIG its active efforts to ensure compliance with applicable legal requirements and describe its corporate compliance program and initiatives. Often, a robust compliance program is the reason providers can detect, investigate, assess, and correct compliance issues when they arise. Although decisions related to the SDP process can be challenging, use of the SDP reflects the providers organizational commitment to compliant practices.

CMS Self-Referral Disclosure Protocol

The physician self-referral statute commonly known as the Stark Law, generally prohibits physicians from referring patients to an entity for designated health services when the physician (or the physician's immediate family member) has a financial relationship with the entity. Under the Patient Protection and Affordable Care Act (ACA) the Secretary of HHS had to establish a self-disclosure protocol for all providers and suppliers to self-disclose actual or potential violations of the Stark Law. In September 2010 HHS created the Self-Referral Disclosure Protocol (SRDP) to allow providers to self-disclose such violations and enter into a settlement with CMS. An SRDP submission and later settlement with CMS is intended to resolve the entity's overpayment liability exposure under the arrangement or conduct identified in the self-disclosure.

A. Initial Implementation of SRDP

In March 2012, CMS released two SRDP settlements. In addition to these two new settlements, CMS released its statutorily required *Report to the Congress:*

Implementation of the Medicare Self-Referral Disclosure Protocol. Combined, the settlements and Report offered additional, though limited, insight into the process for disclosing violations of the federal Stark Law to CMS.

In March 2012, CMS reported that it settled violations of the Stark Law disclosed by a physician group practice in Iowa for $74,000. The physician group disclosed under the SRDP that it violated the Stark Law because the compensation methodology for certain employed physicians did not satisfy the requirements of the Stark Law bona fide employment relationship exception.

The same day, CMS also reported that it had settled a Stark Law violation disclosed under the SRDP by an Arizona acute–care hospital. The hospital disclosed a single arrangement with a physician for the provision of *locum tenens* hospitalist services that did not meet the personal services arrangements exception. The violation was settled for $22,000.

One day after announcing the settlements, CMS posted on its website the statutorily required Report describing the implementation of the SRDP and the status of the disclosures under the SRDP to date.[252] As required by the ACA, the SRDP was developed by CMS to allow healthcare providers to disclose violations of the federal Stark Law. According to the Report, CMS had received 150 disclosures from 148 providers, including 125 hospitals, since the SRDP was first published in 2011. Seven of the disclosures were resolved through settlements, 50 were still under CMS review, 61 required more information from the disclosing party, nine disclosures were withdrawn by the disclosing party, three had been referred to law enforcement for resolution and 20 were in "administrative hold." The Report provided little more information about the disclosed arrangements, other than to note that the most common violations involve a failure to comply with the Stark Law personal services exception, nonmonetary compensation exception, rental of office space exception and physician recruitment arrangement exception.[253]

The Report reiterated that CMS has the authority to "reduce disclosed overpayments in a manner that is proportional to the nature of the disclosed violations."[254] Before the enactment of the ACA, CMS had limited authority to compromise overpayments associated with violations of the Stark Law, and alternative avenues to disclose violations were not appropriate in all circumstances or were foreclosed because of the violation. As discussed in the

---

[252] *Report to the Congress: Implementation of the Medicare Self-Referral Disclosure Protocol*, United States Department of Health and Human Services, https://www.cms.gov/Medicare/Fraud-and-Abuse/PhysicianSelfReferral/Downloads/CMS-SRDP-Report-to-Congress.pdf, last viewed on September 11, 2019.
[253] *Id.* at 9.
[254] *Id.* at 1.

Report, CMS reviewed the facts and circumstances surrounding each disclosed matter to determine an appropriate resolution consistent with the criteria set forth in the SRDP.[255]

Because CMS released little information about the 150 disclosed arrangements and seven settlements, it remained difficult for disclosing parties to predict how CMS might settle other SRDP cases. The settlement amounts did seem to provide some preliminary indications that CMS was using its authority under the ACA to reduce the penalties for providers that voluntarily come forward and disclose Stark Law violations under the SRDP. In addition, the Report and other communications and education from CMS related to the SRDP did reveal some best practices when disclosing under the SRDP. For instance, providers should make sure their disclosures are structured in conformity with the SRDP, include an element-by-element legal analysis of each applicable exception under the Stark Law and detail both its ongoing corporate responsibility activities and how each disclosed arrangement was terminated or remedied.[256]

B. <u>CMS's Voluntary Physician-Owned Hospital SRDP</u>

In 2015, CMS announced a voluntary SRDP allowing physician-owned hospitals and rural providers an alternative way to remedy certain issues of noncompliance with the Stark Law.[257] CMS provided special instructions for a voluntary SRDP for physician-owned hospitals that have been noncompliant with the requirement that physician ownership and investment interests must be disclosed on hospital websites and other advertisements.

To be eligible for the SRDP opportunity, the physician-owned or rural hospital cannot disclose noncompliance with any other Stark Law requirements. The CMS guidance lists the information that would need to be submitted with the disclosure, including identifying information for the hospital, any period of noncompliance and other certifications for the hospital's period of noncompliance. CMS does not require any Medicare referral dollar calculations to be submitted along with this voluntary SRDP submission.[258]

Physician-owned hospitals that believe they may have had a lapse in compliance with the website and advertising requirements of the Stark Law are encouraged to use the SRDP. Because Medicare referral information is not required as a part

---

[255] *Id.* at 7.
[256] *Id.* at 5.
[257] *Instructions for Disclosures of Noncompliance with the Physician Self-Referral Law Arising* Solely *from a Violation of 42 C.F.R. § 411.362(b)(3)(ii)(C)*, https://www.cms.gov/Medicare/Fraud-and-Abuse/PhysicianSelfReferral/Downloads/Disclosures-Noncompliance-Instructions.pdf, last viewed September 11, 2019.
[258] *Id.* at 1.

of the disclosure, preparation of such disclosures and review by CMS should be more efficient than under the traditional SRDP model. Even so, physician-owned hospitals, with additional Stark Law compliance issues, should consider a potential disclosure to CMS under the traditional SRDP process.

C. The Updated SRDP

In 2016, CMS updated its SRDP when it posted a new form to be used as part of the SRDP process.[259] According to CMS, the SRDP Form tries to "streamline and simplify" the SRDP process. CMS cited a need to "reduce the burden on disclosing parties by reducing the amount of information…required for submissions to the SRDP."[260] The SRDP Form became mandatory (with limited exceptions) for all voluntary Stark Law self-disclosures on June 1, 2017.[261] While the SRDP Form streamlines some aspects of the SRDP process, certain questions on the SRDP Form may present challenges for healthcare entities when disclosing potential or actual violations of the Stark Law.

D. Key Changes and Challenges Related to the Updated SRDP Form

The updated SRDP process provides both CMS and healthcare providers with a standardized (and mandatory) means of disclosing potential or actual Stark Law violations. Under this updated process, the disclosing party must include in any disclosure:

1. a SRDP Disclosure Form;

2. a Physician Information Form(s);

3. a Financial Analysis Worksheet (with certain exceptions); and

4. a certification about the accuracy and truthfulness of the information submitted with the disclosure. A disclosing party may also submit an optional cover letter with more information surrounding the self-disclosure.

While requiring the information in a different format, the updated SRDP Form continues to request much of the same information from the previous SRDP. There are several key changes that may present challenges for healthcare entities in assembling the requisite information for a self-disclosure. A discussion of these

---

[259] *CMS Voluntary Self-Referral Disclosure Protocol*, Form CMS-10328 (XX/XX).
[260] 81 Fed. Reg. 88 p. 27451-27452 (May 6, 2016).
[261] https://www.cms.gov/Medicare/Fraud-and-Abuse/PhysicianSelfReferral/Self_Referral_Disclosure_Protocol.html, last viewed September 11, 2019.

key changes and the potential challenges the changes may present for providers follows.

E.   Pervasiveness of Noncompliance

Perhaps most notably, the SRDP Form now requires providers to identify the "pervasiveness of noncompliance" as part of any disclosure to CMS. For the purposes of the SRDP, "pervasiveness means how common or frequent the disclosed noncompliance was in comparison with similar financial relationships between the disclosing party and physicians." Providers may report based on the type of noncompliance (e.g., lease arrangements) or in the aggregate, but they must explain how the calculations were determined. CMS also states that the pervasiveness question should be answered with a quantitative analysis and provides examples of that pervasiveness analyses in the SRDP Form. For example, an entity may disclose that eight percent of the entity's medical director arrangements were potentially noncompliant and were therefore disclosed on the SRDP Form. Depending on the size of the organization, it can be a cumbersome process to identify all financial arrangements in place during the applicable lookback period and may require a thorough review of historical documentation and records. Strategies for calculating the pervasiveness of noncompliance may also vary based on the facts and circumstances. While CMS does not provide details on how it calculates proposed settlements under the SRDP, CMS will likely consider the pervasiveness of noncompliance as a factor when calculating a proposed settlement amount and when considering imposition of a corporate integrity agreement related to the disclosed inappropriate arrangements.[262]

F.   Physician Information Form

The new SRDP Form includes a Physician Information Form (PIF). Providers must submit a separate PIF for each physician involved in a noncompliant arrangement. While prior CMS self-disclosures may have only identified an inappropriate arrangement by the physician group involved, CMS notes now that for any stand–in–the–shoes scenario, each physician must have a separate PIF. The PIF must include a narrative explanation of the arrangement, information on the rate of compensation or the amount of remuneration provided under the problematic arrangement, and the date of discovery of the arrangement. Healthcare entities often contract with physician groups but may not have specific information about the ownership structures or individual physician owners of the group. This information is also rarely available from public resources. This may present challenges in the self-disclosure process as providers work to identify all physicians that must be in the PIFs and may require providers to have potentially sensitive discussions with the physician groups involved to obtain this information. Explicit identification of the date of discovery of a potentially

---

[262]   *CMS Voluntary Self-Referral Disclosure Protocol*, Form CMS-10328 (XX/XX).

problematic arrangement may also have implications for disclosing entities as the information may implicate the 60-day retained overpayment rule.

G.   Financial Analysis Worksheet

Any disclosing provider must also submit a financial analysis of the potential overpayment in Excel-compatible format. For each physician in the disclosure, the worksheet must include:

1. the physician's name;

2. NPI;

3. the date that the overpayment associated with the physician was identified; and

4. the overpayment arising from the physician's prohibited referrals, itemized by calendar year.

The worksheet must also describe the methodology used and specifically address whether estimates were used and, if so, how they were calculated. This new formatting requirement will make it easier for CMS to verify the data provided by the disclosing party and thus make it all the more important for the disclosing party to provide thorough and accurate data. The Financial Analysis Worksheet may also provide an opportunity for CMS to more easily use data mining or perform their own financial calculations as part of their settlement analysis.

The updated SRDP Form, while providing some administrative clarity for both disclosing providers and CMS, raises concerns about the proper documentation and tracking of physician arrangements. In many ways, the new SRDP Form requires more factual background about each arrangement and how each arrangement connects with the provider's other physician contracts than was previously necessary. It will be important for providers to assess how to best present this information in a self-disclosure.

Healthcare entities entering into arrangements with physician organizations should be careful to request sufficient information about the physician owners to enable the entity to consider the potential scope of disclosure upon noncompliance. Asking for this information at the onset of a relationship with a physician entity may avoid potentially tense discussions with the physicians if a self-disclosure is required. And all healthcare providers will want to keep thorough and accurate records of all financial relationships with physicians.

10. THE STARK LAW AND THE ANTI-KICKBACK STATUTE

By Ritu Kaur Cooper and Alyssa James

The federal Stark Law is a civil statute which prohibits a physician (or a physician's immediate family member) who has a direct or indirect financial relationship with an entity from referring to the entity for the provision of certain designated health services (DHS) payable by Medicare, unless the financial relationship meets a specific exception to the Stark Law. The term "financial relationship" is broad and includes almost any remuneration or thing of value provided to a physician. If an arrangement subject to the Stark Law does not comply with every element of the particular exception applicable to the arrangement, then a violation of the Stark Law has occurred.[263]

The AKS prohibits the knowing offer, payment, solicitation, or receipt of a direct or indirect payment in return for referrals for items or services paid for, in whole or in part, under a federal healthcare program.[264]

Alleged violations of the Stark Law and the AKS are common footholds for FCA lawsuits, particularly by whistleblowers. These cases arise both as *qui tam* lawsuits and as retaliation lawsuits. (i.e., those alleging that an employee was fired for investigating unlawful kickbacks or compensation arrangements).

It is clear from recent cases that courts are looking carefully at FCA cases based on the AKS and the Stark Law. Courts are viewing these cases through the lens of safe harbors under AKS and exceptions under the Stark Law provided by regulations and, perhaps even more important, are rejecting cases based on procedural missteps and technical issues with the complaints. These recent cases may provide peace of mind to providers in response to prior trends that often seemed to side with the Government and whistleblowers being more lenient on procedural missteps and technical issues.

But nearly all of potential Stark Law and AKS cases brought under the FCA do not end up shaping the caselaw landscape at all. Many FCA cases are settled between the defendant and the Government before trial. A primary reason for this is the uncertainty associated with the healthcare FCA landscape and the high dollar damages that may be awarded by juries.

An unprecedented update to the fraud and abuse landscape is the passage of Section 8122 of the SUPPORT for Patients and Communities Act, also referred to as the Eliminating Kickbacks in Recovery Act of 2018 (EKRA). EKRA

---

[263] 42 C.F.R. § 1395nn(a)(2).
[264] 42 USC § 1320a-7b(b) (2011).

provides for criminal penalties for taking or paying any remuneration (including kickbacks). EKRA applies to laboratories, recovery homes, and clinical treatment facilities and is expected to have vast implications for healthcare organizations that deal with these provider types. Because of the recent passage of EKRA in October 2018, it remains to be seen what the overall impact of this law may be.

A.   Fraud Against Another Provider is not Fraud Against the Government.

In *Fakorede v. Mid-South Heart Center, P.C.*,[265] the Sixth Circuit ruled that alleged fraud against another healthcare provider does not necessarily allege fraud against the Government. The case, brought as a FCA retaliation case, involved a physician who had been recruited by the local county hospital district and employed by Mid-South Heart Center. The physician claimed that his employment was terminated after he raised issues to his employer about AKS and Stark Law violations. Under the recruitment arrangement among Mid-South Heart Center, the county hospital district, and Dr. Fakorede, the hospital district agreed to provide an income guarantee for the physician. Dr. Fakorede discovered that Mid-South Heart Center improperly attributed over $200,000 in expenses to him during the first year, resulting in the hospital district providing additional assistance beyond what would have been required.

While Dr. Fakorede was terminated after raising concerns about the expense allocation, the Sixth Circuit determined that he failed to state a claim because there was no evidence that he had alerted his employer before his termination of any potential fraud against the federal government. The Sixth Circuit thus concluded that the FCA's anti-retaliation provisions did not protected him.[266]

The dissenting opinion noted that Dr. Fakorede did make many references to an "illegal kickback scheme" and a "violation of Stark Laws." The physician knew that these types of violations can "taint" providers' claims submitted to federal healthcare programs. The dissenting opinion also noted that FCA retaliation claims do not require that the pleading be made with particularity.

B.   Advice of Counsel Defense may be Insufficient.

In *United States ex rel. Lutz v. Berkeley HeartLab, Inc.*,[267] the whistleblower and the Government alleged that the Defendants violated the AKS by participating in three separate schemes: 1) physicians were paid process and handling (P&H) fees to induce the ordering of additional blood tests; 2) Defendants waived TriCare copayments and deductibles to induce the ordering of tests reimbursable by TriCare; and 3) laboratories paid defendants commissions for marketing blood

---

[265] Fakorede v. Mid-South Heart Center, P.C., 2017 WL 4217230 (6th Cir. Sep 22, 2017).

[266] *See* 31, U.S.C. § 3730(h).

[267] *United States ex rel. Lutz v. Berkeley HeartLab, Inc.*, 225 F. Supp. 3d 460 (D.S.C. 2016).

tests with the intent to induce physicians to order blood tests reimbursable by federal healthcare programs. As a result, the Governmen alleged Defendants induced the physicians to order medically unnecessary blood tests paid for by federal healthcare programs.

The Defendants presented an advice of counsel defense, stating that their counsel had advised them on the arrangements at issue. But the court barred this theory because counsel had advised on sales agreements between the Defendants and not about healthcare compliance.[268]

C. Physician Speaking Engagements may Fit into Safe Harbors.

In *United States ex rel. Booker v. Pfizer, Inc.*,[269] the relator claimed that Pfizer engaged physicians to provide event speaking services to induce the physicians to increase prescriptions for a particular Pfizer drug. Pfizer contracted with the physicians for these speaking services and the contracts satisfied the requirements of the AKS personal services and management contracts safe harbors.

The First Circuit held that the whistleblower could not prove that the speaking services arrangements fell outside the applicable AKS safe harbor. While the whistleblower alleged that Pfizer tracked the prescription habits of the event attendees, the First Circuit distinguished this from tracking prescribing practices of event speakers. Tracking speakers rather than attendees may have pointed to that the speaking engagements were intended to increase prescribing patterns.[270]

D. Allegations of False Claims must be Stated with Particularity.

In *United States ex rel. Hirt v. Walgreen Company*,[271] an independent pharmacy owner filed a *qui tam* action against Walgreen Company alleging that Walgreen offered gift cards to potential customers to lure them from competitor pharmacies. The district court held, and Sixth Circuit affirmed, that the whistleblower's complaint failed to identify a single false claim with particularity.

To identify a false claim had been submitted, whistleblowers must be able to provide: names of customers, dates in which customers filled prescriptions, and dates in which claims were submitted to federal healthcare programs.

In contrast, in *United States ex rel. Booker v. Schaeffer*,[272] the district court held that the whistleblowers did plead with sufficient particularity. In *Booker*, the whilstleblower alleged that clinical laboratories and their owners submitted false

---

[268] *Lutz*, 225 F. Supp. 3d at 468.
[269] United States *ex rel.* Booker v. Pfizer, Inc., 847 F.3d 52 (1st Cir. 2017).
[270] *Id.*
[271] United States *ex rel.* Hirt v. Walgreen Co., 846 F.3d 879 (6th Cir. 2017).
[272] United States *ex rel.* Booker v. Schaeffer, 328 F. Supp. 3d 550 (M.D. La. 2018).

claims to Medicare and Medicaid as a result of physicians, who had ownership interests in the laboratories, referring specimens to the clinical laboratories and receiving payments from the laboratories in proportion to the number of private insurance specimens referred to the laboratory. Although the whistleblowers could not plead the exact amounts paid, billing numbers, or dates of the fraudulent billings, the court determined that a strong inference could be made that the claims were submitted to the Government because of the whistleblowers' allegations that the physicians were encouraged to send specimens paid by Medicare and Medicaid to the defendant.[273]

E.   Continued Scrutiny for <u>Arrangements Perceived to Influence Referrals.</u>

Settlements from 2017 to present, including those with Corporate Integrity Agreements (CIAs), continue to emphasize and analyze arrangements that may be perceived as providing remuneration to an individual or entity in exchange for referrals:

- DOJ announced that four San Diego area nursing homes entered into a settlement for $6.9 Million to resolve disputes that nursing home employees offered kickbacks to discharge planners at the hospital in exchange for patient referrals;[274]

- In another DOJ settlement with a healthsystem for $18 million, the parties resolved allegations that the health system offered an interest-free line of credit to HealthNet Inc., Indiana's largest federally qualified health center, in exchange for referrals to a hospital within the health system.[275]

- Two physician groups, EmCare, Inc. and Physician's Alliance Ltd., agreed to pay $29.6 Million and $4 Million respectively for allegedly receiving illegal remuneration in exchange for patient referrals to hospitals. EmCare physicians allegedly received remuneration from hospitals to recommend patients be admitted as inpatients when they should have been treated on an outpatient basis.[276]

---

[273] *Id.* at 557.
[274] Department of Justice, San Diego Nursing Homes Owned by L.A.-Based Brias Management, https://www.justice.gov/usao-cdca/pr/san-diego-nursing-homes-owned-la-based-brius-management-pay-69-million-resolve-kickback.
[275] Department of Justice, Indiana University Health and HealthNet to Pay $18 Million to Resolve Allegations of False Claims, https://www.justice.gov/opa/pr/indiana-university-health-and-healthnet-pay-18-million-resolve-allegations-false-claims.
[276] DOJ, Two Physician Groups Pay Over $33 Million to Resolve Claims Involving HMA Hospitals, https://www.justice.gov/opa/pr/two-physician-groups-pay-over-33-million-resolve-claims-involving-hma-hospitals.

The past three years have brought settlements involving illegal remuneration with laboratories. For example, the OIG concluded that several providers' receipt of point of care test cups at no charge from Millennium Health, LLC f/k/a Millennium Laboratories, Inc. resulted in prohibited referrals.[277] And similarly, Dr. Josette Maria and Maria Medical Center entered into a $60,000 settlement agreement with OIG for among other things, receiving remuneration from laboratory companies in the form of "process and handling" payments in exchange for referring patients for laboratory testing services, paid by Medicare. Going forward, similar arrangements with laboratories likely will be scrutinized under EKRA as well.

While whistleblowers continue to file FCA cases based on alleged Stark Law and AKS violations, courts may be more likely to scrutinize the facts and circumstances to ensure that it is appropriate for the case to continue on procedural grounds. Because of increased enforcement actions over recent years and lucrative settlements awarded to *qui tam* relators, it is no surprise that the number of FCA cases based on Stark Law and AKS violations continues to increase. The checks and balances offered by the courts ensure that only cases that appropriately allege misconduct within the appropriate procedural framework will be permitted to move forward.

---

[277] Here is a listing of the settlements involving Millennium: Advanced Pain Management (APM), a pain management practice with several locations in Arizona, entered into a $186,210.20 settlement agreement with OIG. Parallax Center, Inc. (Parallax), New York, New York, entered into a $64,203.30 settlement agreement with OIG. Addiction Medical Care of Norwalk, Practice Management Associates Norwalk, LLC, Addiction Medical Care of Columbus, and Practice Management Associates, LLC, with locations in Norwalk and Columbus, Ohio, entered into a $79,880.50 settlement agreement with OIG. The Pain Institute, Inc. d/b/a Space Coast Pain Institute, Stanley Golovac, M.D. and Richard Gayles, M.D, Merritt Island, Florida, entered into a $95,302.50 settlement agreement with OIG. AMC - Affordable Medical Care f/k/a Andalusia Medical Center and Dr. Kevin Diel, Opp, Alabama, entered into a $40,500.50 settlement agreement with OIG. Recovery Pathways, LLC (Recovery Pathways), Essexville, Michigan, entered into a $64,555 settlement agreement with OIG. Milind V. Tilak, M.D., Suwarna Tilak, M.D., Doctor's Inlet Pediatrics and Primary Care, P.A., and Avenues Pediatrics and Internal Medicine (collectively, "Doctor's Inlet"), Middleburg and Jacksonville, Florida, entered into a $58,370 settlement agreement with OIG. Ronald Burns, M.D. (Dr. Burns), Phoenix, Arizona, entered into a $75,409.15 settlement agreement with OIG. Tulsa Pain Consultants, Inc., Martin Martucci, M.D., and Andreas Revelis, M.D., Tulsa, Oklahoma, entered into a $98,942.50 settlement agreement with OIG.

11. THE NEW TAX LAW AND THE FCA

By David Honig

The Tax Cuts and Jobs Act (TCJA) was signed into law in 2017. Tucked in the TCJA was a section that made a huge change in how False Claims Act settlements must be structured to preserve deductibility.

FCA settlements usually include compensatory damages as well as fines and penalties. Before the TCJA, compensatory damages paid to the Government in an FCA settlement were deductible as ordinary and necessary business expenses.[278] Fines and penalties were not deductible.[279] In 2014 the First Circuit ruled that, absent an agreement between parties, the taxpayer could prove that an amount greater than single damages could have a compensatory purpose, and therefore be deductible.[280] The Supreme Court also noted that an amount beyond the single damages "is usually necessary to compensate the Government completely for the costs, delays, and inconveniences occasioned by fraudulent claims."[281] It later observed that the FCA's treble damages provision was more than a penalty, as it could include money to pay the whistleblower's share, to make up for the statute's lack of prejudgment interest, and to provide for consequential damages "that typically come with recovery for fraud."[282]

Under the new law, 26 U.S.C. § 162(f), settlement agreements with the Government must explicitly identify the paid as restitution or to come into compliance with the law. In the past, the Government's settlement agreements were specifically agnostic about the tax treatment of amounts paid in FCA settlements, leaving it to the taxpayer to assert what was deductible. Since the passage of the TCJA, the parties entering into an FCA settlement must also specify dollars paid as restitution or for compliance. If an FCA case goes to verdict, the court order must specify the same. The costs of investigation, litigation, and money paid to the Government to reimburse for the costs of investigation or litigation, are no longer deductible. The amended statute is silent on money paid for a whistleblower's fees and costs. Ultimately, the IRS and the Tax Court will need to resolve that issue.

The changes in the Tax Cut and Jobs Act that touch upon the FCA got little attention, but are critical to parties entering into settlements that can reach into the hundreds of millions, and even billions of dollars. Settlements and verdicts now must itemize, with specificity, the amount that is reimbursement or directed

---

[278] 26 U.S.C. § 162(a).
[279] 26 U.S.C. § 162(f).
[280] Fresenius Medical Care Holdings, Inc. v. United States, 763 F.3d 64, 71 (1st Cir. 2014).
[281] United States v. Bornstein, 423 U.S. 303, 315 (1976).
[282] Cook County v. United States *ex rel.* Chandler, 538 U.S. 119, 131 (2003).

to compliance for an FCA defendant to get the benefit of the proper and allowable tax deductions.

12. Attorney's Fees

By David Honig

The FCA includes several subsections addressing costs and attorney's fees. A party liable under the FCA is also "liable to the United States Government for the costs of a civil action brought to recover any such penalty or damages."[283] It awards a successful whistleblower with "an amount for reasonable expenses which the court finds to have been necessarily incurred, plus reasonable attorneys' fees and costs," to be awarded against the defendant.[284] And when the Government does not intervene, it awards a prevailing defendant "its reasonable attorneys' fees and expenses if the defendant prevails in the action and the court finds that the claim of the person bringing the action was clearly frivolous, clearly vexatious, or brought primarily for purposes of harassment."[285] If the Government does intervene the Equal Access to Justice Act[286] can provide an award of fees and costs to certain defendants. That statute allows a party in civil litigation against the Government to recover costs, fees, and other expenses if the party prevails and the Government's position was not substantially justified,[287] or in a civil action in which the Government prevails, but its demand was so "substantially in excess of the judgment finally obtained" that it is "unreasonable when compared with such judgment."[288]

A. The Equal Access to Justice Act and the FCA.

The interplay between the FCA and the Equal Access to Justice Act was addressed recently in *United States ex rel. Wall v. Circle C Construction, LLC*.[289] Circle Construction was a family-owned general contractor that built warehouses for the U.S. Army.[290] One of Circle C's subcontractors, Phase Tech, paid two of its electricians $9,900 less than the wages required by the Davis-Bacon Act and the relator brought an FCA case alleging false certification rendering all the work done by Phase Tech "tainted … and therefore worthless."[291] The Government demanded $1.66 million and ultimately won a judgment for $763,000.[292] That judgment was reversed by the Sixth Circuit, which noted, "the problem with [the Government's] theory was that in all of these warehouses, the Government turns

---

[283] 31 U.S.C. § 3729(a)(3).
[284] 31 U.S.C. § 3730(d)(1) and (2).
[285] 31 U.S.C. § 3730(d)(4).
[286] 31 U.S.C. § 3730(g).
[287] 28 U.S.C. § 2412(d)(1)(A).
[288] 28 U.S.C. § 2412(d)(1)(D).
[289] 868 F.3d 466 (6th Cir. 2017).
[290] *Id.* at 468.
[291] *Id.*
[292] *Id.*

on the lights every day." The Court remanded the case for entry of an award of $14,748.

Circle C, which incurred attorney's fees of more than $450,000, sought fees under the Equal Access to Justice Act, based on the disparity between the Government's demand and the final award. The trial court found that the Government's position had not been unreasonable because the trial court agreed with the Government. The Court of Appeals did not agree. The Government argued that the EAJA did not apply because the FCA's attorney's-fee section was entitled "Fees and expenses to prevailing defendant,"[293] and Circle C did not prevail. The Court rejected that argument because the basic rules of statutory construction instruct that a title "cannot limit the plain meaning of the text,"[294] and the text incorporates all of the EAJA.[295]

The Sixth Circuit did not mince words in its determination that the Government's demand was not reasonable, and thus Circle C was entitled to fees. First, it noted that "the Government's demand for $1.66 million as compensation for Phase Tech's $9,900 underpayment of its electricians, in a project spanning seven years, [was] fairyland rather than actual."[296] It went on to say, "a longer answer begins with the observation that actual damages are a simple concept, familiar to any first-year student in law school. [They are] the difference in value between what the Government bargained for and what the Government received."[297] The Government got the buildings and all but $9,900 of the wages, so that was the proper measure of damages.[298]

The Government next argued that Circle C was barred from recovery because, by the very definition of the FCA, it had been found to "knowingly" make false claims against the Government. The Sixth Circuit just as easily swatted that argument down, noting that "knowledge" under the FCA includes recklessness, which is "a less stringent standard than bad faith."[299]

---

[293] 31 U.S.C. § 3730(g).
[294] *Wall*, 868 F.3d at 469. citing *Penn. Dep't of Corr. v. Yeskey*, 524 U.S. 206, 212, 118 S. Ct. (1952).
[295] *Id.*
[296] *Id.* at 470. (quoting *Wall*, 813 F.3d at 618).
[297] *Id.* (quoting United States *ex rel.* Roby v. Boeing Co., 302 F.3d 637, 646 (6th Cir. 2002)).
[298] *Id.*
[299] *Id.*, (quoting United States v. Wallace, 964 F.2d 1214, 1219 (D.C. Cir. 1992)).

Finally, in response to the Government's argument that a fee award "would have a chilling effect on its efforts to vigorously enforce the False Claim Act,"[300] the court simply responded, "one should hope so."[301]

B. Attorney's Fees and Frivolous Pleadings.

As noted above, fee-shifting may also occur from whistleblower to defendant, if the defendant can show that the action "was clearly frivolous, clearly vexatious, or bought primarily for the purposes of harassment."[302] In *In re: Natural Gas Royalties Qui Tam Litigation*[303] the Tenth Circuit considered more than $20 million in attorney's fees awards in a case that lasted more than 20 years.

Jack Grynberg, the whistleblower, originally sued 70 different natural gas companies, alleging they under-measured gas extracted under federal lease agreements, thereby paying less than what was owed to the Government. The original complaint was dismissed for misjoinder—the whistleblower alleged the same scheme but no connection between Defendants, and failure to plead fraud with particularity. Grynberg then filed 73 different lawsuits against more than 300 natural gas companies. The cases were consolidated in Multi-District Litigation in the federal district court for the District of Wyoming. The second complaint included a misleading attachment that inaccurately alleged royalty payments to the named defendants, and as a result the Defendants' motion to dismiss was denied. But their motion for summary judgment alleging Grynberg was not an original source, and was therefore barred, was granted.[304] The trial court awarded Defendants more than $20 million in attorney's fees, both for their actions at the trial court level and on the first appeal. Grynberg appealed, arguing both that his lawsuit was not frivolous and that the trial court lacked statutory authority to impose appellate attorney's fees.

The Tenth Circuit found that the trial court did not abuse its discretion in finding that the claims were frivolous. Grynberg's disclosure to the Government did not show that any Defendants did anything to cause mismeasurement, and the exhibit that allowed him to survive a motion to dismiss "intentionally distorted the ... data," leading the Court to conclude it was an "outright fabrication designed to mislead [the court] into believing Grynberg's allegations were based on something more than complete speculation."[305] Grynberg continued to press his case, even after warnings from an expert group with applicable experience and after failing to comply with the Government's request for factual support for his

---

[300] *Id.* at 472.
[301] *Id.*
[302] 31 U.S.C. § 3730(d)(4).
[303] 845 F.3d 1010 (10th Cir. 2017).
[304] *In re Nat. Gas Royalties*, 562 F.3d 1032, 1038 (10th Cir. 2009).
[305] 845 F.3d at 1018. (quoting *In re Nat. Gas Royalties Qui Tam Litigation*, 2011 WL 12854134 at *6-7 ¶ 25-26).

allegations.[306] The Court affirmed the award of attorney's fees to Defendants on their motions to dismiss and for summary judgment. But it reversed the award of appellate-related fees, ruling that no statute authorized the trial court to enter such an award–the fees should have been requested from the Court of Appeals.[307]

In *Amphastar Pharmaceuticals Inc. v. Aventis Pharma SA*,[308] a case brought under the pre-2010 version of the FCA and thus subject to the public disclosure bar, the trial court dismissed Amphastar's claims, finding that the underlying allegations had been publicly disclosed and Amphastar was not the original source. The trial court refused to award Aventis its attorney's fees as the prevailing party, finding that was bound by *Branson v. Nott*[309] and it could not do so unless the decision was on the merits. The Ninth Circuit reversed, finding that the "on the merits" rule of *Branson* was superseded by Supreme Court decision in *CRST Van Expedited Inc. v. E.E.O.C.*[310] It also found granting attorney's fees for the filing of a lawsuit subject to the public disclosure bar would help meet "one of the key purposes of the 1986 amendments to the False Claims Act, ... discourag[ing] parasitic lawsuits."[311]

Even where a whistleblower's action is not frivolous, a prevailing defendant is entitled to certain taxable costs.[312] In *United States ex rel. King v. Solvay Pharmaceuticals, Inc.*,[313] the whistleblower appealed the prevailing defendant's award of more than $230,000 in costs. The whistleblower argued that documents were only "necessarily obtained for use in the case," the proper standard, if they were used at trial or as exhibits in a motion for summary judgment. The Fifth Circuit rejected that argument, finding that a document a party "reasonably expected to be used for trial or trial preparation at the time it was obtained" also met the standard.[314]

C.   Reduced Fees for Reduced Results.

That a whistleblower prevails in an FCA case does not necessarily require an award of all requested attorney's fees. Courts apply the lodestar method to determine the reasonable fee for services, and sometimes that can lead to a

---

[306] *Id.* at *8 ¶¶34-35.
[307] 845 F.3d at 1025.
[308] 856 F.3d 696 (9th Cir. 2017).
[309] 62 F.3d 287, 293 (9th Cir. 1995).
[310] 578 U.S. ___, 136 S. Ct. 1642, 1646 (2016).
[311] *Amphastar*, 856 F.3d at 710. (quoting United States v. Johnson Controls, Inc., 457 F.3d 1009, 1017 (9th Cir. 2006)).
[312] 28 U.S.C. § 1920; Fed.R.Civ.P. 54(d)(1).
[313] 871 F.3d 318 (5th Cir. 2018).
[314] *Id.* at 335. (quoting United States *ex rel.* Long v. GSDMIdea City, LLC, 807 F.3d 125, 130 (5th Cir. 2015)).

lowered fee award. This was seen in two recent appellate cases: *United States ex rel Sant v. Biotronik, Inc.*[315] and *United States ex rel. Christiansen v. Everglades College, Inc.*[316]

In *Christiansen*, the Government first refused to intervene and the whistleblowers took the case to trial, where they won no damages and a mere $11,000 in penalties. While on appeal, the Government settled the case with the defendant for $335,000. The whistleblowers sought more than $1 million in attorney's fees and $76,000 in litigation costs. The trial court awarded them $60,000 in fees and $27,000 in costs, given their limited success at trial.[317] The whistleblowers sought additional fees after the settlement with the Government, arguing the settlement occurred because of their appeal.[318]

Whistleblowers alleged the court should consider the amount of recovery in awarding fees for whistleblower cases. They argued reducing awards in successful FCA cases would contradict public policy, as it would deter potential whistleblowers and their attorneys.[319] The Eleventh Circuit rejected the argument, noting that civil-rights cases, too, serve important public needs, and questioning "even why that alleged difference should matter for the award of attorneys' fees."[320]

The decision in *Sant* was more straightforward. The Government intervened and settled the case for a low amount. Sant's attorneys submitted a fee request for more than $1 million, which the trial court reduced both because the whistleblower achieved only limited success, and because of whistleblower's attorneys' "vague billing entries, unnecessary tasks, block billing, and work which should have been delegated to a non-attorney."[321] The whistleblower appealed.

The Ninth Circuit, also relying on *Hensley*, approved the reduction for limited success.[322] It also approved the reduction for deficiency in the billing records.[323]

A different type of attorneys' fees dispute can arise when the whistleblower and the Government disagree about the whistleblower's share of an award. In *Taxpayers Against Fraud*, the whistleblowers argued they should receive a larger percentage of the settlement, and then claimed they were entitled to their attorneys' fees for litigating that dispute.[324] The Ninth Circuit noted that the

---

[315] 2017 WL 4978775, Case Nos. 15-17320, 17391 (9th Cir. Oct. 31, 2017).
[316] 855 F.3d 1279 (11th Cir. 2017).
[317] *Id.* at 1285.
[318] *Id.*
[319] *Id.* at 1293.
[320] *Id.*
[321] 2017 WL 4978775, *1.
[322] *Id.*
[323] *Id.*
[324] 41 F.3d at 1045.

dispute was between the whistleblower and the government, and the defendant, which settled the case to minimize loss and avoid additional litigation, "had no legal standing or right to participate in the proceedings."[325] The Court thus ruled, the Defendant should not need to pay the fees for the prevailing parties' collateral litigation.[326]

D. Attorney's Fees for Attorney Relators

As discussed in Chapter 4, *A New Kind of Whistle Blower*, attorneys are now taking on the role of whistleblower, as well as counsel. That raises a new question, how are whistleblowers who act as counsel to be rewarded, by the whistleblower's share, by attorney's fees, or both? That question was answered recently by the Illinois Supreme Court, interpreting Illinois FCA, which closely mirrors the Federal statute.

In *Illinois ex rel. Schad, Diamond & Shedden, P.C. v. My Pillow, Inc.*,[327] the Court considered the case of a *qui tam* suite brought by Stephen Diamond.[328] Diamond brought the action based on My Pillow's failure to collect state taxes for sales at craft shows, online, and by telephone.[329] All the purchases identified in the complaint were made by Diamond, either to the firm or to his home.[330] Diamond, as well as two other attorneys in the firm, testified as witnesses. Diamond's ultimate petition for attorney's fees included time as whistleblower, e.g., purchasing pillows, attending craft shows, checking credit card statements, and did not separate that time from the time spent drafting legal pleadings or preparing witness examinations.[331]

The trial court granted Diamond's petition for about $600,000 in fees,[332] in addition to the $266,891 awarded as 30% of the recovery on behalf of the State.[333] On appeal, the appellate court ruled Diamond was entitled to the attorney's fees for outside counsel who assisted in the lawsuit,[334] about $1800,[335] but not those incurred by the himself or his law firm.

The Illinois Supreme Court affirmed the ruling of the appellate court. It began its analysis with Illinois's long-standing ruling barring an attorney from charging fees

---

[325] *Id.*
[326] *Id.*
[327] 2018 IL 122487, 115 NE 3d 923 (2018).
[328] *Id.* at *1.
[329] *Id.* at *2.
[330] *Id.*
[331] *Id.* at *3.
[332] *Id.* at *4.
[333] *Id.* at *2.
[334] *Id.* at *3.
[335] *Id.* at *2.

for representing himself, "This is forbidden by every sound principle of professional morality as well as by the policy of the law."[336] The law did not change over the ensuing centuries. The Court, in *Hamver v. Lentz*,[337] ruled "a lawyer representing himself or herself simply does not incur legal fees."[338] And the United States Supreme Court found similarly, ruling that awarding fees to attorney *pro se* litigants would encourage self-representation, putting into play "the adage that 'a lawyer who represents himself has a fool for a client.'"[339]

While the *Diamond* case was based on Illinois law, the similarity between the state and the federal FCA, as well as controlling U.S. Supreme Court caselaw, suggests that *pro se qui tam* relators will not have any more luck double-dipping in federal court.

E.   Conclusion

Attorneys' fees are a significant portion of any False Claims Act lawsuit. Given both the complexity of the cases and the volume of discovery generated in an action that invites the review of all the claims generated by a defendant, fees in the millions of dollars are not unusual. The FCA and other federal statutes create additional risks and rewards that all litigants, including the Government, should consider when bringing or intervening in FCA actions, when making settlement demands and determining whether to take a case to trial.

---

[336]   Quoting *Willard v. Bassett*, 27 Ill. 37, 38 (Ill. 1861).
[337]   547 N.E.2d 191 (Ill. 1989).
[338]   *Id.* at 62.
[339]   Kay v. Ehrler, 499 U.S. 432, 437 (1991).

13. THE FCA STATUTE OF LIMITATIONS

By David Honig

A statute of limitations is a time limit on the filing of a lawsuit. Such statutes generally run from the event that is the basis for a lawsuit and after the time expires a new action cannot be filed.

Several policy arguments support statutes of limitations. First, a defendant may lose the ability to defend itself when memories have faded and records have been lost because of the passage of time. Second, an alleged victim has his or her own responsibility to bring a timely action, both to allow defense and because, if the act caused sufficient harm to justify a lawsuit, it should also be enough to justify a timely lawsuit. Finally, a party should eventually be allowed to move forward without having to look infinitely backwards at the same time.

The FCA raises unique problems when it comes to its statute of limitations. While such statutes stop running when a case is filed, whistleblower cases are filed under seal. It may be years from the filing date before an FCA defendant even discovers they have been sued. The combination of the seal provision and the statute can mean an FCA defendant may be forced to answer to actions a decade or more before they first hear of a lawsuit. Time is now even longer, because of a recent decision by the United States Supreme Court.

The FCA contains two different statutes of limitations:

> (b) A civil action under section 3730 may not be brought—
>
> 1. more than six years after the alleged false claim, or
>
> 2. more than three years after the date when the Government knew or should have known about the false claim, with a limit of 10 years,

whichever occurs last.[340]

In *United States ex rel. Hunt v. Cochise Consultancy, Inc.*,[341] a whistleblower lawsuit originally filed in Alabama, the trial court considered whether a whistleblower was limited to the six–year statute of limitations, or if he could get the benefit of the additional three–year period. Hunt filed his case, under seal, seven years after the alleged fraud but less than three years after he reported the alleged fraud to the

---

[340] 31 U.S.C. § 3731(b) (2009).
[341] 887 F.3d 1081 (11th Cir. 2018).

Government.³⁴² The Government declined intervention.³⁴³ The trial court dismissed, finding that the additional three years were unavailable to him and that, even if it were, it expired three years from the time Hunt learned of the fraud.³⁴⁴

On appeal, the Eleventh Circuit Court of Appeals began by noting that the statute did not say the additional three–year period could not be applied by whistleblowers when the Government did not intervene.³⁴⁵ The Defendant argued that the extension could not apply to whistleblowers because it is triggered by the Government's knowledge, and thus Congress must have intended that it only apply when the Government is a party.³⁴⁶ The Defendant argued that to rule otherwise would lead to an absurd result.³⁴⁷ The Court disagreed. While in most cases a statute of limitations begins to run when the plaintiff learns about the fraud or claim, in FCA cases the Government is the real party in interest. Thus, it is not unwarranted to peg the statute to the Government's knowledge.³⁴⁸ The Court held that a whistleblower could file a case three years after alerting the Government to the alleged fraud, but no later than 10 years after it occurred.³⁴⁹ The Court recognized that its ruling contradicted decisions in the Fourth Circuit³⁵⁰ and Tenth Circuit.³⁵¹

In May 2019, the Supreme Court published its unanimous opinion affirming the decision of the Eleventh Circuit.³⁵² The Court based its ruling on "fundamental rules of statutory interpretation,"³⁵³ Cochise argued that the additional limitations time in §3731(b)(2) applied only when the Government was a party.³⁵⁴ The Court rejected the argument, finding it would require courts to give different meaning to the phrase "civil action under section 3730," depending on the parties.³⁵⁵ If, on the other hand, "civil action under section 3730" means the same thing at all

---

[342] *Id.* at 1085.
[343] *Id.*
[344] *Id.*
[345] *Id.* at 1089.
[346] *Id.* at 1091.
[347] *Id.*
[348] *Id.*
[349] *Id.* at 1097.
[350] United States *ex rel.* Sanders v. North American Bus Industries, Inc., 546 F.3d 288 (4th Cir. 2008).
[351] United States *ex rel.* Sikkenga v. Regence Bluecross Blueshield of Utah, 472 F.3d 7092 (10th Cir. 2006).
[352] Cochise Consultancy, Inc. et al. v. United States *ex rel.* Hunt, 139 S. Ct. 1507 (2019).
[353] *Id.* p. 5.
[354] *Id.*
[355] *Id.*

times, subsections (1) and (2) apply to all such cases, whether prosecuted by the Government or a whistleblower.[356]

Justice Thomas, writing for the Court, argued that such a literal reading could lead to what Cochise called "counterintuitive results,"[357] allowing a whistleblower who is fully aware of the alleged fraud at the moment it occurred to have up to 10 years to sue, so long as the government did not discovery it in the interim.[358] Quoting *Exxon Mobile Corp. v. Allapattah Services, Inc.*,[359] Justice Thomas observed, "a result that 'may seem odd . . . is not absurd.'"[360] If the result is merely odd, but there is "no other plausible interpretation of the text ... the judicial inquiry is complete."[361]

The Court rejected Cochise's secondary argument, that the whistleblower was an official of the United States for the FCA's statute of limitations, because the FCA itself describes whistleblolwer suits as "Actions by Private Persons."[362]

The *Cochise* case is the final word on the FCA's statute of limitations, absent Congressional action. For healthcare providers, this means they may need to answer for events more than a decade before they are served. Document retention policies should be adjusted thus, and changes in information systems should consider the possible need to reach far back in time for the evidence needed to defend against whistleblower lawsuits.

---

[356] *Id.*
[357] *Id.* p. 7.
[358] *Id.* pp. 7-8.
[359] 545 U.S. 546 (2005).
[360] *Cochise*, 139 S. Ct. 1507 at 1513.
[361] *Id.* (quoting *Barnhart v. Sigmon Coal Co.*, 534 U.S. 438, 462 (2002)).
[362] *Id.*, citing 31 U.S.C. §3730(b).

14. Retaliation

By Jonathon A. Rabin

In 1986 a retaliation provision was added to the FCA. The goal was to protect whistleblowers and encourage them to file FCA cases when they discovered fraud against the Government. The retaliation provision was limited to employees and was only directed at actions related to bringing an FCA lawsuit. The 2009 FCA amendments expanded retaliation protections to nonemployees that have enough of a relationship with a defendant to have meaningful knowledge of false claims. A less noticed change also expanded the activity protected under the retaliation provision.

The 1986 version of the FCA stated:

> Any employee who is discharged, demoted, suspended, threatened, harassed, or in any other manner discriminated against in the terms and conditions of employment by his or her employer because of lawful acts done by the employee on behalf of the employee or others in furtherance of an action under this section, including investigation for, initiation of, testimony for, or assistance in an action filed or to be filed under this section, shall be entitled to all relief necessary to make the employee whole.[363]

In 2009, that provision was amended to read:

> Any employee, **contractor, or agent** shall be entitled to all relief necessary to make that employee, **contractor, or agent** whole, if that employee, **contractor, or agent** is discharged, demoted, suspended, threatened, harassed, or in any other manner discriminated against in the terms and conditions of employment . . . because of lawful acts done by the employee, contractor, agent or associated others in furtherance of an action under this section **or other efforts to stop 1 or more violations of this subchapter**.[364]

Much attention focused upon the expansion of the FCA's retaliation provision to include contractors and agents in addition to employees. Since 1986, many retaliation claims were barred when brought by contractors, co-owners, and other

---

[363] 31 U.S.C. § 3730(h) (1986).
[364] 31 U.S.C. § 3730(h)(1) (2009) (emphasis added).

associates, because the statute explicitly applied only to employees.[365] The new provision not only added the words "contractor" and "agent," it also removed the language "by his or her employer."[366]

A. Applying the 2009 Amendments to an "Agent," not just an Employee.

In *United States ex rel. Bias v. Tangipahoa Parish School Bd.*,[367] the Fifth Circuit gave some definition to the 2009 FCA amendments. While the FCA formerly prohibited retaliation by an "employer," the *Bias* case in 2016 turned on the new language prohibiting retaliation against a "contractor" or "agent." Bias was employed and paid by the Marine Corps (having been employed by the school board itself).[368] He served as an instructor for a high school's Junior Reserve Officer Training Corps.[369] Bias reported acts of alleged misappropriation by a subordinate to the high school principal.[370] After receiving orders from the Marine Corps for a transfer to a distant school, he retired from the Corps and sued the School Board and two individual defendants.[371]

The district court dismissed the lawsuit because only the Marine Corps, his employer, could be liable for retaliation. On appeal, Bias argued, that the high school principal and his own subordinate retaliated against him directly and, as a result the school board was liable for their alleged retaliation.

The Fifth Circuit observed that, under the 2009 amendments, "courts must expand the class of defendants beyond just employers but not interpret that expansion as a license to sue anyone."[372] Although Bias admitted that he was not a "contractor," the Court held that he had adequately alleged facts to suggest that he was in the scope of individuals protected from retaliation.[373] In this regard, the Court noted that Bias alleged he was assigned to the same school as when the school board employed him previously and that he performed teacher-like functions and attended meetings with school officials.[374] Given those allegations,

---

[365] United States *ex rel.* Siewick v. Jamieson Science and Engineering, Inc., 322 F.3d 738, 740 (D.C. Cir. 2003) (noting "We have interpreted [§3730(h)] to impose liability only upon employers.").
[366] 31 U.S.C. § 3730(h) (1986).
[367] 816 F.3d 315 (5th Cir. 2016).
[368] *Id.* at 320.
[369] *Id.*
[370] *Id.*
[371] *Id.*
[372] *Id.* at 324.
[373] *Id.* at 325.
[374] *Id.*

the Court found that it was plausible that he was an "agent" of the School Board and thus protected from retaliation by the School Board itself.[375]

B.   Reasonable Belief Includes Both Subjecting and Objecting Components.

In *United States ex rel Uhlig v. Fluor Corp.*,[376] the whistleblower directed concerns to the Government that his employer was using unlicensed electricians in violation of its government contract. After his employer questioned him about why he directed his concerns to the Government rather than raise the issue internally first, he was terminated from his job. The district court granted summary judgment of Uhlig's FCA retaliation claim because Uhlig lacked an objective basis to assert that his employer committed fraud. His complaint, therefore, was not protected activity.

The Seventh Circuit affirmed and rejected Uhlig's FCA retaliation claim because he lacked a reasonable belief to believe that the conduct about which he complained was fraudulent. In reaching this conclusion, the Court explained that it would look at both subjective and objective factors. First, the Court said it would look to whether the employee believes in good faith that the employer was committing fraud against the Government.[377] With respect to the objective consideration, the Court said it would ask whether a reasonable employee "in the same or similar circumstances" might reach that same conclusion.[378] The Court disagreed with Uhlig's contention that the contract mandated the use of licensed electricians and that the employer had become bound by an option to do so. The Court emphasized that Uhlig lacked first-hand knowledge of the contractual obligations because he had not read pertinent terms.[379] As for second-hand knowledge, the Court held that Uhlig's reliance on reading two emails which did not suggest an obligation to use licensed electricians, was inadequate to lead a reasonable employee in Uhlig's shoes, to suspect fraud on the Government.[380]

C.   The Employer need not be the Target of False Claims Reporting.

The Fourth Circuit considered, in *O'Hara v. Nika Technologies, Inc.*,[381] whether an employer could be liable for retaliation where the employer was not itself a target of the employee's complaint. The district court had ruled that the plaintiff could not pursue a retaliation claim against his employer on the theory that the employer

---

[375] *Id.*
[376] 839 F.3d 628 (7th Cir. 2016).
[377] *Id.* at 635.
[378] *Id.*
[379] *Id.*
[380] *Id.*
[381] 878 F.3d 470 (4th Cir. 2017).

fired him for reporting alleged fraud by *another* company.[382] The court held that the employer itself must be the target of the alleged protected activity.[383]

The Fourth Circuit reversed and looked to the plain language of FCA's anti-retaliation provision which, it said, "protects disclosures in furtherance of a viable FCA action against any person or company."[384]

D. Proof of Causation Requires a "But-For" Analysis, not Merely Whether Protected Activity was a "Motivating Factor."

In *DiFiore v. CSL Behring, LLC*,[385] a pharmaceutical company's marketing director, DiFiore, alleged that she was constructively discharged for expressing concerns to her supervisors about the company's marketing of drugs for off-label use. The district court had instructed the jury on the "but-for" causation standard, that her protected activity was the but-for cause of the actions taken against her.[386] DiFiore maintained that the trial court should have instructed the jury that the protected activity need only be a "motivating factor" in the actions taken.[387]

In announcing that the "but-for" standard was proper, the Third Circuit explained that the language in the FCA was like that used in the Age Discrimination in Employment Act and the anti-retaliation provisions of Title VII of the Civil Rights Act of 1964.[388] When interpreting both statutes, the Supreme Court had concluded that the but-for standard, rather than the "motivating factor" standard, applied.[389] The Third Circuit was convinced that the but-for standard likewise applied to the FCA's anti-retaliation clause.[390]

The Fifth Circuit also concluded in *United States ex rel. King v. Solvay Pharmaceuticals, Inc.*,[391] that "but-for" proof of causation is required in FCA retaliation claims.

E. Protected Activity Requires Conduct that "Reasonably Could Lead" to an FCA Action.

In *United States ex rel. Booker v. Pfizer*,[392] Booker testified that he objected when his superiors instructed employees to promote off-label use of a drug even after a

---

[382] *Id.* at 474.
[383] *Id.*
[384] *Id.* at 475.
[385] 879 F.3d 71 (3d Cir. 2018).
[386] *Id.* at 73.
[387] *Id.* at 75.
[388] *Id.* at 76-78.
[389] *Id.*
[390] *Id.*
[391] 871 F.3d 318, 333 (5th Cir. 2017).
[392] 847 F.3d 52 (1st Cir. 2017).

prior FCA settlement over the issue.³⁹³ He claimed that he was fired in retaliation for that objection. The district court denied summary judgment and the First Circuit reversed.³⁹⁴ The Court of Appeals held that objection to an employer's conduct, absent evidence that it related to activity in violation of the FCA, such as the fraudulent submission of claims, was not protected activity.³⁹⁵ The Court explained that only such conduct "reasonably could lead" to an FCA action.³⁹⁶

F.   Timing Alone is not Proof of Causation.

In *King, supra,* two former employees claimed they were discharged three and a half months after making their complaints. The Fifth Circuit explained, consistent with a long line of cases, that timing alone cannot establish the requisite causal connection.³⁹⁷

G.   FCA Retaliation does not Apply to Job Applicants.

Several whistleblowers have asked courts to extend the FCA retaliation provision to cover job applicants, as well as employees. Courts, so far, have refused to accept this expansion of the FCA.

In *Vander Boegh v. Energysolutions, Inc.*,³⁹⁸ the plaintiff worked as a landfill manager at a gaseous diffusion plant. He reported environmental violations that would be protected under the FCA retaliation provision. When the Department of Energy awarded the contract to a new company, he applied for the same job with the new contractor. He was not hired, and he brought suit alleging retaliation.

The trial court dismissed Vander Boegh's claim, ruling he was not an employee, contractor, or agent of the new company, and so the statute did not apply. The plaintiff argued the term "employee" was ambiguous, and should be interpreted consistent with the Energy Reorganization Act,³⁹⁹ as both the Department of Labor⁴⁰⁰ and the Third Circuit⁴⁰¹ had included applicants under the definition of "employee."

---

[393] *Id.* at 59.
[394] *Id.* at 59-60.
[395] *Id.* at 60.
[396] *Id.*
[397] *Id.* at 334.
[398] 772 F.3d 1056 (6th Cir. 2014).
[399] 42 U.S.C. § 5851.
[400] Samodurov v. Gen. Physics, Corp., No 89-ERA-20, 1993 WL 832030, at *3 (Dep't. of Labor Nov. 16, 1993).
[401] Doyle v. Secretary of Labor, 285 F.3d 243, 251 n. 13 (3d Cir. 2002).

The Sixth Circuit rejected his arguments. It found that the term "employee" was not ambiguous.[402] It also found that the legislative history of the 2009 amendment did not support expansion to job applicants. Instead, Congress was trying to include employee-like relationships of contractors and agents.[403]

The issue was revisited most recently in *Heath v. Indianapolis Fire Department*.[404] Heath's father, a Fire Department employee, filed a whistleblower suit against the Department while Quinn Heath's job application was pending.[405] When he was not hired, he joined his father's FCA suit, alleging retaliation for his father's complaint.[406] The trial court granted summary judgment on the retaliation claim and Quinn Heath appealed.[407]

The Seventh Circuit declined to address whether the retaliation provision of the FCA covered job applicants.[408] Instead, it found that Heath failed to demonstrate causation, as the other people hired ranked higher on various merit-based metrics considered by the Department.[409]

Whether job applicant may bring action based on the FCA's retaliation provision remains an open question in most Circuits, and will likely be the subject of continuing litigation until it is resolved.

H.   Employer Intent May be General, not Specific.

The most curious recent FCA retaliation case, and one that is sure to launch a whole new wave of retaliation claims, was decided in March 2018. In *Smith v. LHC Group, Inc.*,[410] the whistleblower argued that she voluntarily resigned from the defendant company because of its fraudulent activity, both "as a matter of conscience and to avoid suspicion in any future investigation by the Government."[411] The trial court dismissed, because there was no allegation that the employer acted with the intent to force her to resign.[412]

The Sixth Circuit noted that the retaliation portion of the FCA[413] did not identify whether the intent element was general or specific. Thus, it was up to a jury to

---

[402] *Vander Boegh*, 772 F.3d at 1059.
[403] *Id.* at 1063.
[404] 889 F.3d 872 (7th Cir. 2018).
[405] *Id.* at 873.
[406] *Id.*
[407] *Id.*
[408] *Id.* at 874.
[409] *Id.* at 875.
[410] 727 F.App'x 100 (6th Cir., 2018).
[411] *Id.* at *1.
[412] *Id.*
[413] 31 U.S.C. § 3730(h).

consider "all of the factors that led to the plaintiff's resignation"[414] and decide whether the employer's fraudulent behavior "would cause a reasonable employee to resign."[415] The Court drew its reasoning from constructive discharge cases, not FCA retaliation cases. Should other courts follow the decision in *Smith*, FCA retaliation claims will likely become much more common companion claims in healthcare related employment litigation.

I. <u>Retaliation Claims need not be Pleaded with Particularity.</u>

While FCA allegations must be pleaded with Rule 9(b) specificity, retaliation claims under the statute need only meet the general pleading requirements of Rule 8. In *United States ex rel. Crockett v. Complete Fitness Rehab.*,[416] the whistleblower filed a complaint alleging both false claims and retaliation under the Act.[417] The trial court dismissed the entire claim for failure to plead fraud with particularity.[418] The Sixth Circuit affirmed the dismissal of the fraud counts but reversed the dismissal of the retaliation claim, stating "such claims are not subject to Rule 9(b)'s heightened standards."[419] It was enough that the plaintiff contended she was fired for trying to prevent fraud.[420] This was acceptable even though the plaintiff had "still not pleaded a specific FCA violation."[421]

J. <u>Conclusion</u>

Claims of retaliation under the FCA often accompany an underlying whistleblower lawsuit. Whether independently or together with a *qui tam* action, a claim of retaliation can present sticky issues for employers. The FCA's cause of action for retaliation represents one of many methods for encouraging the reporting of false claims. Together with the attorney fee-shifting provisions, and the percentages of Government recovery available to whistleblowers, the anti-retaliation clause in the FCA packs a potent punch.

---

[414] *Smith* at *2.
[415] *Id.*
[416] 721 F.App'x 451 (6th Cir. 2018).
[417] *Id.* at 452.
[418] *Id.*
[419] *Id.* at 460.
[420] *Id.*
[421] *Id.*

16. THE FCA AND EVALUATION AND MANAGEMENT CODES

By David Honig

Evaluation and Management codes, known in the healthcare industry as "E/M codes," have long been one of the most common bases for whistleblower lawsuits under the FCA. That might soon end.[422]

Evaluation and Management codes are the basic codes used to identify interactions between patients and physicians, both office and hospital visits. There is an E/M code for each type of visit, e.g., New Patient Office or Outpatient (99201-99205), Established Patient Office or Outpatient (99211-99215), Initial Hospital Care (99221-99223), Subsequent Hospital Care (99231-99233).[423] Each code type is divided into three or five levels, turning on the intensity of the visit. Whistleblowers have used E/M codes as the basis for FCA cases across the country. The codes have specific documentation guidelines and suggested average times per visit, allowing a whistleblower to state the factual basis for an FCA suit that is not easily dismissed in the early stages of litigation.

Medicare's proposed Physician Fee Schedule for 2019[424] retains the same codes, but creates only two payment levels for office E/M visits, rather than five. Physicians would still use CPT codes 99201-99205 and 99211-99215, but would be paid for either a level one visit (99201 or 99211), or an upper level visit. There would be no distinction between the amount paid for a level two visit (99202 or 99212) and level five visit (99205 or 99215).[425] The justifications for the change are misevaluation of the codes,[426] confusing documentation guidelines,[427] and disproportionate administrative burdens.[428]

The proposal allows more streamlined documentation based on time or medical decision making, rather than requiring compliance with the existing, and

---

[422] CMS announced it would delay implementing the new E/M codes until January 1, 2021. *CMS Finalizes Changes to Advance Innocation, Restore Focus on Patients*, Nov. 1, 2018. https://www.cms.gov/newsroom/press-releases/cms-finalizes-changes-advance-innovation-restore-focus-patients.

[423] *CPT 2018 Professional*, American Medical Association, 2018, p. 11-17.

[424] *Medicare Program; Revisions to Payment Policies under the Physician Fee Schedule and Other Revisions to Part B for CY 2019; Medicare Shared Savings Program Requirements; Quality Payment Program; and Medicaid Promoting Interoperability Program*, 42 CFR Parts 405, 410, 411, 414, 415, and 495, Department of Health and Human Services, Centers for Medicare and Medicaid Services, July 27, 2018.

[425] *Id.* at 335.

[426] *Id.* at 323.

[427] *Id.* at 324.

[428] *Id.* at 327.

confusing, guidelines.[429] The proposal sets just two payment levels, one for the lowest intensity visit and another for all other visits. The proposed payments would be based on a work RVU of 1.90 for new patient visits (99202-99205) and 1.22 for established patient visits (99212-99215).[430] The proposed plan included charts comparing the payments under the existing scheme and under the proposed scheme:[431]

HCPCS Code	CY 2018 Non-facility Payment Rate	CY 2018 Non-facility Payment Rate under the proposed Methodology
99201	$45	$44
99202	$76	$135
99203	$110	
99204	$167	
99205	$211	

HCPCS Code	CY 2018 Non-facility Payment Rate	CY 2018 Non-facility Payment Rate under the proposed Methodology
99211	$22	$24
99212	$45	$93
99213	$74	
99214	$109	
99215	$148	

---

[429] *Id.* at 334.
[430] *Id.* at 348.
[431] *Id.* at 349.

The proposed change in the fee schedule would significantly increase payments for the lower intensity office visits, but would cut compensation for seeing patients with the most difficult and complex symptoms and diseases.

CMS has suggested that all providers will benefit from the change, even those specialists with the most complex visits, because of the reduced administrative obligations.[432] But it also recognized that the change may not cover the costs of certain E/M visits, particularly those associated with a 0-day global procedure, primary care visits, and certain specialist visits. It addressed those concerns by reducing by 50% the lower visit associated with a global procedure, and by creating new add-on codes to allow providers to recover the additional costs for certain primary care visits and for inherently complex evaluation and management related to endocrinology, rheumatology, hematology/oncology, urology, neurology, obstetrics/gynecology, allergy/immunology, otolaryngology, cardiology, and interventional pain management.[433]

The proposed change will significantly reduce healthcare providers' risk of being the subject of an FCA whistleblower lawsuit. Evaluation and Management codes have provided the basis for a continual stream of whistleblower lawsuits around the country. A quick perusal of the caselaw reveals almost fifty reported FCA cases based on E/M coding since 2000, and many more were filed, then dismissed or settled, without ever being reported.

Attorneys for whistleblowers have already argued that the change would allow providers to "potentially circumvent potential FCA cases because the consolidation of the codes would be bringing more services into one category."[434] In truth, there would be no circumvention, because the claim for an E/M service would not be false. The change would simply offer less opportunities for whistleblowers to bring their lawsuits. While some providers might see a reduction in income based on the lower compensation for complex office visits, the reduction in the risk of a whistleblower lawsuit, with the tremendous cost of defense and the draconian penalties, should more than compensate for that loss.

---

[432] *Id.* at 348.
[433] *Id.* at 357.
[434] *Payment Code Change May Hinder Medicare Whistleblowers*, Matt Phifer, Bloomberg Law, August 20, 2018.

17. Conclusion

By David Honig

The False Claims Act remains the Government's primary tool to combat fraud, including fraud in public healthcare programs. In recent years a change in focus, from institution to individuals, increased the risk for healthcare executives, who must now protect themselves through aggressive compliance programs. With the change in landscape, there has also been a change in whistleblowers, as plaintiff's attorneys have discovered the FCA for themselves, rather than just their clients. This should force healthcare providers to be cautious in every lawsuit, recognizing that even the most mundane contract or malpractice case can lead to whistleblower litigation.

The ongoing development of caselaw, particularly surrounding materiality and public disclosures, leads to a pastiche of rules, differing by Circuit and changing continually. Healthcare providers can no longer rely on their knowledge of the law from last year, or even last month. An affirmative focus on compliance, along with a relationship with dedicated FCA counsel, is essential in today's healthcare environment.

Finally, the FCA is manageable. Healthcare providers acting in good faith, dedicated to providing quality care for their patients and their communities, and continually working within the confines of the ever-evolving rules, can significantly reduce their risks from the Government and from whistleblowers. *Healthcare and the False Claims Act, 2nd Edition*, describes the most important events and trends since 2016, and should help providers avoid the onerous costs and penalties of the FCA.

APPENDIX A: LESLIE R. CALDWELL REMARKS[435]

Thank you, for that kind introduction. And thanks to everyone at Taxpayers Against Fraud for inviting me to speak to you today.

It has been my privilege, over the past several months, to serve as Assistant Attorney General for the Criminal Division of the Department of Justice.

. . .

Today, I want to announce that we will be stepping up our use of one tool, and that is the fine work done by all of you in investigating and filing cases under the False Claims Act.

Through our Fraud Section, we will be committing more resources to this vital area, so that we can move swiftly and effectively to combat major fraud involving government programs.

To that end, when you are thinking of filing a *qui tam* case that alleges conduct that potentially could be criminal, I encourage you to consider reaching out to criminal authorities, just as you now do with our civil counterparts in the department and the U.S. Attorney's Offices.

We in the Criminal Division have unparalleled experience prosecuting healthcare fraud, procurement fraud, and financial fraud. We can and we will bring that expertise to bear by increasing our commitment to criminal investigations and prosecutions that stem from allegations in False Claims Act lawsuits.

Fraud Section

Let me tell you a little bit about the Criminal Division's Fraud Section. The section employs approximately 100 attorneys and 70 paralegals and other support staff.

It is divided into specialized units, including a 40 attorney Healthcare Fraud Unit – the largest and most prolific unit of criminal prosecutors dedicated solely to healthcare fraud in the country.

---

[435] *Remarks by Assistant Attorney General for the Criminal Division Leslie R. Caldwell at the Taxpayers Against Fraud Education Fund Conference,* Justice News (September 17, 2014) https://www.justice.gov/opa/speech/remarks-assistant-attorney-general-criminal-division-leslie-r-caldwell-taxpayers-against.

The chief of that unit, Gejaa Gobena, has plenty of False Claims Act experience, as he worked for several years on *qui tam* cases in the department's Civil Fraud Section before joining the Criminal Division.

The Fraud Section also has a team that focuses on government procurement fraud.

And we have renowned experience in corporate and financial fraud cases, including prosecutions of conduct of a global nature, handled by prosecutors in our Securities and Financial Fraud Unit and our Foreign Corrupt Practices Act Unit.

I'd like to talk today in more detail about the work of each of these sections – and I hope that you will see that we have a real opportunity to greatly enhance the effectiveness of our nation's *qui tam* system of fraud prevention.

Medicare Fraud Strike Force

The recent success of the Criminal Division in prosecuting healthcare fraud has been nothing short of extraordinary. Since 2007, most of our healthcare fraud cases have been brought through our Medicare Fraud Strike Force.

The strike force is a coordinated team of investigators and prosecutors from the Department of Justice, Health and Human Services, and state and local law enforcement agencies dedicated to fighting Medicare fraud.

The strike force operates in nine cities that are hot spots for Medicare fraud – Baton Rouge, Brooklyn, Chicago, Dallas, Detroit, Houston, Los Angeles, Miami and Tampa. We focus on the worst offenders engaged in the most pervasive fraud in those regions.

In just 2013 alone, the strike force brought healthcare fraud prosecutions charging 345 individuals, secured 234 guilty pleas, and obtained 46 jury trial convictions, all of which were record numbers.

Since the strike force began operating in 2007, nearly 2,000 people have been charged, who were responsible for approximately $6 billion in false billings. Of those 2,000 people, approximately 1,400 have already been convicted through strike force prosecutions, including almost 200 at trial. The strike force has an overall conviction rate of 95 percent – a spectacular rate of success especially considering the volume of prosecutions.

And rest assured: the defendants who are being charged are not just the low-hanging fruit. The strike force has charged almost 140 licensed doctors – individuals who have breached the public trust and their professional duties of care, selling out their medical licenses for the lure of easy money, often by preying on vulnerable Medicare beneficiaries.

Just yesterday, a medical doctor in Detroit pleaded guilty to Medicare and other fraud, admitting that he put greed before the health and safety of his patients, and that he made them endure unnecessary chemotherapy and other treatments just so that he could collect additional millions from Medicare.

Cases involving fraud by executives at healthcare providers such as hospitals are also a high priority for us, and a growing part of our strike force docket.

Those convicted in these strike force cases face real prison time — an average of 52 months for those sentenced in 2013. Some have received far longer sentences, including a 50-year sentence for the owner of a community mental health center called American Therapeutic Corporation, who masterminded a $205 million fraud.

Notably, that case started with a *qui tam* filing in the Southern District of Florida.

In addition to prison time, we can freeze assets, preventing criminals from enjoying the proceeds of their schemes.

We are determined to root out healthcare fraud. Increasingly, we use cutting-edge, real-time analysis of data from CMS to stay one step ahead of the criminals — including those engaged in new areas of fraud, such as Medicare Part D schemes.

We also are stepping up our prosecutions of corporations involved in healthcare fraud. Corporate healthcare fraud cases are a natural fit for us in light of our healthcare fraud expertise and our prosecutions of corporate cases in the financial fraud and foreign bribery arenas. We have numerous ongoing corporate healthcare fraud investigations, and we are determined to bring more.

. . .

Complexity

Many of these cases are complex and resource-intensive. But our prosecutors are more than up to the challenge. In fact, at the Criminal Division, we seek out the most complex cases — that's what we're here for.

As you know, many engaged in fraud go to extravagant lengths to conceal their schemes, making them difficult to uncover. Many of those schemes involve webs of companies and subsidiaries, and the interplay of numerous bank accounts. Nearly all of our cases involve the analysis of voluminous documents and electronic records.

There are no shortcuts to conducting a full and through investigation. But we have many tools at our disposal that help us work more quickly and effectively to uncover the tracks that sophisticated criminals take such great pains to hide.

Advances in technology have made our review of documentary and electronic evidence faster and more accurate. As criminal prosecutors, we can obtain search warrants and wiretaps, make consensual recordings, conduct undercover operations, use confidential informants, and other evidence-gathering tools that might not be available to other enforcement agencies.

These days, more and more of our cases involve evidence overseas and law enforcement agencies and regulators abroad that are also investigating the misconduct. We have developed relationships with foreign government agencies across the globe, and often conduct parallel investigations alongside those agencies.

The Department of Justice has mutual legal assistance treaties in place with countries around the world that enable us to request evidence abroad for our criminal cases, and no one is better able to navigate those waters than the Criminal Division's own Office of International Affairs.

All of these tools, combined with the factual roadmap laid out in your *qui tam* complaints, can help us to investigate and uncover fraud more quickly and efficiently.

New *Qui Tam* Process

The courageous efforts by relators to bring criminal and civil misconduct to light have driven many of the largest and most important healthcare fraud investigations over the last several decades. And that is thanks to the work of many in this room.

I am here to tell you that the Criminal Division will redouble our efforts to work alongside you. *Qui tam* cases are a vital part of the Criminal Division's future efforts.

I know that you heard yesterday from our new Acting Associate Attorney General Stuart Delery about the Civil Division's ongoing commitment to combating fraud on the Government. And I am confident that those efforts will continue in force under new Acting Assistant Attorney General for the Civil Division Joyce Branda.

We in the Criminal Division have recently implemented a procedure so that all new *qui tam* complaints are shared by the Civil Division with the Criminal Division as soon as the cases are filed. Experienced prosecutors in the Fraud Section are immediately reviewing the *qui tam* cases when we receive them to determine whether to open a parallel criminal investigation.

Those prosecutors then coordinate swiftly with the Civil Division and U.S. Attorney's Offices about the best ways to proceed in the parallel investigations. If a case raises potential criminal issues and needs investigative support, we have ready access to experienced fraud investigators from the FBI, HHS-OIG, the Postal Inspection Service and numerous other law enforcement agencies.

And we have a wealth of experience in successfully bringing parallel investigations. We do this in many contexts, not only with the Civil Fraud section and U.S. Attorney's Offices, but with the SEC and other regulatory agencies, here and abroad. We know how to make it work.

We encourage you to reach out to criminal authorities in appropriate cases, even when you are discussing the case with civil authorities. The sooner we on the criminal side learn about potential criminal conduct, the sooner we can investigate.

And the earlier we begin our investigation, the more legal tools and investigative techniques we have available to us. We can add real value to the investigation, working either in partnership with a U.S. Attorney's Office or on our own.

Relators

We understand what it means for you to represent a relator in a False Claims Act case. When relators come forward, they put a lot at risk — all too often, they have lost their jobs after they raised concerns in their workplace, and may be blacklisted in the industry and unable to find work in that field elsewhere. They invest in their cases their time, their livelihood, and often, their self-worth. And you, as relators' counsel, invest a lot as well.

We want to work with you. We know how much work you do on the front end, when you screen your cases before filing them, and when you obtain information to substantiate your clients' claims. We share your interest in moving investigations along efficiently -- the length of our investigations is often measured in months, not years. And most importantly, we are all interested in bringing wrongdoers to justice.

Working together, and along with our Civil Fraud counterparts, U.S. Attorney's Offices, and investigating agencies, we can bring more cases and hold more companies and individuals responsible for the crimes they commit. I very much look forward to doing just that.

Thank you again for having me.

APPENDIX B: THE YATES MEMO[436]

FROM: Sally Quillian Yates, Deputy Attorney General

SUBJECT: Individual Accountability for Corporate Wrongdoing

Fighting corporate fraud and other misconduct is a top priority of the Department of Justice. Our nation's economy depends on effective enforcement of the civil and criminal laws that protect our financial system and, by extension, all our citizens. These are principles that the Department lives and breathes- as evidenced by the many attorneys, agents, and support staff who have worked tirelessly on corporate investigations, particularly in the aftermath of the financial crisis.

One of the most effective ways to combat corporate misconduct is by seeking accountability from the individuals who perpetrated the wrongdoing. Such accountability is important for several reasons: it deters future illegal activity, it incentivizes changes in corporate behavior, it ensures that the proper parties are held responsible for their actions, and it promotes the public's confidence in our justice system.

There are, however, many substantial challenges unique to pursuing individuals for corporate misdeeds. In large corporations, where responsibility can be diffuse and decisions are made at various levels, it can be difficult to determine if someone possessed the knowledge and criminal intent necessary to establish their guilt beyond a reasonable doubt. This is particularly true when determining the culpability of high-level executives, who may be insulated from the day-to-day activity in which the misconduct occurs. As a result, investigators often must reconstruct what happened based on a painstaking review of corporate documents, which can number in the millions, and which may be difficult to collect due to legal restrictions.

These challenges make it all the more important that the Department fully leverage its resources to identify culpable individuals at all levels in corporate cases. To address these challenges, the Department convened a working group of senior attorneys from Department components and the United States Attorney community with significant experience in this area. The working group examined how the Department approaches corporate investigations, and identified areas in which it can amend its policies and practices in order to most effectively pursue the individuals responsible for corporate wrongs. This memo is a product of the working group's discussions.

---

[436] Yates, Sally, *Individual Accountability for Corporate Wrongdoing*, USDOJ, September 9, 2015, https://www.justice.gov/dag/file/769036/download.

The measures described in this memo arc steps that should be taken in any investigation of corporate misconduct. Some of these measures are new, while others reflect best practices that are already employed by many federal prosecutors. Fundamentally, this memo is designed to ensure that all attorneys across the Department are consistent in our best efforts to hold to account the individuals responsible for illegal corporate conduct.

The guidance in this memo will also apply to civil corporate matters. In addition to recovering assets, civil enforcement actions serve to redress misconduct and deter future wrongdoing. Thus, civil attorneys investigating corporate wrongdoing should maintain a focus on the responsible individuals, recognizing that holding them to account is an important part of protecting the public fisc in the long term.

The guidance in this memo reflects six key steps to strengthen our pursuit of individual corporate wrongdoing, some of which reflect policy shifts and each of which is described in greater detail below: (l) in order to qualify for any cooperation credit, corporations must provide to the Department all relevant facts relating to the individuals responsible for the misconduct; (2) criminal and civil corporate investigations should focus on individuals from the inception of the investigation; (3) criminal and civil attorneys handling corporate investigations should be in routine communication with one another; (4) absent extraordinary circumstances or approved departmental policy, the Department will not release culpable individuals from civil or criminal liability when resolving a matter with a corporation; (5) Department attorneys should not resolve matters with a corporation without a clear plan to resolve related individual cases, and should memorialize any declinations as to individuals in such cases; and (6) civil attorneys should consistently focus on individuals as well as the company and evaluate whether to bring suit against an individual based on considerations beyond that individual's ability to pay.

I have directed that certain criminal and civil provisions in the United States Attorney's Manual, more specifically the Principles of Federal Prosecution of Business Organizations (USAM 9-28.000 el seq.) and the commercial litigation provisions in Title 4 (USAM 4-4.000 et seq.), be revised to reflect these changes. The guidance in this memo will apply to all future investigations of corporate wrongdoing. It will also apply to those matters pending as of the elate of this memo, to the extent it is practicable to do so.

1. **To be eligible for any cooperation credit, corporations must provide to the Department all relevant facts about the individuals involved in corporate misconduct.**

In order for a company to receive any consideration for cooperation under the Principles of Federal Prosecution of Business Organizations, the company must completely disclose to the Department all relevant facts about individual misconduct. Companies cannot pick and choose what facts to disclose. That is, to be eligible for any credit for cooperation, the company must identify all individuals involved in or responsible for the misconduct at issue, regardless of their position, status or seniority, and provide to the Department all facts relating to that misconduct. If a company seeking cooperation credit declines to learn of such facts or to provide the Department with complete factual information about individual wrongdoers, its cooperation will not be considered a mitigating factor pursuant to USAM 9-28.700 el seq. 2 Once a company meets the threshold requirement of providing all relevant facts with respect to individuals, it will be eligible for consideration for cooperation credit. The extent of that cooperation credit will depend on all the various factors that have traditionally applied in making this assessment (e.g., the timeliness of the cooperation, the diligence, thoroughness, and speed of the internal investigation, the proactive nature of the cooperation, etc.).

This condition of cooperation applies equally to corporations seeking to cooperate in civil matters; a company under civil investigation must provide to the Department all relevant facts about individual misconduct in order to receive any consideration in the negotiation. For example, the Department's position on "full cooperation" under the False Claims Act, 31 U.S.C. § 3729(a)(2), will be that, at a minimum, all relevant facts about responsible individuals must be provided.

The requirement that companies cooperate completely as to individuals, within the bounds of the law and legal privileges, see USAM 9-28.700 to 9-28.760, does not mean that Department attorneys should wait for the company to deliver the information about individual wrongdoers and then merely accept what companies provide. To the contrary, Department attorneys should be proactively investigating individuals at every step of the process - before, during, and after any corporate cooperation. Department attorneys should vigorously review any information provided by companies and compare it to the results of their own investigation, in order to best ensure that the information provided is indeed complete and docs not seek to minimize the behavior or role of any individual or group of individuals.

Department attorneys should strive to obtain from the company as much information as possible about responsible individuals before resolving the corporate case. But there may be instances where the company's continued cooperation with respect to individuals will be necessary post-resolution. In these circumstances, the plea or settlement agreement should include a provision that requires the company to provide information about all culpable individuals and that is explicit enough so that a failure to provide the information results in specific consequences, such as stipulated penalties and/or a material breach.

2. **Both criminal and civil corporate investigations should focus on individuals from the inception of the investigation.**

Both criminal and civil attorneys should focus on individual wrongdoing from the very beginning of any investigation of corporate misconduct. By focusing on building cases against individual wrongdoers from the inception of an investigation, we accomplish multiple goals. First, we maximize our ability to ferret out the full extent of corporate misconduct. Because a corporation only acts through individuals, investigating the conduct of individuals is the most efficient and effective way to determine the facts and extent of any corporate misconduct. Second, by focusing our investigation on individuals, we can increase the likelihood that individuals with knowledge of the corporate misconduct will cooperate with the investigation and provide information against individuals higher up the corporate hierarchy. Third, by focusing on individuals from the very beginning of an investigation, we maximize the chances that the final resolution of an investigation uncovering the misconduct will include civil or criminal charges against not just the corporation but against culpable individuals as well.

3. **Criminal and civil attorneys handling corporate investigations should be in routine communication with one another.**

Early and regular communication between civil attorneys and criminal prosecutors handling corporate investigations can be crucial to our ability to effectively pursue individuals in these matters. Consultation between the Department's civil and criminal attorneys, together with agency attorneys, permits consideration of the full range of the Government's potential remedies (including incarceration, fines, penalties, damages, restitution to victims, asset seizure, civil and criminal forfeiture, and exclusion, suspension and debarment) and promotes the most thorough and appropriate resolution in every case. That is why the Department has long recognized the importance of parallel development of civil and criminal proceedings. See USAM 1-12.000.

Criminal attorneys handling corporate investigations should notify civil attorneys as early as permissible of conduct that might give rise to potential individual civil liability, even if criminal liability continues to be sought. Further, if there is a decision not to pursue a criminal action against an individual - due to questions of intent or burden of proof~ for example criminal attorneys should confer with their civil counterparts so that they may make an assessment under applicable civil statutes and consistent with this guidance. Likewise, if civil attorneys believe that an individual identified in the course of their corporate investigation should be subject to a criminal inquiry, that matter should promptly be referred to criminal prosecutors, regardless of the current status of the civil corporate investigation.

Department attorneys should be alert for circumstances where concurrent criminal and civil investigations of individual misconduct should be pursued. Coordination in this regard should happen early, even if it is not certain that a civil or criminal disposition will be the end result for the individuals or the company.

4. **Absent extraordinary circumstances, no corporate resolution will provide protection from criminal or civil liability for any individuals.**

There may be instances where the Department reaches a resolution with the company before resolving matters with responsible individuals. In these circumstances, Department attorneys should take care to preserve the ability to pursue these individuals. Because of the importance of holding responsible individuals to account, absent extraordinary circumstances or approved departmental policy such as the Antitrust Division's Corporate Leniency Policy, Department lawyers should not agree to a corporate resolution that includes an agreement to dismiss charges against, or provide immunity for, individual officers or employees. The same principle holds true in civil corporate matters; absent extraordinary circumstances, the United States should not release claims related to the liability of individuals based on corporate settlement releases. Any such release of criminal or civil liability clue to extraordinary circumstances must be personally approved in writing by the relevant Assistant Attorney General or United States Attorney.

5. **Corporate cases should not be resolved without a clear plan to resolve related individual cases before the statute of limitations expires and declinations as to individuals in such cases must be memorialized.**

If the investigation of individual misconduct has not concluded by the time authorization is sought to resolve the case against the corporation, the prosecution or corporate authorization memorandum should include a discussion of the potentially liable individuals, a description of the current status of the investigation regarding their conduct and the investigative work that remains to be done, and an investigative plan to bring the matter to resolution prior to the end of any statute of limitations period. If a decision is made at the conclusion of the investigation not to bring civil claims or criminal charges against the individuals who committed the misconduct, the reasons for that determination must be memorialized and approved by the United States Attorney or Assistant Attorney General whose office handled the investigation, or their designees. Delays in the corporate investigation should not affect the Department's ability to pursue potentially culpable individuals. While every effort should be made to resolve a corporate matter within the statutorily allotted time, and tolling agreements should be the rare exception, in situations where it is anticipated that a tolling agreement is nevertheless unavoidable and necessary, all efforts should be made either to resolve the matter against culpable individuals before the limitations period expires or to preserve the ability to charge individuals by tolling the limitations period by agreement or court order.

6. **Civil attorneys should consistently focus on individuals as well as the company and evaluate whether to bring suit against an individual based on considerations beyond that individual's ability to pay.**

The Department's civil enforcement efforts are designed not only to return government money to the public fisc, but also to hold the wrongdoers accountable and to deter future wrongdoing. These twin aims - of recovering as much money as possible, on the one hand, and of accountability for and deterrence of individual misconduct, on the other - are equally important. In certain circumstances, though, these dual goals can be in apparent tension with one another, for example, when it comes to the question of whether to pursue civil actions against individual corporate wrongdoers who may not have the necessary financial resources to pay a significant judgment.

Pursuit of civil actions against culpable individuals should not be governed solely by those individuals' ability to pay. In other words, the fact that an individual may not have sufficient resources to satisfy a significant judgment should not control the decision on whether to bring suit. Rather, in deciding whether to file a civil action against an individual, Department attorneys should consider factors such as whether the person's misconduct was serious, whether it is actionable, whether the admissible evidence will probably be sufficient to obtain and sustain a judgment, and whether pursuing the action reflects an important federal interest. Just as our prosecutors do when making charging decisions, civil attorneys should make individualized assessments in deciding whether to bring a case, taking into account numerous factors, such as the individual's misconduct and past history and the circumstances relating to the commission of the misconduct, the needs of the communities we serve, and federal resources and priorities.

Although in the short term certain cases against individuals may not provide as robust a monetary return on the Department's investment, pursuing individual actions in civil corporate matters will result in significant long-term deterrence. Only by seeking to hold individuals accountable in view of all of the factors above can the Department ensure that it is doing everything in its power to minimize corporate fraud, and, over the course of time, minimize losses to the public fisc through fraud.

Conclusion

The Department makes these changes recognizing the challenges they may present. But we are making these changes because we believe they will maximize our ability to deter misconduct and to hold those who engage in it accountable.

In the months ahead, the Department will be working with components to turn these policies into everyday practice. On September 16, 2015, for example, the Department will be hosting a training conference in Washington, D.C., on this subject, and I look forward to further addressing the topic with some of you then.

APPENDIX C: THE GRANSTON MEMO

Introduction

Over the last several years, the Department has seen record increases in *qui tam* actions filed under the False Claims Act (FCA), 31 U.S.C. § 3729 et seq., with annual totals approaching or exceeding 600 new matters. Although the number of filings has increased substantially over time, the rate of intervention has remained relatively static. Even in non-intervened cases, the Government expends significant resources in monitoring these cases and sometimes must produce discovery or otherwise participate. If the cases lack substantial merit, they can generate adverse decisions that affect the Government's ability to enforce the FCA. Thus, when evaluating a recommendation to decline intervention in a *qui tam* action, attorneys should also consider whether the Government's interests are served, in addition, by seeking dismissal pursuant to 31 U.S.C. § 3730(c)(2)(A).

Historically, the Department has utilized section 3730(c)(2)(A) sparingly, in large part because the statutory text makes clear that relators can proceed with certain *qui tam* actions following the Government's declination. Moreover, a decision not to intervene in a particular case may be based on factors other than merit, particularly in light of the Government's limited resources.

Accordingly, we have been circumspect with the use of this tool to avoid precluding relators from pursuing potentially worthwhile matters, and to ensure that dismissal is utilized only where truly warranted.

While it is important to be judicious in utilizing section 3730(c)(2)(A), it remains an important tool to advance the Government's interests, preserve limited resources, and avoid adverse precedent. The Department plays an important gatekeeper role in protecting the False Claims Act, because in *qui tam* cases where we decline to intervene, the relators largely stand in the shoes of the Attorney General. That is why the FCA provides us with the authority to dismiss cases. This memo is intended to provide a general framework for evaluating when to seek dismissal under section 3730(c)(2)(A) and to ensure a consistent approach to this issue across the Department. We reviewed those cases in which the Government moved to dismiss relators pursuant to this statutory provision since 1986, when this provision was added to the FCA. As discussed below, we identified approximately seven factors that the Government has relied upon in seeking to dismiss a *qui tam* action pursuant to section 3730(c)(2)(A). To ensure consistency across the Department, these factors should serve as a basis for evaluating whether to seek to dismiss future matters, though they are not intended to constitute an exhaustive list, and there may be other reasons for concluding that the Government's interests are best served by the dismissal of a *qui tam* action.

Appendix C: The Granston Memo

Finally, as noted below, when the Department is considering dismissal, relators should be advised of this possibility since it will inform their judgment regarding whether to voluntarily dismiss their actions.

Discussion

The False Claims Act authorizes the Attorney General to dismiss a *qui tam* action over the relator's objection:

> The Government may dismiss the action notwithstanding the objections of the person initiating the action if the person has been notified by the Government of the filing of the motion and the court has provided the person with an opportunity for a hearing on the motion.

31 U.S.C. § 3730(c)(2)(A). The FCA does not, however, provide a standard of review for evaluating such a request for dismissal. As a result, courts have developed two differing standards. Compare *United States ex rel. Sequoia Orange Co. v. Baird-Neece Packing Corp.*, 151 F.3d 1139, 1145 (9th Cir. 1998) (holding that the United States must identify a "valid government purpose" that is rationally related to dismissal) with *Swift v. United States*, 318 F.3d 250, 252 (D.C. Cir. 2003) (holding that the United States has an "unfettered right" to dismiss a *qui tam* action).

Moreover, the FCA does not set forth specific grounds for dismissal under section 3730(c)(2)(A). However, below is a non-exhaustive list of factors that the Department can use as a basis for dismissal, along with citations to cases where the Government has previously sought dismissal based on these factors.

1. *Curbing Meritless Qui Tams*

The Department should consider moving to dismiss where a *qui tam* complaint is facially lacking in merit-either because relator's legal theory is inherently defective, or the relator's factual allegations are frivolous. Examples of inherent legal defects include *qui tam* actions where the relator failed to allege an actionable obligation to support a reverse false claim violation, ... or to allege a non-federal defendant that is not covered by sovereign immunity.... Factually frivolous cases can take a number of forms....

In certain cases, even if the relator's allegations are not facially deficient, the Government may conclude after completing its investigation of the relator's allegations that the case lacks merit. In such a case, the Department should consider dismissing the matter.... This is just one of several mechanisms contained in the FCA to ensure that the United States retains substantial control over lawsuits brought on its behalf.... These cases may be rare, in part, because to maximize its resources the Government typically will investigate a *qui tam* action only to the point where it concludes that a declination is warranted. This may not equate to a conclusion that no fraud occurred. If the Department is concerned that a case lacks any merit, but elects to afford the relator an opportunity to further develop the case, the Department attorney may consider advising the relator that dismissal will be considered if the relator is unable to obtain additional support for the relator's claims by a specified date.

2. *Preventing Parasitic or Opportunistic Qui Tam Actions*

The Department should consider moving to dismiss a *qui tam* action that duplicates a preexisting government investigation and adds no useful information to the investigation. In these cases, the Government should consider whether the relator would receive an unwarranted windfall at the expense of the public fisc because Congress intended for the relator share to incentivize and award the provision of meaningful information and assistance instead of merely providing duplicative information already known to the Government.... For example, in *United States ex rel. Amico, et al. v. Citi Group, Inc., et al.*, No. 14-cv-4370 (CS) (S.D.N.Y. August 7, 2015), relators filed a *qui tam* action against Citi Group and its subsidiaries alleging fraud in connection with the marketing and sale of residential mortgage backed securities; however, the Department of Justice had been investigating the same conduct for several years prior to the filing and had engaged in extensive settlement negotiations before relators filed their complaint. The Government successfully moved to dismiss the action under section 3730(c)(2)(A) because, among other factors, relators' belated complaint provided no assistance to the Government in its pre-existing investigation....

3. *Preventing Interference with Agency Policies and Programs*

Dismissal should be considered where an agency has determined that a *qui tam* action threatens to interfere with an agency's policies or the administration of its programs and has recommended dismissal to avoid these effects. For example, in *United States ex rel. Ridenour v. Kaiser-Hill Co., LLC*, 397 F.3d 925 (10th Cir. 2005), relator alleged that a security contractor submitted false claims to the Department of Energy for deficient security services at Rocky Flats, a radiologically-contaminated nuclear weapons manufacturing facility that was slated to undergo decontamination and closure. The Government successfully moved to dismiss the action because, among other things, litigation would delay the clean-up and closure of the facility by diverting agency personnel and resources away from the project. 397 F.3d at 937.... Finally, there may be instances where an action is both lacking in merit and raises the risk of significant economic harm that could cause a critical supplier to exit the Government program or industry....

4. *Controlling Litigation Brought on Behalf of the United States*

Relatedly, the Department should consider dismissing cases when necessary to protect the Department's litigation prerogatives. For example, in *In Re Natural Gas Royalties Qui Tam Litigation*, MDL Docket No. 1293 (D. Wyo. October 9, 2002), relator filed separate *qui tam* actions in various districts against more than 300 defendants accused of underpaying royalties owed to the United States in connection with natural gas produced from federal lands. After intervening as to a limited number of defendants, the Government sought to dismiss certain declined claims to, among other things, avoid interference with the Government's ability to litigate the intervened claims. The court agreed, finding that the interest in avoiding interference with ongoing litigation warranted dismissal of the declined claims.... In addition, in *United States ex rel. Wright v. Agip Petroleum Co.*, No. 5:03-264 (E.D. Tex. Feb. 3, 2005), the Government moved to dismiss, in part, to avoid the risk of unfavorable precedent. See id. Finally, in *United States ex rel. Piacentile*, 2013 WL 5460640, the Government moved to dismiss a declined claim that was serving as an obstacle to the settlement of the Government's intervened claims. But cf *United States ex rel. Schweizer v. Oce*, 677 F.3d 1228 (D.C. Cir. 2012) (once the Government reaches a settlement with defendant of relator's claims, the dismissal of those claims is governed by section 3730(c)(2)(B), requiring a showing that the settlement is fair, adequate, and reasonable, rather than by section 3730(c)(2)(A)).

5. *Safeguarding Classified Information and National Security Interests*

In certain cases, particularly those involving intelligence agencies or military procurement contracts, we should seek dismissal to safeguard classified information. For example, in *United States ex rel. Fay v. Northrup Grumman Corp.*, No. 06-cv-00581-EWN-MJW, 2008 WL 877180 (D. Colo. Mar. 27, 2008), the relator alleged that a defense contractor defrauded the United States in connection with work performed on a classified contract. After declining to intervene, the Department moved to dismiss the action under section 3730(c)(2)(A), asserting that continued litigation would pose "an unacceptable risk to national security" due to the potential for disclosure of classified information. Applying the *Sequoia Orange* standard, the Court agreed, concluding that the claims and defenses were inextricably tied to classified information and dismissal was rationally related to the valid government interest of preventing the disclosure of such information. Id. at * 6-7.... Finally, it should be noted that the Government need not demonstrate that continued litigation will result in the disclosure of classified information. In jurisdictions that apply the "rational basis" basis test, the Government has a strong argument that the risk of disclosure, alone, justifies dismissal....

6. *Preserving Government Resources*

The Department should also consider dismissal under section 3730(c)(2)(A) when the Government's expected costs are likely to exceed any expected gain.... Examples of potential costs may include, among other things, the need to monitor or participate in ongoing litigation, including responding to discovery requests.... In some cases, the Government may also be liable for the defendant's litigation costs if the defendant prevails in the action. See, e.g., FAR §31.205-47(c).

7. *Addressing Egregious Procedural Errors*

The Department may also seek dismissal of a *qui tam* action pursuant to section 3 730(c)(2)(A) based on problems with the relator's action that frustrate the Government's efforts to conduct a proper investigation. For example, in *United States ex rel. Surdovel v. Digirad Imaging Solutions,* No. 07-cv-0458, 2013 WL 6178987

(E.D. Pa. Nov. 25, 2013), the relator ignored repeated requests from the Office of the U.S. Attorney to serve the *qui tam* complaint and disclose material facts as required by 31 U.S.C. § 3730(b). The Court granted the Government's motion to dismiss the action because the "egregious procedural enors completely frustrated the Government's ability to investigate the relator's claims." *Id.* at *4....

* * *

Several additional points are in order with respect to the use of the Government's dismissal authority under section 3730(c)(2)(A). First, while the Department's position has been that the appropriate standard for dismissal under section 3730(c)(2)(A) is the "unfettered" discretion standard adopted by the D.C. Circuit rather than the "rational basis" test adopted by the 9th and 10th Circuits, we should argue that even the latter standard was intended to be a highly deferential one. Moreover, in those jurisdictions where the standard remains unresolved, in many cases the prudent course may be to identify the Government's basis for dismissal and to argue that it satisfies any potential standard for dismissal under section 3730(c)(2)(A).

Second, the factors identified above are not mutually-exclusive, and the Department has often relied on multiple grounds for dismissal (for example, lack of merit and need to safeguard classified information). Nor, as noted above, are the factors identified in this memorandum intended to constitute an exhaustive list-there may be other reasons for concluding that the Government's interests are best served by the dismissal of a *qui tam* action.

Third, in some cases there may be alternative grounds for seeking dismissal other than section 3730(c)(2)(A), such as the first to file bar, the public disclosure bar, the tax bar, the bar on *pro se* relators, or Federal Rule of Civil Procedure 9(b). Although the Department has sometimes moved to dismiss on these grounds under section 3730(c)(2)(A), we believe the better approach is to assert these grounds separately since they can provide alternative, independent legal bases for dismissal. It may sometimes be appropriate, however, to move for dismissal under section 3730(c)(2)(A) in the alternative based on one or more for the factors listed above.

Fourth, section 3730(c)(2)(A) does not require the Government "to proceed in an all or nothing manner." ... In certain situations, it may be appropriate to seek only partial dismissal of some defendants or claims....

Fifth, where a *qui tam* case is a potential candidate for dismissal, Department attorneys should consult closely with the affected agency as to whether dismissal is warranted under any of the factors set forth in this guidance. The agency's recommendation should be obtained in advance of the filing of any request to dismiss. In cases where dismissal under section 3730(c)(2)(A) is opposed by the agency (because, for example, it would require the Government to disclose sensitive information or could result in other collateral consequences), there may be alternative ways to address the deficiencies while accommodating the agency's desire to forego seeking dismissal. For example, if the agency views the alleged falsity as immaterial, the United States can provide an agency declaration to that effect. *See Trinity,* 872 F.3d at 664 (holding that district court erred in concluding alleged falsity was material to agency despite agency memorandum stating that there was "an unbroken chain of eligibility for Federal reimbursement" for the allegedly defective product at issue).

Sixth, although a motion to dismiss under section 3730(c)(2)(A) will often be filed at or near the time of declination, there may be cases where dismissal is warranted at a later stage, particularly when there has been a significant intervening change in the law or evidentiary record. However, if one waits until the close of discovery or trial, there is a risk that the court may be less receptive to the request given the expenditure of resources by the court and parties. The court may also be less receptive to a motion filed at a later stage when doing so undercuts a claimed desire to avoid or reduce costs associated with discovery or safeguard information in discovery. Attorneys considering dismissal should therefore allow for sufficient time to consult with the affected agency and, in delegated cases, to provide appropriate notice to the Fraud Section.

Finally, attorneys planning to recommend declination or dismissal should, to the extent possible, consider advising relators of perceived deficiencies in their cases as well as the prospect of dismissal so that relators may make an informed decision regarding whether to proceed with the action. In many cases, relators may choose to voluntarily dismiss their actions, particularly if the Government has advised the relator that it is considering seeking dismissal under section 3730(c)(2)(A).

APPENDIX D: THE BRAND MEMO

Limiting Use of Agency Guidance Documents In Affirmative Civil Enforcement Cases

On November 16, 2017, the Attorney General issued a memorandum ("Guidance Policy") prohibiting Department components from issuing guidance documents that effectively bind the public without undergoing the notice-and-comment rulemaking process. Under the Guidance Policy, the Department may not issue guidance documents that purport to create rights or obligations binding on persons or entities outside the Executive Branch (including state, local, and tribal governments), or to create binding standards by which the Department will determine compliance with existing statutory or regulatory requirements.

The Guidance Policy also prohibits the Department from using its guidance documents to coerce regulated parties into taking any action or refraining from taking any action beyond what is required by the terms of the applicable statute or lawful regulation. And when the Department issues a guidance document setting out voluntary standards, the Guidance Policy requires a clear statement that noncompliance will not in itself result in any enforcement action.

The principles from the Guidance Policy are relevant to more than just the Department's own publication of guidance documents. These principles also should guide Department litigators in determining the legal relevance of other agencies' guidance documents in affirmative civil enforcement ("ACE").

Guidance documents cannot create binding requirements that do not already exist by statute or regulation.

Accordingly, effective immediately for ACE cases, the Department may not use its enforcement authority to effectively convert agency guidance documents into binding rules.

Likewise, Department litigators may not use noncompliance with guidance documents as a basis for proving violations of applicable law in ACE cases.

The Department may continue to use agency guidance documents for proper purposes in such cases. For instance, some guidance documents simply explain or paraphrase legal mandates from existing statutes or regulations, and the Department may use evidence that a party read such a guidance document to help prove that the party had the requisite knowledge of the mandate.

However, the Department should not treat a party's noncompliance with an agency guidance document as presumptively or conclusively establishing that the party violated the applicable statute or regulation. That a party fails to comply with agency guidance expanding upon statutory or regulatory requirements does not mean that the party violated those underlying legal requirements; agency guidance documents cannot create any additional legal obligations.

This memorandum applies only to future ACE actions brought by the Department, as well as (wherever practicable) those matters pending as of the date of this memorandum. This memorandum is an internal Department of Justice policy directed at Department components and employees. Accordingly, it is not intended to, does not, and may not be relied upon to, create any rights, substantive or procedural, enforceable at law by any party in any matter civil or criminal.

Appendix E: Department of Justice Cooperation Credit Gudelines

4-4.112 - GUIDELINES FOR TAKING DISCLOSURE, COOPERATION, AND REMEDIATION INTO ACCOUNT IN FALSE CLAIMS ACT MATTERS

Introduction

These guidelines identify factors that will be considered and the credit that will be provided by Department of Justice attorneys when entities or individuals voluntarily self-disclose misconduct that could serve as the basis for False Claims Act (FCA) liability and/or administrative remedies, take other steps to cooperate with FCA investigations and settlements, or take adequate and effective remedial measures.

In addition to the factors discussed below, the Department of Justice, in its discretion, takes into account many considerations when evaluating the appropriate resolution of FCA matters, including the nature and seriousness of the violation, the scope of the violation, the extent of any damages, the defendant's history of recidivism, the harm or risk of harm from the violation, whether the United States' interests will be adequately served by a compromise, the ability of a wrongdoer to satisfy an eventual judgment, and litigation risks presented if the matter proceeds to trial. Some of these considerations may reduce the credit available to an entity or individual, or in egregious circumstances, may render the entity or individual ineligible for any credit. The discussion in these guidelines does not limit Department attorneys' discretion to consider all appropriate factors in determining whether and on what basis to resolve an FCA matter.

Disclosure, Cooperation, and Remedial Action

Voluntary Disclosure. The Department has a strong interest in incentivizing companies and individuals that discover false claims to voluntarily disclose them to the government. Voluntary self-disclosure of such misconduct benefits the government by revealing, and enabling the government to make itself whole from, previously unknown false claims and fraud, and may also enable the government to preserve and gather evidence that would otherwise be lost. Entities or individuals that make proactive, timely, and voluntary self-disclosure to the Department about misconduct will receive credit during the resolution of a FCA case. During the course of an internal investigation into the government's concerns, moreover, entities may discover additional misconduct going beyond

Appendix E: DOJ's Cooperation Credit Guidelines

the scope of the known concerns, and the voluntary self-disclosure of such additional misconduct will qualify the entity for credit.

Other Forms of Cooperation. In addition to voluntarily self-disclosing misconduct, an individual or entity can earn credit by taking steps to cooperate with an ongoing government investigation. A comprehensive list of activities that constitute such cooperation is not feasible because of the diverse factual and legal circumstances involved in FCA investigations. However, the following measures illustrate the type of activities by entities or individuals under investigation that will be taken into account. These measures are not mandatory and an entity or individual does not have to satisfy all of them to qualify for some cooperation credit.

i. Identifying individuals substantially involved in or responsible for the misconduct;

ii. Disclosing relevant facts and identifying opportunities for the government to obtain evidence relevant to the government's investigation that is not in the possession of the entity or individual or not otherwise known to the government;

iii. Preserving, collecting, and disclosing relevant documents and information relating to their provenance beyond existing business practices or legal requirements;

iv. Identifying individuals who are aware of relevant information or conduct, including an entity's operations, policies, and procedures;

v. Making available for meetings, interviews, examinations, or depositions an entity's officers and employees who possess relevant information;

vi. Disclosing facts relevant to the government's investigation gathered during the entity's independent investigation (not to include information subject to attorney-client privilege or work product protection), including attribution of facts to specific sources rather than a general narrative of facts, and providing timely updates on the organization's internal investigation into the government's concerns, including rolling disclosures of relevant information;

vii. Providing facts relevant to potential misconduct by third-party entities and third-party individuals;

viii. Providing information in native format, and facilitating review and evaluation of that information if it requires special or proprietary technologies so that the information can be evaluated;

ix. Admitting liability or accepting responsibility for the wrongdoing or relevant conduct; and

x. Assisting in the determination or recovery of the losses caused by the organization's misconduct.

In considering the value of any voluntary disclosure or additional cooperation, government counsel will consider the following factors: (1) the timeliness and voluntariness of the assistance; (2) the truthfulness, completeness, and reliability of any information or testimony provided; (3) the nature and extent of the assistance; and (4) the significance and usefulness of the cooperation to the government.

Remedial Measures. Department attorneys will also consider whether an entity has taken appropriate remedial actions in response to the FCA violation. Such remedial actions may include:

i. demonstrating a thorough analysis of the cause of the underlying conduct and, where appropriate, remediation to address the root cause;
ii. implementing or improving an effective compliance program designed to ensure the misconduct or similar problem does not occur again;1
iii. appropriately disciplining or replacing those identified by the entity as responsible for the misconduct either through direct participation or failure in oversight, as well as those with supervisory authority over the area where the misconduct occurred; and
iv. any additional steps demonstrating recognition of the seriousness of the entity's misconduct, acceptance of responsibility for it, and the implementation of measures to reduce the risk of repetition of such misconduct, including measures to identify future risks.

Credit for Disclosure, Cooperation, and Remediation

An entity or individual that seeks to earn maximum credit in a False Claims Act matter generally should undertake a timely self-disclosure that includes identifying all individuals substantially involved in or responsible for the misconduct, provide full cooperation with the government's investigation, and take remedial steps designed to prevent and detect similar wrongdoing in the future. However, even if an entity or individual does not qualify for maximum credit, they may receive partial credit if they have meaningfully assisted the government's investigation by engaging in conduct qualifying for cooperation credit. See Department of Justice Manual, § 4-3.100(3).

Where the conduct of the entity or individual warrants credit, the Department has discretion in FCA cases to reward such credit. Most often, this discretion will be exercised by reducing the penalties or damages multiple sought by the Department.

The maximum credit that a defendant may earn may not exceed an amount that would result in the government receiving less than full compensation for the losses caused by the defendant's misconduct (including the government's damages, lost interest, costs of investigation, and relator share).

The Department may consider, in appropriate circumstances, additional avenues that would permit an entity or individual to claim credit in FCA cases, including:

- Notifying a relevant agency about an entity's or individual's disclosure, other cooperation, or remediation, so that the agency in its discretion may consider such factors in evaluating its administrative options, such as suspension, debarment, exclusion, or civil monetary penalty decisions;
- Publicly acknowledging the entity's or individual's disclosure, other cooperation, or remediation; and
- Assisting the entity or individual in resolving qui tam litigation with a relator or relators.

The foregoing options are ways in which the Department may in its discretion credit disclosure, other cooperation, or remediation; they are not entitlements that arise whenever these factors are present. As noted above, the value of credit awarded to an entity or individual will vary depending on the facts and circumstances of each case.

Other Considerations

Nothing in these guidelines changes any preexisting obligation an entity or individual has under the law to report to or cooperate with the federal government.2

Cooperation does not include disclosure of information required by law, or merely responding to a subpoena, investigative demand, or other compulsory process for information. However, cooperation credit may be awarded where an entity or individual meaningfully assists the government's investigation by, for example, disclosing additional relevant documents or information, or otherwise proactively aiding the government in understanding the context or significance of the documents or information produced. Cooperation also does not include the disclosure of information that is under an imminent threat of discovery or investigation.

The Department will not award any credit to an entity or individual that conceals involvement in the misconduct by members of senior management or the board of directors, or to an entity or individual that otherwise demonstrates a lack of good faith to the government during the course of its investigation. See Department of Justice Manual, § 4-3.100(3).

Entities and individuals are entitled to assert their legal rights and, unless required by law, do not have to cooperate with a government investigation. Nothing about the guidelines herein changes those rights. Entities and individuals remain free to reject these options and forgo any potential credit consistent with the law.

Eligibility for credit for voluntary disclosure or other forms of cooperation is not predicated on waiver of the attorney-client privilege or work product protection, and none of the guidelines herein require such a waiver.

The measures set forth in these guidelines are intended solely to guide attorneys for the government in accordance with their statutory responsibilities and federal law. They are not intended to, do not, and may not be relied upon to create a right or benefit, substantive or procedural, enforceable at law by any party.

[1] In addition to considering a company's decision to implement or improve a compliance program after an alleged violation, the Department may take into account the prior existence of a compliance program in evaluating a defendant's liability under the False Claims Act. For example, the Department may consider the nature and effectiveness of such a compliance program in evaluating whether any violation of law was committed knowingly. In making such an evaluation, the criteria to be considered may include those set forth in the Department of Justice Manual at § 9-28.800.

[2] For example, the Federal Acquisition Regulation requires contractors to self-disclose credible evidence of certain violations of law and significant overpayments in connection with the award or performance of a federal contract or subcontract. Contractor Business Ethics Compliance Program and Disclosure Requirements, 48 C.F.R. pts. 2, 3, 9, 42 and 52.

[new May 2019]

Appendix F: OIG's Provider Self-Disclosure Protocol

Updated OIG's Provider Self-Disclosure Protocol

I. Background

In 1998, the Office of Inspector General (OIG) of the United States Department of Health and Human Services (HHS) published the Provider Self-Disclosure Protocol (the SDP) at 63 Fed Reg. 58399 (October 30, 1998) to establish a process for health care providers to voluntarily identify, disclose, and resolve instances of potential fraud involving the Federal health care programs (as defined in section 1128B(f) of the Social Security Act (the Act), 42 U.S.C. 1320a–7b(f)). The SDP provides guidance on how to investigate this conduct, quantify damages, and report the conduct to OIG to resolve the provider's liability under OIG's civil monetary penalty (CMP) authorities. Over the past 15 years, we have resolved over 800 disclosures, resulting in recoveries of more than $280 million to the Federal health care programs.

Since the original publication, we identified areas where additional guidance would be beneficial to the health care community and would improve the efficient resolution of SDP matters. To that end, we issued three Open Letters to Health Care Providers in 2006, 2008, and 2009. Since the last Open Letter, we continued to evaluate our SDP process. We also solicited comments about the SDP on June 18, 2012, and we received numerous helpful comments from the public. On the basis of our experience and the comments we received, we have decided to revise the SDP in its entirety at this time. This revised SDP supersedes and replaces the 1998 *Federal Register* Notice and the Open Letters, as described below.

A. Why Disclosure Is Important

For many years, OIG has emphasized the importance of dealing with the Federal health care programs with integrity. All members of the health care industry have a legal and ethical duty to do so. This duty includes an obligation to take measures to detect and prevent fraudulent and abusive activities, including implementing specific procedures and mechanisms to investigate and resolve instances of potential fraud involving the Federal health care programs. Whether as a result of voluntary self-assessment or in response to external forces, participants in the health care industry must be prepared to investigate such instances, assess the potential losses suffered by the Federal health care programs, and make full disclosure to the appropriate authorities.

B. Benefits of Disclosure

We recognize that whether to disclose potential fraud to OIG is a significant decision. However, there are significant benefits to disclosing potential fraud to OIG that should make that decision easier.

First, we believe that good faith disclosure of potential fraud and cooperation with OIG's review and resolution process are typically indications of a robust and effective compliance program. As a result, we have instituted a presumption against requiring integrity agreement obligations in exchange for a release of OIG's permissive exclusion authorities in resolving an SDP matter. Since 2008, we have resolved 235 SDP cases through settlements. In all but one of these cases, we have released the disclosing parties from permissive exclusion without requiring any integrity measures.

Second, we believe that individuals or entities that use the SDP and cooperate with OIG during the SDP process deserve to pay a lower multiplier on single damages than would normally be required in resolving a Government-initiated investigation. The specific multiplier that we accept may vary depending on the facts of each case. OIG's general practice in CMP settlements of SDP matters is to require a minimum multiplier of 1.5 times the single damages, although we determine in each individual case whether a higher multiplier may be warranted.

Third, we believe that using the SDP may mitigate potential exposure under section 1128J(d) of the Act, 42 U.S.C. 1320a-7k(d). Section 1128J(d)(2) of the Act requires that a Medicare or Medicaid overpayment be reported and returned by the later of (1) the date that is 60 days after the date on which the overpayment was identified or (2) the date any corresponding cost report is due, if applicable. Any overpayment retained by a "person," as defined in section 1128J(d)(4)(C) of the Act after this deadline may create liability under the Civil Monetary Penalties Law (CMPL), section 1128A of the Act, and the False Claims Act (FCA), 31 U.S.C. 3729. In its Notice of Proposed Rulemaking, 77 Fed. Reg. 9179-9187 (February 16, 2012), the Centers for Medicare & Medicaid Services (CMS) proposes to suspend the obligation to report overpayments under section 1128J(d) of the Act when OIG acknowledges receipt of a submission to the SDP so long as the submission is timely made. CMS also proposes to suspend the obligation to return overpayments until a settlement agreement is entered into, or the provider or supplier withdraws or is removed from the SDP. As necessary, we will provide additional guidance on OIG's web site concerning section 1128J of the Act and the SDP after CMS issues its final rule.

Finally, we commit to working with individuals and entities that use the SDP in good faith and cooperate with OIG's review and resolution process. OIG created the SDP to provide a specific and detailed process that can be relied upon by all participants in the health care industry as one that OIG will consistently follow. As part of this commitment, we streamlined our internal process to reduce the average time a case is pending with OIG to less than 12 months from acceptance into the SDP. To further facilitate timely resolutions of SDP matters, we are changing the timeframe to submit the findings of the completed internal investigation and damages calculation from 90 days from acceptance into the SDP to 90 days from the date of the initial submission.

II. Eligibility Criteria and Guidance

This section explains the eligibility criteria for the SDP, including who may use the SDP and what conduct is and is not eligible for acceptance into the SDP.

A. Who May Use the SDP

All health care providers, suppliers, or other individuals or entities who are subject to OIG's CMP authorities found at 42 C.F.R. Part 1003 are eligible to use the SDP. The SDP is not limited to any particular industry, medical specialty, or type of service. For example, a pharmaceutical or medical device manufacturer may use the SDP to disclose potential violations of the Federal anti-kickback statute (AKS), section 1128B(b) of the Act, because such violations trigger CMP liability under section 1128A(a)(7) of the Act, a provision of the CMPL. For purposes of the SDP, we refer to all individuals or entities that make a submission to the SDP as "disclosing parties." The disclosing party should disclose conduct for which it may be liable, including potential successor liability based on its purchase of another entity. For example, a disclosing party could have liabilities as the result of a merger or an acquisition. However, disclosing parties should not use the SDP to disclose conduct of another, unrelated party. OIG's hotline should be used to report potential misconduct of other parties (1-800-OIG-TIPS or https://oig.hhs.gov/fraud/report-fraud/index.asp).

Disclosing parties already subject to a Government inquiry (including investigations, audits, or other oversight activities) are not automatically precluded from using the SDP. The disclosure, however, must be made in good faith and must not be an attempt to circumvent any ongoing inquiry. Disclosing parties under Corporate Integrity Agreements (CIA) with OIG may also use the SDP in addition to making any reports required in the CIA.

B. Conduct Eligible for the SDP

The SDP is available to facilitate the resolution of matters that, in the disclosing party's reasonable assessment, potentially violate Federal criminal, civil, or administrative laws for which CMPs are authorized. In making a disclosure, a disclosing party must acknowledge that the conduct is a potential violation. Disclosing parties must explicitly identify the laws that were potentially violated and should not refer broadly to, for example, "Federal laws, rules, and regulations" or "the Social Security Act." OIG has found that disclosing parties who avoid acknowledging that there is a potential violation are more likely to have unclear or incomplete submissions or unrealistic expectations about resolutions, which result in a lengthier review and resolution process. In addition, statements such as "the Government may think there is a violation, but we disagree" raise questions about whether the matter is appropriate for the SDP. The resulting back-and-forth over these issues can create unnecessary delays in reaching a resolution and may result in the disclosing party's removal from the SDP.

C. Conduct Ineligible for the SDP

First, the SDP is not available for a matter that does not involve potential violations of Federal criminal, civil, or administrative law for which CMPs are authorized, such as one exclusively involving overpayments or errors. In this situation, the matter should be disclosed directly to the appropriate CMS or other responsible contractor under the payor's voluntary refund process.

Second, the SDP is not available to request an opinion from OIG regarding whether an actual or potential violation has occurred. For example, a disclosure that broadly describes a business arrangement and requests a determination from OIG regarding whether the arrangement violates the AKS is not appropriate for the SDP. The Advisory Opinion process is the only vehicle to obtain an OIG opinion, as described at https://oig.hhs.gov/compliance/advisory-opinions/index.asp.

Third, the SDP is not available for disclosure of an arrangement that involves only liability under the physician self-referral law, section 1877 of the Act (the Stark Law), without accompanying potential liability under the AKS for the same arrangement. Disclosing parties must analyze each arrangement involving a physician to determine whether it raises potential liability under the AKS, the Stark Law, or both laws. Stark-only conduct should be disclosed to CMS through its Self-Referral Disclosure Protocol (SRDP), which can be found at: http://www.cms.gov/PhysicianSelfReferral/. OIG reserves the right to determine whether an arrangement is appropriate for resolution in the SDP.

D. Tolling the Statute of Limitations

As described above, one of the benefits of disclosure is that CMS has proposed that the time for repayment of an identified overpayment under section 1128J(d) of the Act will be tolled for the disclosing party. To preserve the rights of the parties while the matter is being resolved through the SDP, OIG expects disclosing parties to disclose with a good faith willingness to resolve all liability within the CMPL's six year statute of limitations as described in section 1128A(c)(1) of the Act. Accordingly, the disclosing party agrees, as a condition precedent to the OIG's acceptance into the SDP, to waive and not to plead statute of limitations, laches, or any similar defenses to any administrative action filed by OIG relating to the disclosed conduct, except to the extent that such defenses would have been available to the disclosing party had an administrative action been filed on the date of submission.

E. Corrective Action

Prior to disclosure, the disclosing party should ensure that the conduct has ended or, at least, in the case of an improper kickback arrangement, that corrective action will be taken and the improper arrangement will be terminated within 90 days of submission to the SDP. Additionally, all other necessary corrective action should be complete and effective at the time of disclosure.

III. Submission Content

To be considered for admission into the SDP, the disclosing party must include the following information in its submission:

A. Requirements for All Disclosures

The disclosing party is expected to conduct an internal investigation and report its findings to OIG in its submission. If the disclosing party is unable to complete its internal investigation before sending its submission, the disclosing party must certify in its submission that it will complete the internal investigation within 90 days of the date of its initial submission.

Disclosures may be submitted through OIG's Web site at https://oig.hhs.gov/compliance/self-disclosure-info/index.asp. Disclosures may also be submitted by mail to the Chief of the Administrative and Civil Remedies Branch, Office of Counsel to the Inspector General, Office of Inspector General, Department of Health and Human Services, 330 Independence Avenue, SW, Cohen Building, Room 5527, Washington, DC 20201. Submissions by facsimile or other means will not be accepted. The narrative submission must include:

1. The name, address, type of health care provider, provider identification number(s), and tax identification number(s) of the disclosing party and the Government payors (including Medicare contractors) to which the disclosing party submits claims or a statement that the disclosing party does not submit claims.

2. If the disclosing party is an entity that is owned or controlled by or is otherwise part of a system or network, an organizational chart, a description or diagram describing the pertinent relationships; the names and addresses of any related entities; and any affected corporate divisions, departments, or branches.

3. The name, street address, phone number, and email address of the disclosing party's designated representative for purposes of the voluntary disclosure.

4. A concise statement of all details relevant to the conduct disclosed, including, at minimum, the types of claims, transactions, or other conduct giving rise to the matter; the period during which the conduct occurred; and the names of entities and individuals believed to be implicated, including an explanation of their roles in the matter.

5. A statement of the Federal criminal, civil, or administrative laws that are potentially violated by the disclosed conduct.

6. The Federal health care programs affected by the disclosed conduct.

7. An estimate of the damages, as described in the applicable section below, to each Federal health care program relevant to the disclosed conduct, or a certification that the estimate will be completed and submitted to OIG within 90 days of the date of submission. When a disclosing party can determine the amount of actual damages to Federal health care programs, the actual damages amount must be provided instead of an estimate.

8. A description of the disclosing party's corrective action upon discovery of the conduct.

9. A statement of whether the disclosing party has knowledge that the matter is under current inquiry by a Government agency or contractor. If the disclosing party has knowledge of a pending inquiry, it must identify any involved Government entity and its individual representatives. The disclosing party must also disclose whether it is under investigation or other inquiry for any other matters relating to a Federal health care program and provide similar information relating to those other matters.

10. The name of an individual authorized to enter into a settlement agreement on behalf of the disclosing party.

11. A certification by the disclosing party, or, in the case of an entity, an authorized representative on behalf of the disclosing party, stating that to the best of the individual's knowledge, the submission contains truthful information

and is based on a good faith effort to bring the matter to the Government's attention for the purpose of resolving potential liability to the Government and to assist OIG in its resolution of the disclosed matter.

B. Requirements for Conduct Involving False Billing

When a disclosure involves the submission of improper claims to Federal health care programs, the disclosing party must conduct a review to estimate the improper amount paid by the Federal health care programs (referred to as "damages") and prepare a report of its findings that follows the requirements in this section. OIG will verify a disclosing party's calculation of damages.

The disclosing party's estimation of damages must consist of a review of either: (1) all the claims affected by the disclosed matter or (2) a statistically valid random sample of the claims that can be projected to the population of claims affected by the matter. A disclosing party may not extend the time to resubmit claims to Federal health care programs through the SDP; therefore, the damages estimation must not include a reduction, or "netting" for any underpayments discovered in the review.

When using a sample to estimate damages, the disclosing party must use a sample of at least 100 items and use the mean point estimate to calculate damages. If a probe sample was used, those claims may be included in the 100-item sample if statistically appropriate. To avoid unreasonably large sample sizes, the SDP does not require a minimum precision level for the review of claims. As a result, the disclosing party may select an appropriate sample size to estimate damages as long as the sample size is at least 100 items. As a general rule, smaller sample sizes (closer to 100) will suffice where the population has a high level of homogeneity, and larger sample sizes will be necessary where the population contains a more diverse mixture of claim types. The disclosing party should keep in mind that a careful and complete definition of the population will assist in making accurate findings.

The disclosing party's report must include, at a minimum, the following information:

1. Review Objective: A statement clearly articulating the objective of the review.

2. Population: A description of the group of claims about which information is needed, an explanation of the methodology used to develop the population, and the basis for this determination.

3. Sources of Data: A full description of the source of the data reviewed and the information upon which the review was based, including the sources of payment data, and the documents that were relied upon.

4. Personnel Qualifications: The names and titles of the individuals who conducted the review. The review should be conducted by qualified individuals, e.g., statisticians, accountants, auditors, consultants, and medical reviewers, and the review report should describe their qualifications.

5. Characteristics Measured: The review report should identify the characteristics used for testing each item. For example, in a review designed to estimate the value of overpayments due to duplicate payments, the characteristics used are those that must exist for an item to be a duplicate. The amount of the duplicate payment is the measurement of the overpayment. The report must also explain the method for determining whether an item entirely or partially meets the criterion for having the characteristics measured.

If the financial review was based upon a sample, the review report must also include the Sampling Plan that was followed. At a minimum, this includes:

1. Sampling Unit: Any of the designated elements that constitute the population of interest.

2. Sampling Frame: The totality of the sampling units from which the sample was selected and the way in which the audit population differs from the sampling frame (and the effect this difference has on conclusions reached as a result of the audit).

3. Sample Size: The size of the sample reviewed to reach the estimate of the damages. The sample size must be at least 100 claims.

4. Source of Random Numbers: The sample must be selected through random numbers. The source of the random numbers used must be shown in the report. We strongly recommend the use of OIG's Statistical Sampling Software, also known as "RAT-STATS," which is currently available free of charge at https://oig.hhs.gov/compliance/rat-stats/index.asp.

5. Method of Selecting Sampling Units: The method for selecting the sample units.

6. Sample Design: Unless the disclosing party demonstrates the need to use a different sample design, the review should use simple random sampling. If necessary, the disclosing party may use stratified or multistage sampling. Details about the strata, stages, and clusters should be included in the review report.

7. Missing Sample Items and Other Evidence: If the review was based on a sample, missing sample items should be treated as errors, pursuant to Federal health care program rules requiring the retention of supporting information for submitted claims. Missing sample items should be noted in the report. The report must also describe any evidence, other than the sample results, that was considered in arriving at the review results.

8. Estimation Methodology: If the review was based on a sample, because the general purpose of the review is to estimate the monetary losses to the Federal health care programs, the methodology to be used must be variables sampling (treating each individual item in the population as a sampling unit) using the difference estimator (estimates of the total errors in the population are made from the sample differences by multiplying the average audited difference by the number of units in the population).

C. Requirements for Conduct Involving Excluded Persons

Many SDP submissions disclose the employment of, or contracting with, individuals who appear on OIG's List of Excluded Individuals and Entities (LEIE) (available online at https://exclusions.oig.hhs.gov). We are providing additional guidance here to help disclosing parties gather the necessary information for a complete disclosure.

Specific Information

In addition to providing the general information required by section III.A, the disclosure must provide the following information:

1. The identity of the excluded individual and any provider identification number.

2. The job duties performed by that individual.

3. The dates of the individual's employment or contractual relationship.

4. A description of any background checks that the disclosing party completed before and/or during the individual's employment or contract.

5. A description of the disclosing party's screening process (including any policy or procedure that was in place) and any flaw or breakdown in that process that led to the hiring or contracting with the excluded individual.

6. A description of how the conduct was discovered.

7. A description of any corrective action (including a copy of any revised policy or procedure) implemented to prevent future hiring of excluded individuals.

In addition, before disclosing the employment of an excluded individual, a disclosing party must screen all current employees and contractors against the LEIE. Once this has been done, the disclosing party should disclose all excluded persons in one submission.

Calculating Damages

Federal health care programs may not pay, directly or indirectly, for items or services furnished, ordered, or prescribed by excluded individuals or entities. If a disclosing party employed or contracted with an excluded person who was a direct provider, such as a physician or a pharmacist, and the items or services furnished, ordered, or prescribed by that person were separately billed to Federal health care programs, the disclosure must include the total amounts claimed and paid by the Federal health care programs for those items or services.

We understand that when an excluded individual provided items or services that are not billed separately to Federal health care programs, such as many items or services furnished by nurses, respiratory therapists, and billing and other administrative personnel, the damages amounts can be difficult to quantify. For purposes of resolving SDP matters involving such non-separately-billable items or services, we use the disclosing party's total costs of employment or contracting during the exclusion to estimate the value of the items and services provided by that excluded individual. The costs of employment or contracting include, but are not limited to, all salary and benefits and other money or items of value, health insurance, life insurance, disability insurance, and employer taxes paid related to employment of the individual (e.g., employer's share of FICA and Medicare taxes). This total amount should be multiplied by the disclosing party's revenue-based Federal health care program payor mix for the relevant time period. (If a disclosing party can measure the Federal payor mix for the department or unit in which the excluded person worked, it is appropriate to apply that payor mix. If the departmental payor mix cannot reasonably be measured, the disclosing party must apply the payor mix for the whole entity.) The resulting amount will be used, for purposes of compromising OIG's CMP authorities in a settlement, as a proxy for the amount paid and the single damages to the Federal health care programs resulting from the employment of the excluded individual. When the disclosing party is using a Federal payor mix, the disclosure must include a separate calculation for each Federal health care program. For example, if the disclosing party's Federal payor mix is 60 percent, the disclosure should break down how the Federal health care programs make up that 60 percent, such as 40 percent Medicare, 10 percent Medicaid State A, 5 percent Medicaid State B, and 5 percent TRICARE.

D. Requirements for Conduct Involving the Anti-Kickback Statute and Physician Self-Referral Law

Another large category of SDP submissions relates to potential violations of the AKS (including conduct that violates both the AKS and the Stark Law). This section provides further guidance to help disclosing parties gather the necessary information for complete disclosure.

Specific Information

In this section, we provide additional guidance on submitting the information described in section III.A. Any disclosure must clearly acknowledge that in the disclosing party's reasonable assessment of the information available at the time of the disclosure, the subject arrangement(s) constitute potential violations of the AKS and, if applicable, the Stark Law. In the past, some disclosing parties have failed to include this acknowledgment in their submissions to the SDP while others have phrased their acknowledgments as suggestions that OIG could view the disclosed conduct as potential violations. OIG will not accept any disclosing party into the SDP that fails to acknowledge clearly that the disclosed arrangement constitutes a potential violation of the AKS and, if applicable, the Stark Law.

As with other self-disclosed conduct, OIG needs to understand the precise nature of the disclosed conduct that creates potential AKS liability or both AKS and Stark Law liability. Therefore, the disclosing party must include in its narrative submission (not by reference to attachments or other documents) a concise statement of all details directly relevant to the disclosed conduct and a specific analysis of why each disclosed arrangement potentially violates the AKS and Stark Laws. The description should include the participants' identities, their relationship to one another to the extent that the relationship affects their potential liability (e.g., hospital-landlord, referring physician-tenant); the payment arrangements; and the dates during which each suspect arrangement occurred.

Further, the disclosure should explain the relevant context and the features of the arrangement that raise potential AKS or both AKS and Stark Law liability.

Below are several examples of the type of information OIG finds helpful in assessing and resolving disclosed conduct involving potential AKS and, if applicable, Stark Law violations. These illustrations are by no means comprehensive or exclusive; rather, they reflect some common issues that have arisen in SDP submissions. For example:

1. How fair market value was determined and why it is now in question.

2. Why required payments from referral sources, under leases or other contracts, were not timely made or collected or did not conform to the negotiated agreement and how long such lapses existed.

3. Why the arrangement was arguably not commercially reasonable (e.g., lacked a reasonable business purpose).

4. Whether payments were made for services not performed or documented and, if so, why.

5. Whether referring physicians received payments from Designated Health Service entities that varied with, or took into account, the volume or value of referrals without complying with a Stark Law exception. Finally, the submission must describe the corrective action taken to remedy the suspect arrangement(s), as well as any safeguards implemented by the disclosing party to prevent the conduct from reoccurring.

Calculating Damages

AKS compliance is a condition of payment of the Federal health care programs. Under section 1128B(g) of the Act, claims that include items or services resulting from an AKS violation constitute false or fraudulent claims for purposes of the FCA. Stark Law compliance is also a condition of payment under section 1877 of the Act. Thus, a disclosing party must submit an estimate of the amount paid by Federal health care programs for the items or services associated with potential violations of the AKS and, if applicable, the Stark Law. A disclosing party may use the methodology in section III.B to calculate the estimate. Alternatively, a disclosing party may identify another reliable methodology to calculate this claims-based estimate and explain that methodology in its submission.

Consistent with OIG's CMPL authorities, a disclosing party must include the total amount of remuneration involved in each arrangement without regard to whether the disclosing party believes a portion of the total remuneration was offered, paid, solicited, or received for a lawful purpose. A disclosing party may also explain what it believes is the value of the financial benefit conferred under the arrangement and whether it believes any portion of the total remuneration should not be considered by OIG in determining an appropriate settlement of OIG's CMP authorities. Given the various legal authorities at issue, OIG has broad discretion in determining an appropriate resolution in these cases. For purposes of resolving SDP matters, we generally exercise this discretion by compromising our CMP authorities for an amount based upon a multiplier of the remuneration conferred by the referral recipient to the individual or entity making the referral. While this is our general approach, OIG's determination of the appropriate settlement amount depends on the facts and circumstances of each matter. We generally use this remuneration-based methodology in the SDP as an incentive to encourage disclosure of potential AKS violations. OIG's use of a remuneration-based methodology in the SDP settlement context does not govern OIG's position in other situations, such as Government-initiated investigations, in which the Government may use any legally supportable measure of damages, multipliers, and penalties.

IV. Resolution

Resolution of a matter in the SDP depends on cooperation, realistic expectations, and clear communication between OIG and the disclosing party. This section provides some basic information about successful resolution of SDP matters.

A. Cooperation Is Essential

The benefits of self-disclosure, such as a speedy resolution, lower multiplier, and an exclusion release without integrity agreement obligations, depend on the disclosing party's willingness to work cooperatively with OIG throughout the process. Cooperation includes, for example, conducting a thorough investigation, submitting all necessary information, communicating through a consistent point of contact, being responsive to OIG requests for additional information, and being willing to pay a penalty or multiplier of damages for self-disclosed conduct. Disclosing parties who fail to cooperate with OIG in good faith will be removed from the SDP.

B. OIG Coordination With DOJ on Civil Matters

OIG will coordinate with the Department of Justice (DOJ) on in resolving SDP matters. If OIG is the sole agency representing the Federal Government, the matter will be settled under OIG's applicable CMP authorities. In some cases, disclosing parties may request release under the FCA, and in other cases, DOJ may choose to participate in the settlement of the matters. If DOJ participates in the settlement, the matter will be resolved as DOJ determines is appropriate consistent with its resolution of FCA cases, which could include a calculation of damages resulting from violations of the AKS based on paid claims. OIG will advocate that the disclosing party receive a benefit from disclosure under the SDP and the matter be resolved consistent with OIG's approach in similar cases. However, DOJ determines the approach in cases in which it is involved.

C. OIG Coordination With DOJ on Criminal Matters

OIG encourages disclosing parties to disclose potential criminal conduct though the SDP process. OIG's Office of Investigations investigates criminal matters, and any disclosure of criminal conduct through the SDP will be referred to DOJ for resolution. As in civil cases referred to DOJ, OIG will advocate that the disclosing parties receive a benefit from disclosure under the SDP.

D. OIG Coordination With the SRDP

Disclosing parties need to decide whether OIG's SDP or CMS's SRDP is the appropriate protocol to disclose potential Stark Law violations. Both protocols should not be used for the same arrangement. As stated above, disclosing parties must analyze each arrangement to determine whether the arrangement raises potential violations of the AKS, the Stark Law, or both. If the arrangement raises a potential violation of only the AKS or of both the AKS and the Stark Law, the arrangement should be disclosed to OIG under the SDP. If the arrangement raises a potential violation of only the Stark Law, the arrangement should be disclosed to CMS under the SRDP. OIG coordinates with CMS on the review and resolution of matters disclosed to either agency as appropriate. However, OIG does not participate in SRDP settlements.

E. Minimum Settlement Amounts

While OIG does not demand an admission of liability in settlement agreements, disclosing parties should expect to pay above single damages for disclosed conduct that potentially violates Federal law. OIG's general practice is to require a minimum multiplier of 1.5 times the single damages, although in each case, we determine whether a higher multiplier is appropriate. As a general practice, for purposes of settlement in the SDP, OIG applies this multiplier to the amount paid by Federal health care programs, not the amount claimed.

To better allocate disclosing party and OIG resources in resolving matters through the SDP and to promote transparency and realistic expectations in the SDP process, we require minimum settlement amounts for self-disclosed matters. For kickback-related submissions accepted into the SDP, OIG will require a minimum $50,000 settlement amount to resolve the matter. This minimum amount is consistent with OIG's statutory authority to impose a penalty of up to $50,000 for each such transaction and an assessment of up to three times the total remuneration. See section 1128A(a)(7) of the Act. For all other matters accepted into the SDP, OIG will require a minimum $10,000 settlement amount to resolve the matter. This minimum amount is consistent with OIG's statutory authority to impose a penalty of at least up to $10,000 for each improper claim submitted as described in the CMPL, section 1128A(a) of the Act. These minimum amounts account for Federal health care program damages and any relevant multiplier.

In the unusual instance when OIG determines that no potential fraud liability exists for conduct disclosed under the SDP, OIG will refer the matter to the appropriate payor for acceptance of the overpayment and no CMP release will be provided.

F. Financial Inability To Pay

In some situations, disclosing parties may be unable to pay otherwise appropriate settlement amounts. In preparing the disclosure, disclosing parties should determine whether an inability to pay may be an issue. If a disclosing party asserts that it cannot pay a proposed settlement amount (i.e., damages plus a multiplier or penalty amount), OIG will require extensive financial information, including audited financial statements, tax returns, and asset records. Disclosing parties must certify to the truthfulness and completeness of the financial disclosure. In addition to submitting the financial forms, disclosing parties should include an assessment of how much they believe they can afford to pay.

Disclosing parties should raise potential inability-to-pay issues at the earliest possible time, preferably in the SDP submission. Doing so enables OIG to promptly send the disclosing party the financial disclosure forms and consider that information in determining an appropriate resolution.

G. Overpayment Reconciliation

If, prior to resolving an SDP matter, a disclosing party refunds an overpayment related to the same conduct disclosed under the SDP, OIG will credit the amount paid toward the ultimate settlement amount. However, OIG is not bound by any amount that is repaid outside the SDP process. OIG may question the methodology of the overpayment calculation, particularly if the disclosing party estimated the overpayment amount by some method other than as described in the SDP. If OIG disputes the methodology used to calculate the overpayment, OIG may require the disclosing party to redo the review or conduct an independent damages review, which may result in a damages or overpayment amount that is higher than the disclosing party's estimate. Moreover, even if OIG agrees with the methodology used to calculate the overpayment, the disclosing party should expect to pay a multiplier on the damages under the SDP.

H. FOIA Implications of Disclosure

Disclosing parties should clearly identify any portion of their submissions that they believe are trade secrets or are commercial, financial, privileged, or confidential and therefore potentially exempt from disclosure under the Freedom of Information Act (FOIA), 5 U.S.C. § 552. Information identified as exempt must meet the criteria for exemption from disclosure under FOIA as determined by an OIG FOIA officer. Consistent with the Department of Health and Human Services' FOIA procedures, set forth in 45 C.F.R. Part 5, OIG will make a reasonable effort to notify a disclosing party prior to any release by OIG of information submitted by a disclosing party and identified upon submission by a disclosing party as trade secrets or as commercial, financial, privileged, or confidential under the FOIA rules. With respect to such releases, a disclosing party will have the rights set forth at 45 C.F.R. § 5.65(d).

APPENDIX G: CASES

Cases are provided in condensed versions for readers who wish for greater insight and understanding into the caselaw which continues to inform, and even create, the operable rules and law under the False Claims Act.

Amphastar Pharmaceuticals Inc. v. Aventis Pharma SA[437]

We must decide whether we have subject matter jurisdiction over a corporate *qui tam* action under the False Claims Act that accuses a competing company of committing fraud against the United States.

. . .

In June 1991, Aventis applied to the U.S. Patent and Trademark Office ("USPTO") for a patent to cover a supposedly new version of enoxaparin ("618 Product").³ Aventis filed a New Drug Application ("NDA") with the Food and Drug Administration ("FDA") a month later.

. . .

Amphastar Pharmaceuticals, Inc., ("Amphastar") a U.S.-based generic pharmaceutical firm founded in 1999 by Yong Feng Zhang, decided that enoxaparin would be a good prospect for a generic product, believing it might be possible to develop a generic version by utilizing information from EP144. . . Amphastar then submitted an Abbreviated New Drug Application ("ANDA") to the FDA on March 4, 2003.

Aventis responded to Amphastar's ANDA by bringing suit five months later, alleging that Amphastar and Teva Pharmaceuticals were infringing on the 618 Patent.

. . .

Amphastar then brought this *qui tam* action against Aventis . . . alleging that by committing fraud against the USPTO, Aventis obtained an illegal monopoly over enoxaparin and then knowingly overcharged the United States. By committing such fraud, Amphastar further alleged, Aventis knew the patent was invalid and thus knowingly defrauded the United States. . . .

On November 14, 2012, the district court ruled that Amphastar's complaint was based on public disclosures, and therefore Amphastar had to show it was the "original source ... of the information on which the allegations are based."[438] Thereafter, Aventis filed a motion for summary judgment contending Amphastar had failed to meet the original source exception to the jurisdictional bar. . . . The district court denied Aventis's summary judgment motion on this issue in a May 2014 ruling, but certified its ruling for interlocutory appeal, which Aventis brought in No. 14-56382.

---

[437] 856 F.3d 696 (9th Cir. 2017).
[438] § 3730(e)(4).

The district court then proceeded to the "direct and independent knowledge" issue. It held a four-day evidentiary hearing to determine if Amphastar had direct and independent knowledge of any of the information underlying its allegations. The district court made various factual findings: Amphastar had no knowledge of Example 6 being false before the *Aventis I* litigation began; Zhang (Amphastar's CEO) was not a credible witness; Amphastar had engaged in inconsistent actions regarding whether it had known of the Example 6 error before the *Aventis I* litigation, and such inconsistent actions undermined its argument. The district court also concluded that Amphastar did not produce enoxaparin by following EP144 in its Pre-Litigation Experiments, but copied key information from Patent 618. For all these reasons the district court held that Amphastar had neither direct nor independent knowledge of any of the elements of fraud supposedly committed by Aventis. The district court then dismissed the case for lack of jurisdiction. Aventis moved for attorneys' fees, which motion was denied.

. . .

If Amphastar's allegations are based on publicly disclosed information, the jurisdictional bar[439] applies unless Amphastar is an "original source." To be an original source, Amphastar must demonstrate that: (1) it had direct and independent knowledge of the information on which it based its allegations, and (2) it satisfied the pre-suit disclosure requirements by providing the necessary information to the Government before filing an action. Amphastar "bears the burden of establishing subject matter jurisdiction by a preponderance of the evidence."[440]

Was the public disclosure bar triggered?

Transactions or allegations are disclosed if they can be found in pleadings or other public filings.[441] Our circuit interprets "allegations" to refer to direct claims of fraud, and, we interpret "transaction to refer to facts from which fraud can be inferred."[442] We have adopted the reasoning of *United States ex rel. Springfield Terminal Railway Co. v. Quinn*, which states that when a critical mass of the underlying facts or of the allegations in the *qui tam* complaint have been disclosed prior to the *qui tam* complaint being filed, the public disclosure bar applies.[443]

. . .

The evidence that the misrepresented facts and the true facts were actually disclosed is overwhelming. The *qui tam* complaint alleges that: (1) Aventis

---

[439] Amphastar's FCA suit was brought under the pre-2010 version of the FCA.
[440] *Alcan*, 197 F.3d at 1018.
[441] Hagood v. Sonoma Cnty. Water Agency, 81 F.3d 1465, 1474 n.13 (9th Cir. 1996).
[442] United States *ex rel.* Mateski v. Raytheon Co., 816 F.3d 565, 571 (9th Cir. 2016).
[443] *Mateski*, 816 F.3d at 571 (citing 14 F.3d 645, 653–54 (D.C. Cir. 1994)).

intentionally made material misrepresentations to the USPTO regarding whether the 618 Product was novel relative to prior art, (2) such misrepresentations allowed it fraudulently to obtain the 618 Patent, (3) Aventis then improperly listed the 618 Patent in the FDA Orange Book, and (4) such listing allowed Aventis to overcharge the Government. The 2004 allegations that were publicly disclosed included all of these facts, except, instead of mentioning overcharging the Government, they mentioned overcharging in general. While the Amended Answer and Counterclaim did not specifically mention Example 6, it did allege material misrepresentations regarding "studies of the pharmacological properties of prior art compounds, including half life."

. . .

Since the public disclosure bar was triggered, did Amphastar qualify as an original source?

The first prong of the original source analysis asks whether Amphastar can show it had "knowledge that is *both* direct and independent."[444] To prove "direct" knowledge, Amphastar "must show that [it] had firsthand knowledge of the alleged fraud, and that [it] obtained this knowledge through [its] own labor unmediated by anything else."[445] To prove "independent" knowledge, relators have to show they had relevant "evidence of fraud prior to the public disclosure of the allegations."[446]

. . .

So the crucial question is whether the district court's factual findings derived from the July 2014 evidentiary hearing are clearly erroneous. . . The district court found that Amphastar had no knowledge Example 6 was false before this fact was publicly disclosed in the *Aventis I* litigation.[447] The court concluded that Zhang's testimony, that he knew Example 6 of the 618 Patent application was false before the *Aventis I* litigation began, was not credible.[448] It also concluded that Amphastar had no direct or independent knowledge that Aventis had made false reports to the FDA about its manufacturing process.[449]

. . .

---

[444] United States *ex rel.* Devlin v. California, 84 F.3d 358, 361 n.5. (9th Cir. 1996).
[445] *Alcan*, 197 F.3d at 1020.
[446] *Devlin*, 84 F.3d at 361 n.5.
[447] *Aventis VI*, 2015 WL 4511573, at *6.
[448] *Id.*
[449] *Id.* at *14 ("Indeed, in argument, Amphastar acknowledged that its only witness regarding its supposed 'direct and independent knowledge,' Zhang, did not offer such evidence.").

In its cross-appeal, Aventis contends that the district court erred in concluding it had no power to award attorneys' fees to Aventis, and we agree. The relevant fee-shifting provision states:

> If the Government does not proceed with the action and the person bringing the action conducts the action, the court may award to the defendant its reasonable attorneys' fees and expenses if the defendant *prevails in the action* and the court finds that the claim of the person bringing the action was clearly frivolous, clearly vexatious, or brought primarily for purposes of harassment.[450]

. . .

The question of whether Aventis is a prevailing party is an easy one: Yes. Aventis has spent eight years, quite a bit of money, and quite a bit of energy, fighting this lawsuit. This lawsuit has probably lasted longer than the vast majority of lawsuits that are resolved on the "merits." If Amphastar brought a frivolous action, the statutory scheme strongly indicates that this is the kind of case for which fee awards should be available to deter future frivolous plaintiffs.[451] Common sense says that Aventis has won a significant victory and permanently changed the "legal relationship of the parties."[452]

Amphastar challenges whether § 3730(d)(4) contains an independent grant of subject matter jurisdiction to award attorneys' fees. We have located independent grants in some cases but not in others, as discussed above, but whether § 3730(d)(4) contains an independent grant of jurisdiction is a matter of first impression for this circuit. . . .

The False Claims Act jurisdictional bar covers a huge number of cases. To rule that a district court cannot award attorneys' fees even when it determines that a Relator brought a frivolous suit just because the jurisdictional bar applies would undermine one of the key purposes of the 1986 amendments to the False Claims Act—"to discourage 'parasitic' suits brought by individuals with no information of their own to contribute to the suit."[453]

---

[450] 31 U.S.C. § 3730(d)(4) (emphasis added).
[451] See *CRST*, 136 S.Ct. at 1652.
[452] *Id.* at 1646.
[453] United States v. Johnson Controls, Inc., 457 F.3d 1009, 1017 (9th Cir. 2006) (quoting Seal 1 v. Seal A, 255 F.3d 1154, 1158 (9th Cir. 2001)).

It is consistent with the statutory scheme that Aventis can receive attorneys' fees from Amphastar if its claim was frivolous, given the immense amount of resources and time this action has cost everyone.[454]

. . .

We are persuaded that the district court had subject matter jurisdiction over the attorneys' fees issue and that Aventis is the prevailing party. As such, the district court may award attorneys' fees to Aventis if it determines that Amphastar's claim "was clearly frivolous, clearly vexatious, or brought primarily for purposes of harassment."[455]

Amphastar's allegations in this action were based on publicly disclosed information, and it lacked the direct and independent knowledge needed to be an original source. We uphold the judgment of the district court in favor of Aventis on the merits. However, because the False Claims Act's fee-shifting provision contains an independent grant of subject matter jurisdiction and because a party who wins a lawsuit on a non-merits issue is a "prevailing party," the conclusion of the district court that it could not award attorneys' fees is erroneous, and the case is remanded for resolution of the attorneys' fees issue.

Therefore, the judgment of the district court in No. 15-56122 is **AFFIRMED**, the appeal in No. 14-56382 is **DISMISSED**, the judgment in No. 15-56209 is **REVERSED**, and the case is **REMANDED** for further proceedings consistent with this opinion.

---

[454] Cf. *CRST*, 136 S.Ct. at 1652–53 (discussing how in the context of Title VII of the Civil Rights Act, "significant attorney time and expenditure may have gone into contesting the claim [in cases like these]" and "Congress could not have intended to bar defendants from obtaining attorney's fees in these cases").

[455] § 3730(d)(4).

Bellevue v. Universal Health Services of Hartgrove, Inc.[456]

Relator and plaintiff-appellant George Bellevue filed a *qui tam* action under the False Claims Act (FCA)[457] and its Illinois analog, the Illinois False Claims Act (IFCA),[458] on behalf of the United States and the State of Illinois against defendant-appellee Universal Health Services of Hartgrove, Incorporated ("Hartgrove"). Bellevue argues that Hartgrove violated the FCA under a number of theories, including false certification and fraudulent inducement. The district court granted Hartgrove's motion to dismiss the complaint for failure to state a claim of fraud with particularity as required by Federal Rules of Civil Procedure 12(b)(6) and 9(b).

. . .

Hartgrove's license, issued by the Illinois Department of Public Health, permits it to maintain 150 beds for patients with acute mental illness, but it actually maintains 152 beds. Prior to September 30, 2009, Hartgrove was permitted to maintain 136 beds for acute mental illness patients. Newly admitted adolescent patients suffering from acute mental illness are placed in a room used for daytime group therapy, known as a "dayroom," rather than patient rooms. These patients sleep on rollout beds until a patient room becomes available. This occurred on 13 separate occasions between January 1, 2011, and June 3, 2011. Hartgrove submitted claims for inpatient care to Medicaid on behalf of these patients even though they were not assigned a room.

Bellevue . . . contends that Hartgrove knowingly submitted fraudulent claims for reimbursement to Medicaid by admitting new patients with acute mental illness in excess of its 150-bed capacity and permitting these patients to sleep in the dayroom rather than in a private room. He further contends that Hartgrove certified, "either explicitly or implicitly," that it was in compliance with licensing standards contained in state law, rules, and regulations, even though it was over capacity.[459]

. . .

Hartgrove argues that Bellevue's claims were publicly disclosed by the IDPH and CMS letters and audit report from March and May 2009. Determining whether to apply the public-disclosure bar requires the court to complete a three-step inquiry. First, we examine whether the relator's allegations have been "publicly disclosed."[460] If so, we next ask whether the lawsuit is "based upon," i.e.,

---

[456] 867 F.3d 712 (7th Cir. 2017).
[457] 31 U.S.C. § 3729 et seq.
[458] 740 Ill. Comp. Stat. 175/1 et seq.
[459] *See* Ill. Admin. Code tit. 77, § 250.230(b).
[460] *Cause of Action*, 815 F.3d at 274 (citation omitted).

"substantially similar to" the publicly disclosed allegations.[461] "If it is, the public-disclosure bar precludes the action unless 'the relator is an original source of the information upon which the lawsuit is based.'"[462] "The relator bears the burden of proof at each step of the analysis."[463]

. . .

Bellevue does not dispute that the information was in the public domain; he contends that the letters and audit report state merely that Hartgrove was over census without any reference to a knowing misrepresentation of facts, which is a critical element of fraud. The district court found that the Government had enough information to infer scienter from the results of its audits. We agree. We have held that the public-disclosure bar applied in instances "where one can infer, as a direct and logical consequence of the disclosed information, that the defendant knowingly — as opposed to negligently — submitted a false set of facts to the Government."[464]

. . .

Moving to the second step, we address whether Bellevue's allegations are substantially similar to the publicly disclosed allegations. . . .

The district court found that Bellevue's allegations concerning Hartgrove's conduct through May 5, 2009 (the issuance date of CMS's letter), are substantially similar to the publicly disclosed allegations. However, it found that Bellevue's allegations that Hartgrove continued its billing practices beyond May 5, 2009, involves a different time period. Thus, it concluded that Bellevue's claims concerning conduct after May 5, 2009, are not substantially similar to the publicly disclosed allegations.

We agree with the district court as to Bellevue's allegations through May 5, 2009. Bellevue's complaint describes the same contested conduct and pertains to the same entity. . . .

As to Bellevue's post-May 5, 2009, allegations, we must disagree with the district court in light of our recent holding in *Cause of Action*. . . . Here, as in *Cause of Action*, Bellevue's allegations pertain to the same entity and describe the same contested conduct as the publicly disclosed information. Therefore, we find that Bellevue's post-May 5, 2009, allegations, are substantially similar to the publicly disclosed allegations.

---

[461] *Id.* (citation omitted).
[462] *Id.* (citation and brackets omitted).
[463] *Id.* (citation omitted).
[464] *Id.* at 279 (citing Absher, 764 F.3d at 709 n.10).

Moving to the third step, we ask whether Bellevue was an original source of the information upon which the allegations in his complaint were based. . . .

After the district court's decision, *Bogina* made clear that the amended definition of "original source" controls.[465] Therefore, Bellevue must show that he "has knowledge that is independent of and materially adds to the publicly disclosed allegations or transactions" and "has voluntarily provided the information to the Government before filing [its] action."[466] It is undisputed that Bellevue voluntarily provided information concerning his allegations to the Government before filing suit.

In order to possess "independent knowledge," the relator must "have learned of the allegation or transactions independently of the public disclosure."[467] As the district court noted, we have permitted an inference of independent knowledge where the relator had an opportunity to observe the contested conduct.[468] However, we need not decide whether Bellevue is entitled to such an inference because he has not "materially add[ed]" to the publicly disclosed allegations.

Bellevue recycles the district court's analysis regarding his material addition to the publicly disclosed allegations. However, this line of reasoning was foreclosed by *Cause of Action*. In that case, we found that because the plaintiff's allegations were "substantially similar to" the publicly disclosed allegations, the plaintiff did not "materially add" to the public disclosure and could not be an original source.[469] This conclusion applies with equal force here, and Bellevue has not provided a reason to diverge from it. Thus, we find that Bellevue is not an original source of the allegations, and his FCA and IFCA claims are precluded by the public-disclosure bar.

III. CONCLUSION

The allegations in this case fall within the public-disclosure bar to the FCA, and, therefore, the district court properly dismissed the amended complaint with prejudice. The judgment of the district court is AFFIRMED.

---

[465] *See* 809 F.3d at 369.
[466] 31 U.S.C. § 3730(e)(4)(B) (2010).
[467] *Cause of Action*, 815 F.3d at 283 (citation omitted).
[468] *See* Leveski v. ITT Educational Services, Inc., 719 F.3d 818, 838 (7th Cir. 2013); United States *ex rel.* Lamers v. City of Green Bay, 168 F.3d 1013, 1017 (7th Cir. 1999).
[469] 815 F.3d at 283 (citation omitted).

Cochise Consultancy, Inc. et al. v. United States ex rel. Hunt[470]

The False Claims Act contains two limitations periods that apply to a "civil action under section 3730"—that is, an action asserting that a person presented false claims to the United States Government. 31 U. S. C. §3731(b). The first period requires that the action be brought within 6 years after the statutory violation occurred. The second period requires that the action be brought within 3 years after the United States official charged with the responsibility to act knew or should have known the relevant facts, but not more than 10 years after the violation. Whichever period provides the later date serves as the limitations period.

This case requires us to decide how to calculate the limitations period for *qui tam* suits in which the United States does not intervene. The Court of Appeals held that these suits are "civil action[s] under section 3730" and that the limitations periods in §3731(b) apply in accordance with their terms, regardless of whether the United States intervenes. It further held that, for purposes of the second period, the private person who initiates the *qui tam* suit cannot be deemed the official of the United States. We agree, and therefore affirm.

I

. . .

At issue here is the Act's statute of limitations, which provides:

> "(b) A civil action under section 3730 may not be brought—
>
> "(1) more than 6 years after the date on which the violation of section 3729 is committed, or
>
> "(2) more than 3 years after the date when facts material to the right of action are known or reasonably should have been known by the official of the United States charged with responsibility to act in the circumstances, but in no event more than 10 years after the date on which the violation is committed,
>
> "whichever occurs last." §3731(b).

. . .

---

[470] USSC, May 13, 2019.

II

The first question before us is whether the limitations period in §3731(b)(2) is available in a relator-initiated suit in which the Government has declined to intervene. If so, the second question is whether the relator in such a case should be considered "the official of the United States" whose knowledge triggers §3731(b)(2)'s 3-year limitations period.

A

Section 3731(b) sets forth two limitations periods that apply to "civil action[s] under section 3730." Both Government-initiated suits under §3730(a) and relator-initiated suits under §3730(b) are "civil action[s] under section 3730." Thus, the plain text of the statute makes the two limitations periods applicable in both types of suits.

Cochise agrees with that view as to the limitations period in §3731(b)(1), but argues that the period in §3731(b)(2) is available in a relator-initiated suit only if the Government intervenes. According to Cochise, starting a limitations period when the party entitled to bring a claim learns the relevant facts is a default rule of tolling provisions, so subsection (b)(2) should be read to apply only when the Government is a party. In short, under Cochise's reading, a relator-initiated, nonintervened suit is a "civil action under section 3730" for purposes of subsection (b)(1) but not subsection (b)(2).

This reading is at odds with fundamental rules of statutory interpretation. In all but the most unusual situations, a single use of a statutory phrase must have a fixed meaning. See *Ratzlaf v. United States*, 510 U. S. 135, 143 (1994). We therefore avoid interpretations that would "attribute different meanings to the same phrase." *Reno v. Bossier Parish School Bd.*, 528 U. S. 320, 329 (2000). Here, either a relator-initiated, nonintervened suit is a "civil action under section 3730"—and thus subject to the limitations periods in subsections (b)(1) and (b)(2)—or it is not. It is such an action. Whatever the default tolling rule might be, the clear text of the statute controls this case.

. . .

Again pointing to *Graham County*, Cochise next contends that our reading would lead to "'counterintuitive results.'" Brief for Petitioners 26. For instance, if the Government discovers the fraud on the day it occurred, it would have 6 years to bring suit, but if a relator instead discovers the fraud on the day it occurred and the Government does not discover it, the relator could have as many as 10 years to bring suit. That discrepancy arises because §3731(b)(2) begins its limitations period on the date that "the official of the United States charged with responsibility to act" obtained knowledge of the relevant facts. But we see nothing unusual about extending the limitations period when the Government official did not know and should not reasonably have known the relevant facts, given that the Government is the party harmed by the false claim and will receive the bulk of any recovery. See §3730(d). In any event, a result that "may seem odd . . . is not absurd." *Exxon Mobil Corp. v. Allapattah Services, Inc.*, 545 U. S. 546, 565 (2005). Although in *Graham County* we sought "a construction that avoids . . . counterintuitive results," there the text "admit[ted] of two plausible interpretations." 545 U. S., at 421, 419, n. 2. Here, Cochise points to no other plausible interpretation of the text, so the "'judicial inquiry is complete.'" *Barnhart v. Sigmon Coal Co.*, 534 U. S. 438, 462 (2002).

B

Cochise's fallback argument is that the relator in a nonintervened suit should be considered "the official of the United States charged with responsibility to act in the circumstances," meaning that §3731(b)(2)'s 3-year limitations period would start when the relator knew or should have known about the fraud. But the statute provides no support for reading "the official of the United States" to encompass a private relator.

· · ·

For the foregoing reasons, the judgment of the Court of Appeals is

Affirmed.

DiFiore v. CSL Behring, LLC[471]

Marie DiFiore asserted claims against her former employer, CSL Behring, for retaliation in violation of the False Claims Act, and for wrongful discharge under a theory of constructive discharge in violation of Pennsylvania state law. . . . The judge instructed the jury that the FCA retaliation provision required that protected activity be the "but-for" cause of adverse actions against DiFiore. The jury found in favor of CSL Behring. DiFiore appeals the District Court's jury instruction using the "but-for" causation standard, the grant of summary judgment, and one additional jury instruction. For the reasons that follow, we affirm and hold that an employee's protected activity must be the "but-for" cause of adverse actions to support a claim of retaliation under the FCA.

DiFiore worked for CSL Behring from 2008 until her resignation in 2012, first as an Associate Director of Marketing/New Products, and then, after a promotion in August 2011, as Director of Marketing. While at CSL, and particularly after her promotion, DiFiore became concerned about the activities of CSL and its employees in marketing drugs for off-label use and including off-label use in sales forecasts. . . . DiFiore expressed her concerns to her supervisors, and she contends that CSL initiated a third-party compliance audit in part because of her complaints.

DiFiore alleges that as a consequence of her protected conduct, she suffered the following six adverse employment actions, all of which took place after her promotion to Director of Marketing.

. . .

The District Court correctly applied Supreme Court caselaw when it instructed the jury using the "but-for" causation standard for DiFiore's FCA relation claim.[472] Under the FCA's anti-retaliation provision, an employee is entitled to relief if she was "discharged, demoted, suspended, threatened, harassed, or in any other manner discriminated against in the terms and conditions of employment because of lawful acts" conducted in furtherance of an FCA action.[473]

The parties dispute what causation standard applies to the statutory language "because of" in § 3730(h). To prove retaliation under the FCA, a plaintiff must show (1) that he engaged in protected conduct, and (2) that he was discriminated

---

[471] 879 F.3d 71 (3d Cir. 2018).
[472] *See* Gross v. FBL Fin. Servs., Inc., 557 U.S. 167, 176, 129 S.Ct. 2343, 174 L.Ed.2d 119 (2009); Univ. of Tex. Sw. Med. Ctr. v. Nassar, 570 U.S. 338, 133 S.Ct. 2517, 2533, 186 L.Ed.2d 503 (2013).
[473] 31 U.S.C. § 3730(h)(1).

against because of his protected conduct.[474] The District Court ruled that DiFiore was required to show that her protected activity was the "but-for" cause of an adverse action, while DiFiore contends that a lower standard applies and she should have only been required to prove that her protected activity was a "motivating factor" in the adverse actions taken by CSL.

. . .

In *Gross*, the Supreme Court held that the ordinary meaning of "because of" in the Age Discrimination in Employment Act required a plaintiff to prove that age was the "but-for" cause of the employer's adverse action.[475] . . . .

After *Gross*, the Supreme Court again addressed causation standards in the context of retaliation claims. In *Nassar*, the Supreme Court held that the use of "because" in the Title VII anti-retaliation provisions requires a plaintiff to prove that the desire to retaliate was the "but-for" cause of the adverse employment action.[476] The majority analyzed Title VII as prohibiting two separate categories of wrongful conduct and applying distinct causation standards to those categories. The first category—status-based discrimination on the basis of race, color, religion, sex or national origin—could be proven using the motivating factor standard because the language prohibiting this type of discrimination expressly required the lower burden.[477] In contrast, the language of the second category of prohibited conduct—employer retaliation on account of an employee having opposed, complained of, or sought remedies for discrimination—contains no language specifying the lower standard of motivating factor.[478]

To interpret Title VII's anti-retaliation provision, the Court looked to its earlier decision in *Gross* for guidance. The Court held that the word "because" in the Title VII anti-retaliation provision had the same meaning as the words "because of" in the ADEA. Consequently, Title VII retaliation claims require proof that the protected activity was the "but-for" cause of the adverse employment action.[479] . . . . Against this background, the Court held that the motivating factor test only applied to status discrimination under Title VII because the language of

---

[474] Hutchins v. Wilentz, Goldman & Spitzer, 253 F.3d 176, 186 (3d Cir. 2001); United States *ex rel.* Hefner v. Hackensack Univ. Med. Ctr., 495 F.3d 103, 110 (3d Cir. 2007).
[475] *Gross*, 557 U.S. at 176, 129 S.Ct. 2343.
[476] *Nassar*, 133 S.Ct. at 2527–28, 2533.
[477] 42 U.S.C. § 2000e-2(a), (m) ("an unlawful employment practice is established when the complaining party demonstrates that race, color, religion, sex, or national origin was a motivating factor for any employment practice, even though other factors also motivated the practice").
[478] 42 U.S.C. § 2000e-3(a).
[479] *Nassar*, 133 S.Ct. at 2533.

the statute explicitly required it. Because such language was not present in the anti-retaliation provisions of Title VII, "but-for" causation applied.

Here, the District Court concluded that it was compelled by *Nassar* to apply "but-for" causation to DiFiore's FCA retaliation claim because of the "identical language" in the FCA, the ADEA, and Title VII. The court relied on *Nassar*'s logic and instructed the jury that DiFiore's protected activity must have been the "but-for" cause of any adverse employment action she suffered.

The District Court's reasoning was sound given not only the Supreme Court's precedent, but also given our own caselaw addressing the effect of *Gross* and *Nassar* in the context of FMLA retaliation claims. In *Egan v. Delaware River Port Authority*, the plaintiff asserted a FMLA retaliation claim,[480] urging that the district court should have given a mixed motive instruction, requiring less than "but-for" causation. The FMLA regulation at issue in Egan prohibited employers from considering the use of FMLA leave as a "negative factor" in an employment decision. . . Based on this language, we applied a lessened causation standard requiring plaintiffs to show only that the use of FMLA leave was a "negative factor" in the adverse employment decision.

Unlike the language of the FMLA anti-retaliation regulation, the language of the FCA anti-retaliation provision uses the same "because of" language that compelled the Supreme Court to require "but-for" causation in *Nassar* and *Gross*. For this reason, the District Court correctly instructed the jury that to find retaliation, it had to find that DiFiore's protected conduct was the "but-for" cause of the adverse employment action.

For the foregoing reasons, retaliation claims under the FCA require proof of "but-for" causation. We affirm the District Court's instruction to the jury employing that standard.

. . .

For the reasons explained above, we affirm the orders of the District Court.

---

[480] 851 F.3d 263, 266–67 (3d Cir. 2017).

Fakorede v. Mid-South Heart Center, P.C.[481]

. . .

Fakorede's relevant pre-termination conduct was related to the calculation of costs attributed to him by Mid-South for which it was effectively reimbursed by the Hospital District. Fakorede requested information related to those expenses, including a year-end financial report and underlying documents and data. After receiving the financial report, he "expressed concerns" about some of the expenses attributed to him. Eventually, he requested an independent review of the report and was told there would be a line-item audit. Although Fakorede was "reassured by the line-item audit," he nonetheless "reminded" the Hospital District that "only expenses permitted by federal law for the [Hospital District] to cover" were properly attributable to Fakorede under his recruiting agreement. He was terminated approximately one week later. To tie his conduct to federal fraud, as is necessary for his claim to survive, Fakorede asserts that, if Mid-South improperly calculated expenses to overdraw from the support account, then any Medicare claims "tainted" by violations of the Stark Law and Anti-Kickback Statute were submitted to Medicare in violation of the FCA. This legal conclusion itself is not unfounded, as the connection between the Anti-Kickback Statute, the Stark Law, and the FCA is statutory.[482] Nonetheless, one cannot reasonably infer from Fakorede's complaint that his efforts were directed toward preventing what he reasonably believed was ongoing federal fraud.

In essence, Fakorede requested information related to expenses attributed to him by his private employer, expressed concerns as to whether those expenses were correctly calculated and reimbursed by a Tennessee entity, and reminded others that an audit should check for compliance with federal law. This fails to allege conduct reasonably related to fraud against the federal government.[483] Accordingly, Fakorede has not pleaded that he engaged in protected activity.

. . .

For the foregoing reasons, we affirm the district court.

---

[481] 709 F.App'x 787 (6th Cir. 2017).
[482] *See* 42 U.S.C. § 1395nn(a)(1)(B); 42 U.S.C. § 1320a-7b(g).
[483] *See* McKenzie v. BellSouth Telecommunications, Inc., 219 F.3d 508, 516–17 (6th Cir. 2000) (protected activity does not include "merely urging compliance with regulations") (citing U.S. *ex rel.* Yesudian v. Howard Univ., 153 F.3d 731, 744 (D.C. Cir. 1998)); see also *Iqbal*, 556 U.S. at 679, 129 S.Ct. 1937 (we do not accept legal conclusions as true absent supporting factual allegations).

Grabcheski v. American International Group, Inc.[484]

Plaintiff-Appellant Alex Grabcheski ("Grabcheski") appeals from the judgment of the United States District Court for the Southern District of New York, denying his motion for leave to file a third amended complaint and dismissing his False Claims Act ("FCA"),[485] case against Defendant-Appellee American International Group, Inc. ("AIG") with prejudice. We assume the parties' familiarity with the underlying facts, the procedural history of the case, and the issues on appeal.

. . .

On the merits, we find that Grabcheski has failed adequately to allege an FCA claim. Under the FCA, any person who "knowingly makes, uses, or causes to be made or used, a false record or statement material to an obligation to pay or transmit money or property to the Government" is liable for a civil penalty.[486] We affirm because, even assuming arguendo that Grabcheski has sufficiently alleged knowing "false ... statement [s]" with the particularity required by Federal Rule of Civil Procedure 9(b), . . . he has not plausibly pleaded that they were material.

The FCA defines materiality as "having a natural tendency to influence, or be capable of influencing, the payment or receipt of money or property."[487] Therefore, in assessing materiality, we "look to the effect on the likely or actual behavior of the recipient of the alleged misrepresentation."[488] Materiality must be pleaded with particularity under Rule 9(b).[489]

. . .

We have considered Grabcheski's remaining arguments and find them to be without merit. Accordingly, we AFFIRM the judgment of the district court.

---

[484] 687 Fed.Appx. 84 (2nd Cir. 2017).
[485] 31 U.S.C. § 3729 et seq.
[486] 31 U.S.C. § 3729(a)(1)(G).
[487] 31 U.S.C. § 3729(b)(4).
[488] *Universal Health Servs.*, 136 S.Ct. at 2002 (alterations omitted) (quoting 26 Richard A. Lord, Williston on Contracts § 69:12 (4th ed. 2003)).
[489] *See*, e.g., id. at 2004 n.6; Minzer v. Keegan, 218 F.3d 144, 151 (2d Cir. 2000).

Heath v. Indianapolis Fire Department[490]

In January 2015, Quinn Heath applied to become an Indianapolis firefighter. Over the next four months, he passed the Indianapolis Fire Department's written examination, oral interview, and Certified Physical Agility Test. Quinn's performance during the application process led to his placement on a ranked list for hiring consideration. The Department hired two academy classes in 2015 from that ranked list, but Quinn was not selected for either class.

Meanwhile, Quinn's father—Rodney Heath—filed a *qui tam* suit under the False Claims Act against the Indianapolis Fire Department, alleging that the Department had made false statements of material fact to the federal government in order to receive federal grant funds. At the time, Rodney was a backup investigator in the Department's arson unit. The same day that Quinn found out he had not been selected for the second academy class, the Department's Deputy Chief told several Department employees they needed to be interviewed by the U.S. Department of Homeland Security in connection with Rodney's suit.

Thereafter, Quinn joined his father's suit, alleging that the Department retaliated against him for his father's complaint, in violation of the False Claims Act. Quinn's retaliation claim alleges that he was not hired as an Indianapolis firefighter because of his father's suit.

The district court granted summary judgment to the Indianapolis Fire Department on Quinn's retaliation claim. Quinn now appeals that decision.

. . .

The district court's dismissal of Quinn's claim turned on its conclusion that the False Claims Act's anti-retaliation provisions do not cover job applicants or prospective employees. This court has not yet addressed that issue, and we decline to do so now. Even assuming that § 3730(h)'s definition of "employee" is broad enough to encompass job applicants or prospective employees, the Indianapolis Fire Department would still be entitled to summary judgment. Section 3730(h)(1) requires that Quinn show he was retaliated against because of his father's protected activity, and he cannot do so.

Recent authority raises a question about what causation standard Quinn must meet to show that he was retaliated against because of his father's protected activity. In *Fanslow v. Chicago Manufacturing Center, Inc.*, relying in part on Title VII principles, we noted that False Claims Act complainants can establish that they were retaliated against because of protected activity by demonstrating that the retaliation was motivated "at least in part" by the protected activity.[491] Nearly ten

---

[490] 889 F.3d 872 (7th Cir. 2018).
[491] 384 F.3d 469, 485 (7th Cir. 2004).

years post-*Fanslow*, the Supreme Court held that Title VII retaliation claims require but-for causation, rather than the lesser mixed-motive standard of causation we described in *Fanslow*. *Univ. of Tex. Sw. Med. Ctr. v. Nassar*.[492] We have not yet revisited *Fanslow* to extend *Nassar's* Title VII holding to § 3730(h)(1), though the similarity of the two provisions might give us reason to do so in a future case. See *United States ex rel. King v. Solvay Pharm., Inc.*[493] But the causation standard makes no difference here. Under any standard, there is no evidence—even when construing the facts in Quinn's favor—from which a jury could conclude that the Department did not hire Quinn because of his father's *qui tam* suit.

. . .

II. CONCLUSION

Quinn's retaliation claim against the Indianapolis Fire Department raises a complicated question about the scope of the False Claims Act's anti-retaliation provisions. We need not resolve that question in this case, however. Even assuming that the meaning of "employee" under § 3730(h) is broad enough to encompass job applicants or prospective employees, there are no facts from which a jury could conclude that Quinn was retaliated against because of his father's *qui tam* suit.

The district court's judgment in favor of the Indianapolis Fire Department on Quinn's retaliation claim is AFFIRMED.

---

[492] 570 U.S. 338, 360, 133 S.Ct. 2517, 186 L.Ed.2d 503 (2013).
[493] 871 F.3d 318, 333 (5th Cir. 2017) (noting that the False Claims Act requires but-for causation).

IN RE: NATURAL GAS ROYALTIES QUI TAM LITIGATION[494]

This is the second appeal in a *qui tam* case lasting over 20 years and initially involving more than 300 natural gas industry defendants. The number of defendants has shrunk significantly, and the issues on this appeal present narrow questions. Specifically, Relator and Appellant Jack J. Grynberg appeals two district court orders awarding attorney fees.

. . .

Mr. Grynberg presents two issues on appeal. First, he argues the district court abused its discretion when it awarded attorney fees under the FCA relating to the district court proceedings. We hold the district court did not abuse its discretion and affirm. Second, Mr. Grynberg argues the district court did not have authority to award appellate-related attorney fees. We agree and reverse. Mr. Grynberg challenges only whether these fees should have been awarded and does not challenge whether the amounts are reasonable.

A. *Attorney Fees for District Court Proceedings*

. . .

2. Legal Standard

The FCA's fee-shifting provision provides:

> If the Government does not proceed with the action and the person bringing the action conducts the action, the court may award to the defendant its reasonable attorneys' fees and expenses if the defendant prevails in the action and *the court finds that the claim of the person bringing the action was clearly frivolous, clearly vexatious, or brought primarily for purposes of harassment.*

31 U.S.C. § 3730(d)(4) (emphasis added).

We focus on the phrase "clearly frivolous," which is the ground for our decision here. The Supreme Court provided guidance on frivolousness in *Christiansburg Garment Co. v. EEOC*, 434 U.S. 412, 98 S.Ct. 694, 54 L.Ed.2d 648 (1978). In *Christiansburg*, the Court addressed "what standard should inform a district court's discretion in deciding whether to award attorney's fees to a successful *defendant* in a Title VII action."[495] The Court said "[t]o the extent that abstract words can deal with concrete cases," attorney fees may be awarded "upon

---

[494] 845 F.3d 1010 (10th 2017).
[495] *Id.* at 417, 98 S.Ct. 694.

a finding that the plaintiff's action was frivolous, unreasonable, or without foundation, even though not brought in subjective bad faith."[496]

4. Analysis

Our review of the record has uncovered no reason to question the district court's findings regarding Mr. Grynberg's handling of the case. The court properly articulated and applied the legal standards under § 3730(d)(4) and *Christiansburg* after reviewing "the entire course of the litigation." The court did not abuse its discretion in determining Mr. Grynberg's FCA claims were clearly frivolous.

Without support from the inaccurate Exhibit Bs, his own personal dealings and investigation of the fraud, or any other supporting evidence, Mr. Grynberg's claims against the FCA Appellees lacked an evidentiary foundation. In the district court's words, the allegations *Grynberg I* deemed critical to the claims' success were based on nothing more than "complete speculation." *In re Nat. Gas Royalties Qui Tam Litig.*, 2011 WL 12854134, at *7 ¶ 26. The district court therefore did not abuse its discretion in awarding fees under § 3730(d)(4) based on the clear frivolousness of Mr. Grynberg's claims against the FCA Appellees. Because the clear frivolousness of his claims is a sufficient ground to affirm, we need not address whether the court abused its discretion in awarding fees either because Mr. Grynberg's original-source position was clearly frivolous or because his claims were clearly vexatious.

We affirm the district court's grant of attorney fees under § 3730(d)(4).

B. *Attorney Fees for the First Appeal*

In *Hoyt v. Robson Cos., Inc.*, we held that a district court lacked authority to award appellate-related fees to a prevailing party absent explicit statutory authorization.[497] The party must first apply to us for appellate-related attorney fees.[498] The Appellate-Fee Appellees did not do so.

---

[496] *Id.* at 421, 98 S.Ct. 694.
[497] 11 F.3d 983, 985 (10th Cir. 1993).
[498] *Id.*

The district court therefore lacked authority to award appellate-related fees. We reverse.

C. *Attorney Fees for this Appeal*

In their brief, Appellees request attorney fees and costs incurred in this appeal under § 3730(d)(4) and Rule 38 of the Federal Rules of Appellate Procedure. Although Appellees seem to equate the two grounds for fees, they apply in different circumstances. Under § 3730(d)(4), attorney fees are appropriate if the district court determines a claim was "clearly frivolous, clearly vexatious, or brought primarily for purposes of harassment." Under Rule 38, in contrast, attorney fees and costs are appropriate if a court of appeals determines "an appeal is frivolous."[499]

Even if a district court does not abuse its discretion in determining fees are appropriate under § 3730(d)(4), it does not necessarily follow that a court of appeals will find an appeal from that award frivolous. Such was the case here — where the district court did not abuse its discretion in awarding fees under § 3730(d)(4), but the appeal was not frivolous because, as we have held above, the district court lacked authority to award appellate-related fees.

Moreover, to the extent Appellees request fees under Rule 38, we deny their request for failure to file a separate motion. . . .

Accordingly, we deny Appellees' request for attorney fees and costs relating to this appeal.

III. CONCLUSION

We (1) affirm the district court's grant of attorney fees under the FCA's fee-shifting provision, 31 U.S.C. § 3730(d)(4); (2) reverse the court's grant of attorney fees relating to the first appeal; (3) remand the case to the district court to enter orders and judgments consistent with this opinion; and (4) deny Appellees' request for attorney fees relating to this appeal.

---

[499] Fed. R. App. P. 38.

O'Hara et al. v. Nika Technologies, Inc.[500]

William C. O'Hara sued his employer, NIKA Technologies, Inc., under the so-called "whistleblower-protection provisions" of the False Claims Act... claiming that NIKA fired him for disclosing another company's alleged fraud on the Government. The district court entered summary judgment for NIKA on the first claim because it determined that § 3730(h) only protects disclosures targeting the whistleblower's employer.... Although we hold that the district court applied the wrong legal standard to the § 3730(h) claim, we affirm its grant of summary judgment because O'Hara's disclosures are not protected under the correct legal standard either....

. . .

Regarding the § 3730(h) claim, the district court held that the statute only protects a whistleblower from negative employment action when his employer had reason to know that the whistleblower was contemplating an FCA action against *the employer*. In this case, NIKA had reason to know that O'Hara was contemplating an FCA action against NTVI. But there was no genuine dispute that NIKA lacked reason to believe that O'Hara was contemplating a lawsuit against NIKA itself. The district court therefore determined that NIKA was entitled to judgment as a matter of law.

. . .

First, we address O'Hara's § 3730(h) argument. We hold that the district court's conclusion that § 3730(h) only protects whistleblowing activity directed at the whistleblower's employer was erroneous, because the plain language of § 3730(h) protects disclosures in furtherance of a viable FCA action against *any person or company*. Nevertheless, we affirm the district court's grant of summary judgment because, applying the correct legal standard, we are compelled to conclude that O'Hara's disclosures were not in furtherance of a viable FCA action.

1.

First, we hold that the district court's determination that § 3730(h) only protects whistleblowing activity directed at the whistleblower's employer was erroneous, because that interpretation is at odds with the statute's plain language. Construction of a statute begins with the statute's text.... "[W]here, as here, the statute's language is plain, 'the sole function of the courts is to enforce it according to its terms.'"[501] "Courts are not free to read into the language [of a

---

[500] 878 F.3d 470 (4th Cir. 2017).
[501] United States v. Ron Pair Enters., Inc., 489 U.S. 235, 241, 109 S.Ct. 1026, 103 L.Ed.2d 290 (1989) (quoting Caminetti v. United States, 242 U.S. 470, 485, 37 S.Ct. 192, 61 L.Ed. 442 (1917)).

statute] what is not there, but rather should apply the statute as written."[502] *Murphy*, 35 F.3d at 145.

The plain language of § 3730(h) reveals that the statute does not condition protection on the employment relationship between a whistleblower and the subject of his disclosures. Section 3730(h) protects a whistleblower from retaliation for "lawful acts done ... in furtherance of an action under this section." 31 U.S.C. § 3730(h)(1). The phrase "an action under this section" refers to a lawsuit under § 3730(b), which in turn states that "[a] person may bring a civil action for a violation of [the FCA]." *Id.* § 3730(b)(1). Therefore, § 3730(h) protects lawful acts in furtherance of an FCA action. This language indicates that protection under the statute depends on the type of conduct that the whistleblower discloses—*i.e.*, a violation of the FCA—rather than the whistleblower's relationship to the subject of his disclosures.

The district court's construction of § 3730(h) improperly reads a limitation into the statute that does not appear in its text. As explained above, the statute describes protected activity in terms of the type of conduct disclosed by the whistleblower. It is silent regarding the relationship between the whistleblower and the subject of his disclosures. Accordingly, the district court's conclusion that § 3730(h) only protects disclosures that reveal information about the whistleblower's employer reads into statute's language a limitation that is not there.

Because the district court's interpretation of § 3730(h) contradicts the statute's plain language, we are compelled to hold that the interpretation was erroneous.

2.

We nevertheless affirm the district court's determination that NIKA was entitled to summary judgment on the § 3730(h) claim. A prima facie case of retaliation under § 3730(h) requires the plaintiff to prove, among other things, that he was engaged in "protected activity."[503] We have previously held that this standard requires the whistleblower to demonstrate that the conduct he disclosed reasonably could have led to a viable FCA action.[504] The undisputed facts in this case demonstrate that O'Hara did not disclose any conduct that could have led to a viable FCA action. We are therefore compelled to hold that NIKA is entitled to judgment as a matter of law.

O'Hara argues that he engaged in protected activity because he revealed that NTVI attempted to charge the Government for unnecessary work by submitting a bid to install a protective slab over pipelines that would be abandoned later in

---

[502] United States v. Murphy, 35 F.3d 143, 145 (4th Cir. 1994).
[503] Zahodnick v. IBM Corp., 135 F.3d 911, 914 (4th Cir. 1997).
[504] Mann v. Heckler & Koch Def., Inc., 630 F.3d 338, 344 (4th Cir. 2010).

the Project. The disclosed conduct, however, could not have led to a viable FCA action, because a contractor is not "liable for defrauding the Government by following the Government's explicit directions,"[505] and it is undisputed that the Government directed NTVI to submit the bid in question. In fact, in a sworn affidavit to the OIG, O'Hara acknowledged that NTVI submitted its bid to construct the protective slab in response to a government RFP for a "[s]tructural [s]lab at [c]ooling [t]ower [l]ines."

For these reasons, there is no genuine dispute that that the Government solicited the bid at issue. Accordingly, we are compelled to hold that O'Hara's disclosure was not protected because it could not have led to a viable FCA action. NIKA is thus entitled to summary judgment on the § 3730(h) claim.

. . .

In sum, we hold that the district court erroneously concluded that § 3730(h) only protects whistleblowing activity directed at the whistleblower's employer, because the plain language of § 3730(h) protects disclosures that reasonably could lead to a viable FCA action against any person or company. NIKA is nevertheless entitled to summary judgment on the § 3730(h) claim, because O'Hara did not disclose any conduct that could have reasonably led to a viable FCA claim. . . . For these reasons, the judgment of the district court is

AFFIRMED.

---

[505] United States *ex rel.* Becker v. Westinghouse Savannah River Co., 305 F.3d 284, 289 (4th Cir. 2002) (quoting United States *ex rel.* Durcholz v. FKW, Inc., 189 F.3d 542, 545 (7th Cir.1999)),

Smith v. LHC Group[506]

I. Introduction

This case under the False Claims Act, 31 U.S.C. §§ 3729–31, arises from plaintiff Sue Smith's allegations against the defendants, her employers, LHC Group, Inc., and Kentucky LV, LLC, for perpetrating health care fraud on the federal government by seeking and receiving fraudulent reimbursements. Rather than participate in the fraud, she quit her job as Director of Nursing with the defendants. She apparently did so as a matter of conscience and to avoid suspicion in any future investigation by the Government. She then sued her employers for damages under a theory of "constructive discharge," or discrimination "in the terms and conditions of employment because of lawful acts done by the employee ... to stop 1 or more violations" of the False Claims Act by her employers.

The district court dismissed Smith's case as failing to state a valid cause of action as follows:

> Even accepting all of Smith's claims as true, as the Court must, and assuming arguendo that such a theory could constitute "intolerable working conditions" ... her claim must fail. Smith's theory focuses solely on the allegedly insufferable working conditions she faced, but it ignores that a prima facie case of constructive discharge requires that an employer also act with an intention to force an employee to quit his or her job. ... Smith's complaint tells the story of an employee who unwittingly became trapped working for a company who adopted a business model based on fraud, and despite efforts to follow protocol, had no real control over the decisions being made. Quite reasonably, Smith felt like she had to quit her job. But where her claims fails is that she has not alleged that Defendants perpetrated the alleged fraud ... with the specific intention of forcing her to do so.

Smith v. LHC Grp., Inc., No. CV 5:17-15-KKC, 2017 WL 2838048, at *3–4 (E.D. Ky. June 30, 2017) (emphasis added) (citations omitted).

The meaning of the federal statute is not clear on the question of interpretation before us. The federal question before us is whether under § 3730(h) the district court is correct that an employer like the LHC Group, Inc., here must have a conscious "specific intention," or a subjective intent, for the employee to resign.

---

[506] --- Fed.Appx. ----, 2018 WL 1136072 (6th Cir. March 2, 2018).

We conclude that the intent required by the statute is a more general intent that takes into account all of the circumstances in addition to the employer's "specific intention." The case must therefore be remanded for trial not limited to the defendant corporation's "specific" or subjective intent but including all of the factors that led to the plaintiff's resignation.

If the employee is left to think she may be charged with fraud by the Government if she remains as Director of Nursing, a jury may find that her employer's fraudulent behavior is imposing on her fear that would cause a reasonable employee to resign. The jury may find that the employer's alleged fraudulent behavior plus the employee's moral conscience and reasonable fear of being accused of participating in the employer's fraud is enough to justify quitting. Whether we call her resignation a "constructive discharge," "harassment" or a form of discrimination, the employee should be made "whole" under the statute and accorded the "relief" set out in section (2) of § 3730(h) if the jury finds in her favor.

.   .   .

The question in this appeal is whether the plaintiff, Smith, adequately alleged that she suffered a discharge or adverse employment action when she felt it necessary to resign her job as Director of Nursing because her employer continued to defraud the Government. LHC did not fire or demote Smith. LHC claims that it did not seek her resignation and took no adverse employment action that could constitute a discharge, demotion, or other action for which it should be held liable under § 3730(h). Smith alleges that her employer ignored her complaints and required her to continue working as she had prior to her report while LHC continued defrauding the Government. Smith quit to avoid being implicated in what she perceived to be an illegal and unethical scheme and because she could not in good conscience remain an employee.

Smith acknowledges that she was not fired but argues that her claim survives because LHC "constructively discharged" her. Constructive discharge occurs when "working conditions would have been so difficult or unpleasant that a reasonable person in the employee's shoes would have felt compelled to resign."[507]

The district court found that Smith's complaint fails to allege the elements of intolerable working conditions and employer intent to force the employee to quit.[508] We disagree. First, taking Smith's allegations as true, we find that a jury could find that LHC created intolerable conditions by ignoring Smith's complaints of illegal activity. Her conditions must be analyzed "from the

---

[507] Held v. Gulf Oil Co., 684 F.2d 427, 432 (6th Cir. 1982) (quoting Bourque v. Powell Elec. Mfg., 617 F.2d 61, 65 (5th Cir. 1980)).
[508] LHC Grp., 2017 WL 2838048, at *4.

perspective of a reasonable person in the position that [the plaintiff] was in at the time of her discharge."[509] A jury may conclude that it is damaging to a professional to require her to engage in activity she considers illegal and immoral with the threat of prosecution and loss of her nursing license looming in the background.

. . .

The next question before us is whether the district court is correct in the opinion quoted above that the constructive discharge doctrine requires that the employer must have a conscious "specific intention," i.e., a subjective intent, for the employee to resign.[510]

We disagree with the district court's narrow reading of intent because it focuses only on the outcome LHC specifically desired—profits from the scheme—and fails to take into account the foreseeable consequences of their actions. The Restatement (Second) of Torts § 8A cmt. b (Am. Law Inst. 1965), states:

> Intent is not ... limited to consequences which are desired. If the actor knows that the consequences are certain, or substantially certain, to result from his act, and still goes ahead, he is treated by the law as if he had in fact desired to produce the result.

This circuit has adopted a similarly broad definition: in constructive discharge cases, an employer's "[i]ntent can be shown by demonstrating that quitting was a foreseeable consequence of the employer's actions."[511] Our constructive discharge caselaw is rooted in the "well recognized rule in labor relations law that 'a man is held to intend the foreseeable consequences of his conduct.' "[512]

. . .

We therefore clarify that the standard described by *Held* is ultimately an objective one. The employee alleging constructive discharge need not prove that his or her employer undertook actions with the subjective intention of forcing the employee to quit. Rather, the *Held* intent requirement can be satisfied so long as the employee's resignation was a reasonably foreseeable consequence of the employer's actions.[513] Taking the facts of the complaint as true and drawing all reasonable inferences in favor of Smith, her repeated complaints to management

---

[509] Williams v. Caterpillar Tractor Co., 770 F.2d 47, 50 (6th Cir. 1985).
[510] *See* LHC Grp., 2017 WL 2838048, at *3–4 (emphasis added) (citations omitted).
[511] Moore v. KUKA Welding Sys. & Robot Corp., 171 F.3d 1073, 1080–81 (6th Cir. 1999).
[512] *Held*, 684 F.2d at 432.
[513] *Held*, 684 F.2d at 432; Moore, 171 F.3d at 1080.

concerning illegal activity should have enabled LHC to foresee that failure to take action against the fraudulent scheme would compel Smith to leave.

The defendants support the district court's requirement of subjective intent also by arguing that the statute itself, § 3730(h)(1), requires the employer to have a "retaliatory" motive when it says that the employer must take adverse employment action "because of lawful acts done by the employee" to counteract the employer's fraud. But the statute also states that a court adjudicating such a fraud claim should provide "all relief necessary to make that employee ... whole" if she is "discriminated against in the terms and conditions of employment." Here the jury may find that the employee is seriously harmed when the defendant continues its fraud and subjects the plaintiff to possible prosecution as Director of Nursing and to the loss of her nursing license and reputation. This court can hardly be said to provide "all relief necessary" if it should impose a subjective intent requirement.

. . .

For the foregoing reasons, the judgment of the district court is REVERSED and the case remanded for further proceedings consistent with this opinion.

Illinois ex rel. Schad, Diamond & Shedden, P.C. v. My Pillow, Inc.[514]

This appeal presents a single issue: where the relator in a successful *qui tam* action brought against a corporation for the benefit of the State of Illinois under the Illinois False Claims Act (Act)[515] is a law firm, does section 4(d)(2) of the Act[516] entitle the firm to an award of both a reasonable amount "for collecting the civil penalty and damages" from the corporation on behalf of the State and an additional amount in attorney fees for the services performed by the firm's own lawyers for the same work? . . . .

BACKGROUND

In July 2013, the law firm of Schad, Diamond and Shedden, P.C., subsequently known as Stephen B. Diamond, P.C. (Diamond), filed a *qui tam* action against My Pillow, Inc. (My Pillow), a Minnesota corporation, pursuant to the Act. . . . The gist of its claim was that My Pillow had "knowingly conceal[ed] or knowingly and improperly avoid[ed] or decrease[d] an obligation to pay or transmit money or property to the state" in violation of section 3(a)(1)(G) of the Act.[517]

. . .

From filing of the complaint to final judgment, Diamond the relator was represented by Diamond the law firm. . . .

. . .

In addition to receiving 30% of the proceeds as compensation for its bringing the action against My Pillow on the State's behalf, Diamond asserted that, under section 4(d)(2) of the Act, My Pillow was also required to pay it "an amount for reasonable expenses which the court finds to have been necessarily incurred, plus reasonable attorneys' fees and costs." Diamond submitted a lengthy fee petition in support of its claim. The total amount requested was $748,383.

. . .

More than 150 years ago, our court expressly rejected the notion that an attorney who represents himself or herself in a legal proceeding may charge a fee for professional services in prosecuting or defending the case. "To allow him to become his own client and charge for professional services in his own cause, although in a representative or trust capacity, would be holding out inducements for professional men to seek such representative place to increase their

---

[514] --- N.E.3d ----, 2018 IL 122487, 2018 WL 4501033 (Ill. 2018).
[515] 740 ILCS 175/1 et seq. (West 2012).
[516] *Id.* § 4(d)(2).
[517] *Id.* § 3(a)(1)(G).

professional business, which would lead to most pernicious results. This is forbidden by every sound principle of professional morality as well as by the policy of the law."[518]

While notions of "professional morality" have evolved since the mid-nineteenth century, our court has continued to adhere to the principle that it is contrary to public policy of Illinois to allow an attorney "to become his own client and charge for professional services in his own cause."[519] This rule has not been limited to individual lawyers. It has also been extended to their law partners.[520]

The most complete modern pronouncement on the subject by our court was made in *Hamer v. Lentz*.[521] In that case, we expressly held that "[a] lawyer representing himself or herself simply does not incur legal fees."[522] To the extent that a lawyer elects to proceed *pro se* in a case for which the legislature has provided statutory authorization for an award of attorney fees, he or she therefore has no attorney fees to claim and is not entitled to an award of fees under the statute.[523] Although not binding on our construction of the Illinois statute at issue in this case, the United States Supreme Court reached the same conclusion when applying a federal fee-shifting statute: a lawyer who represents himself or herself should be treated like any other pro se litigant and may not be awarded attorney fees for the work done by that lawyer on his or her own case.[524]

In *Hamer*, our court explained that there are several reasons why self-represented lawyers should be treated the same as any other *pro se* litigant when it comes to the award of attorney fees. First, where a fee-shifting statute is intended to remove a burden that might otherwise deter litigants from pursuing a legitimate action and was not meant to serve as a reward to successful plaintiffs or a punishment against the Government, the rationale for the law is absent when a lawyer is self-represented. Because a *pro se* lawyer incurs no fees, fees present no barrier to the lawyer's ability to bring his or her cause of action.[525]

Fee-shifting statutes may also advance the goal of avoiding unnecessary litigation by encouraging citizens to seek legal advice before filing suit. Again, however, such objectivity is lacking—and this goal is therefore not advanced—when a litigant, lawyer or otherwise, represents himself or herself. Id. In addition, allowing attorneys to collect fees for representing themselves may engender abusive fee generation practices. The most effective way to deter such potential

---

[518] Willard v. Bassett, 27 Ill. 37, 38 (1861).
[519] Cheney v. Ricks, 168 Ill. 533, 549, 48 N.E. 75 (1897).
[520] Stein v. Kaun, 244 Ill. 32, 38, 91 N.E. 77 (1910).
[521] 132 Ill.2d 49, 138 Ill.Dec. 222, 547 N.E.2d 191 (1989).
[522] *Id.* at 62, 138 Ill.Dec. 222, 547 N.E.2d 191.
[523] *Id.* at 62-63, 138 Ill.Dec. 222, 547 N.E.2d 191.
[524] Kay v. Ehrler, 499 U.S. 432, 437-38, 111 S.Ct. 1435, 113 L.Ed.2d 486 (1991).
[525] *Hamer*, 132 Ill.2d at 62, 138 Ill.Dec. 222, 547 N.E.2d 191.

fee generation, we have held, "is to deny fees to lawyers representing themselves."[526]

. . .

We agree with the appellate court that the line of precedent running through Hamer and its progeny leads directly to the case before us today and determines its outcome. To the extent that Diamond prosecuted its own claim using its own lawyers, the law firm was proceeding *pro se*. Under the foregoing authority, the firm was therefore not entitled to an award of attorney fees for the services those lawyers performed in prosecuting the law firm's claim.

. . .

In its arguments before our court, Diamond directs our attention to the significant revenues it has recovered for the State through this and numerous other actions it has brought under the Act. Those successes have doubtlessly benefitted the people of our State. They are not, however, justification for paying Diamond twice for the same work. Having elected to assume the dual role of litigant and lawyer, Diamond must be content with the percentage share of the award it was granted by the circuit court to compensate it for its efforts in collecting that sum. As would be the case with any other pro se litigant, the law does not permit it to claim an additional amount as attorney fees for the work it did itself. The appellate court was therefore correct when it reversed that portion of the circuit court's judgment awarding Diamond attorney fees for work it performed by the firm's own lawyers and remanded the cause for recalculation of the attorney fee award to include only fees for services performed by the firm's outside counsel.

CONCLUSION

For the foregoing reasons, the judgment of the appellate court is affirmed.

Affirmed.

---

[526] *Id.* at 62-63, 138 Ill.Dec. 222, 547 N.E.2d 191.

Appendix G: Cases

United States ex rel. Ambrosecchia v. Paddock Laboratories, LLC[527]

Relator Shara Ambrosecchia appeals the district court's[3] dismissal of claims she brought against two pharmaceutical manufacturers under the False Claims Act ("FCA"). For the following reasons, we affirm.

. . .

First, Ambrosecchia contends that it is not appropriate to resolve whether the public disclosure bar applies on a motion to dismiss because the public disclosure bar, as amended in 2010, is no longer jurisdictional. Prior to 2010, 31 U.S.C. § 3730(e)(4) removed a court's subject matter jurisdiction where the allegations and transactions of an FCA action previously had been publicly disclosed. . . In 2010, Congress amended § 3730(e)(4) as part of the Patient Protection and Affordable Care Act. . . The amended section 3730(e)(4) provides:

> The court shall dismiss an action or claim under this section, unless opposed by the Government, if substantially the same allegations or transactions as alleged in the action or claim were publicly disclosed—
>
> (i) in a Federal criminal, civil, or administrative hearing in which the Government or its agent is a party;
>
> (ii) in a congressional, Government Accountability Office, or other Federal report, hearing, audit, or investigation; or
>
> (iii) from the news media....[528]

Ambrosecchia argues that this amended language does not pose a jurisdictional question. Therefore, she argues, whether the public disclosure bar applies is a factual question that cannot be resolved prior to summary judgment.

However, this court has already determined that the amended public disclosure bar is appropriately resolved on a motion to dismiss, even assuming that it no longer poses a jurisdictional question.[529] We are not at liberty to disregard this authority as Ambrosecchia advocates. Indeed, neither party disagrees with the conclusion that the amended public disclosure bar is not jurisdictional. Defendants filed their motion to dismiss under Rule 12(b)(6), not 12(b)(1), and the key case Ambrosecchia cites held that the amended public disclosure bar

---

[527] 855 F.3d 949 (8th Cir. 2017).
[528] 31 U.S.C. § 3730(e)(4)(A).
[529] United States *ex rel.* Paulos v. Stryker Corp., 762 F.3d 688, 696 (8th Cir. 2014); United States *ex rel.* Kraxberger v. Kan. City Power & Light Co., 756 F.3d 1075, 1083 (8th Cir. 2014).

173

should be evaluated under Rule 12(b)(6).[530] Accordingly, we proceed to the merits of Defendants' Rule 12(b)(6) motion.

. . .

A relator who qualifies as an original source is exempt from the public disclosure bar.[531] An original source is

> an individual who either (i) prior to a public disclosure under subsection (e)(4)(a) [sic], has voluntarily disclosed to the Government the information on which allegations or transactions in a claim are based, or (2) [sic] who has knowledge that is independent of and materially adds to the publicly disclosed allegations or transactions, and who has voluntarily provided the information to the Government before filing an action under this section.[532]

The record reflects only that Ambrosecchia provided information concerning her contemplated suit to the Government prior to filing her lawsuit, not prior to the public disclosures. Ambrosecchia provided information to the Government in mid-November 2012, a short time before filing her initial complaint on November 20, 2012. The federal reports the district court found to publicly disclose Ambrosecchia's claims were published in the second quarter of 2012 or earlier. Accordingly, Ambrosecchia does not qualify as an original source under subsection (i).

To qualify under subsection (2), Ambrosecchia must have (1) independent knowledge that (2) "materially adds to the publicly disclosed allegations or transactions," in addition to providing the information to the Government before filing.[533] "Independent knowledge is knowledge not derived from the public disclosure."[534] Although the court is obligated to take the allegations in the complaint as true, it is not obligated to accept legal conclusions, and "[a] pleading that offers labels and conclusions or a formulaic recitation of the elements of a cause of action will not do."[535] Ambrosecchia conclusorily alleges that she has independent knowledge that materially adds to publicly available information but does not provide more. This is not sufficient. The complaint also conclusorily

---

[530] *Moore*, 812 F.3d at 297 ("We agree that the public disclosure bar is no longer jurisdictional and that the motion therefore should have been decided under Rule 12(b)(6) rather than Rule 12(b)(1).").
[531] 31 U.S.C. § 3730(e)(4)(A).
[532] *Id.* § 3730(e)(4)(B).
[533] 31 U.S.C. § 3730(e)(4)(B)(2).
[534] *Newell*, 728 F.3d at 797 (quotations omitted).
[535] Ashcroft v. Iqbal, 556 U.S. 662, 678, 129 S.Ct. 1937, 173 L.Ed.2d 868 (2009) (quotations omitted).

asserts that she gained the information from her employment with Defendants, but the complaint does not detail the nature of that information or explain how it relates to her employment. The complaint merely implies that because of her employment in the pharmaceutical industry, she was familiar with the regulatory framework underlying Medicare reimbursement. Thus, when a relative asked her whether a certain drug could be reimbursed, she knew that the drug in question was not eligible. The only independent knowledge in the complaint comes from this relative, who purportedly received reimbursement for an ineligible Paddock drug. This allegation only provides an example of a false claim; it does not materially add to information regarding how Defendants perpetrated the alleged fraud.

Ambrosecchia claims that her information materially adds to the existing information by demonstrating scienter. However, the complaint provides no more than the simple, conclusory allegation that Defendants' actions were knowing. The complaint does not elaborate, and this "formulaic recitation of the elements of [the] cause of action" alone is not sufficient.[536] Accordingly, Ambrosecchia's complaint is insufficient to plausibly state that she qualifies as an original source.

As a result, the public disclosure bar applies, and the district court was correct to dismiss Ambrosecchia's FCA claims.[6] Because we find in Defendants' favor on these grounds, we need not address their argument that Ambrosecchia's complaint does not satisfy Rule 9(b).

. . .

For the foregoing reasons, we affirm.

---

[536] *See Iqbal*, 556 U.S. at 678, 129 S.Ct. 1937 (quotations omitted).

United States ex rel. Armes v. Garman[537]

Relator Jason Armes brought this *qui tam* action on behalf of the United States and the State of Tennessee against two Tennessee hospitals owned by Select Medical Corporation, and several hospital employees and executives ("the Select Medical defendants"). Armes alleged that the Select Medical defendants violated the False Claims Act and the Tennessee Medicaid False Claims Act by submitting false claims for payment to Medicare and Tenncare, Tennessee's Medicaid program. The district court dismissed Armes's claims with prejudice. We AFFIRM, albeit on grounds different from those on which the district court relied.

. . .

District courts must generally give plaintiffs "at least one chance to amend the complaint" before dismissing it with prejudice.[538] Where a plaintiff engages in undue delay or where an amendment would be futile, denial may be appropriate.[539] When a district court denies a motion to amend based on undue delay, we look to see whether the plaintiff had sufficient notice that his complaint was deficient, and if so, whether the plaintiff had an adequate opportunity to cure the deficiencies.[540]

Here, the Select Medical defendants filed a motion to dismiss in November 2015, relying on the first-to-file bar, the public-disclosure bar, and Rule 9(b), putting Armes on notice that his complaint might require amendment. Armes sought and received an extension of time to respond, and responded in January 2016.... He then waited until April 2016, nearly five months after the motion to dismiss and three days before oral argument on that motion, to file a motion to amend his complaint. Even then, Armes did not allege any new schemes that were not barred by the FCA's first-to-file or public-disclosure bars in his proposed amended complaint. The district court did not abuse its discretion by denying Armes's motion to amend his complaint based on undue delay.

. . .

For the foregoing reasons, we AFFIRM the judgment of the district court. We DENY the Select Medical defendants' October 9, 2017, motion to take judicial notice.

---

[537] 719 F.App'x 459 (6th Cir. 2017).
[538] United States *ex rel.* Bledsoe v. Cmty. Health Sys., Inc., 342 F.3d 634, 644 (6th Cir. 2003) (internal quotation marks and citation omitted).
[539] *Id.*
[540] *Id.*

United States ex rel. Bias v. Tangipahoa Parish School Board, et al.[541]

Ronald Bias, a high school JROTC instructor, brought suit against the Tangipahoa Parish School Board and two school employees. The district court dismissed Bias's False Claims Act retaliation, Section 1983, and state law claims pursuant to Federal Rule of Civil Procedure 12(b)(6). We AFFIRM in part, and REVERSE and REMAND in part.

FACTS AND PROCEDURAL BACKGROUND

In August 2008, Ronald Bias, a retired lieutenant colonel in the United States Marine Corps, began working for the Tangipahoa Parish School Board as the Junior Reserve Officers' Training Corps' ("JROTC") senior Marine Corps instructor at Amite High School. One year later, the Marine Corps recalled Bias to active duty but allowed him to retain his position at Amite High. The Marine Corps paid and employed Bias. Bias alleged, however, that he was "in effect" a contractor or agent for the School Board because he was supervised by Amite High Principal Michael Stant.

. . .

II. False Claims Act Retaliation Claim

Bias filed an FCA retaliation claim against the School Board and Stant and Foster in their official capacities. The district court dismissed the official capacity claims as redundant of Bias's claim against the School Board. . . . It also dismissed the claim against the School Board, finding that the Marine Corps was "responsible for the terms and conditions of [Bias's] employment." Therefore, only the Marine Corps or its agents or employees, not the School Board, could have retaliated against Bias.

. . .

A. Required Statutory Relationship

Initially, we examine whether Bias has alleged the kind of relationship with the School Board required by statute. In 2009, Congress amended the FCA retaliation statute by omitting the word "employer" as the only potentially culpable party, and adding "contractor" or "agent" to "employee" as identifiers of a possible aggrieved party.[542] There is little available caselaw discussing the amendment. Most district courts, including some in this circuit, reason that the amendment expanded the range of plaintiffs in FCA retaliation actions while still requiring

---

[541] 816 F.3d 315 (5th Cir. 2016).
[542] Fraud Enforcement and Recovery Act of 2009, Pub.L. No. 111-21, § 4, 123 Stat. 1617, 1624.

that a defendant have "some employer-type relationship with the plaintiff." We factor into our analysis that Section 3730(h)(1) is designed to protect individuals who expose unlawful use or handling of the property of the federal government.[543] Because the FCA is "remedial," its provisions are to be construed "broadly to effectuate its purpose."[544]

. . . . We . . . conclude that the 2009 amendment requires that courts must expand the class of defendants beyond just employers but not interpret that expansion as a license to sue anyone. To discern the outer boundary of liability, we look "to the plain language of the statute, reading it as a whole and mindful of the linguistic choices made by Congress."[545] One of the district courts recognized there still must be an "employer-type relationship,"[546] an articulation we can accept if the meaning is confined to the three types of relationships listed in the statute. Defendants, then, must be those by whom plaintiffs are employed, with whom they contract, or for whom they are agents. In addition, the retaliatory action must be related to "terms and conditions of employment," or the contract or agency relationship.[547]

. . .

"Contractor" requires the existence of some form of contract between parties. Although Bias alleged in his complaint that he was effectively a contractor for the School Board, he did not plead that he entered into a contract with the defendants. Also, counsel conceded in oral argument that no such contract exists.

As for "employee," courts should look to the "conventional master-servant relationship as understood by common-law agency doctrine" where a statute leaves the word undefined.[548] To determine whether an employment relationship exists in other contexts, this circuit applies a "hybrid economic realities/common law control test."[549] . . . .

Similarly, the common law definition of "agency" anticipates "a consensual relationship in which one person ... acts as a representative ... of another ... with power to affect the legal rights and duties of the other person."[550] The person

---

[543] 31 U.S.C. § 3730(h).
[544] United States ex rel. Rigsby v. State Farm Fire & Cas. Co., 794 F.3d 457, 468 (5th Cir.2015), petition for cert. filed (Oct. 21, 2015) (No. 15-513).
[545] *In re Universal Seismic Assocs., Inc.*, 288 F.3d 205, 207 (5th Cir.2002).
[546] *Wuestenhoeffer*, 2014 WL 7409760, at *7 (emphasis added)
[547] 31 U.S.C. § 3730(h)(1).
[548] Community for Creative Non-Violence v. Reid, 490 U.S. 730, 739-40, 109 S.Ct. 2166, 104 L.Ed.2d 811 (1989).
[549] Muhammad v. Dallas Cnty. Cmty. Supervision & Corr. Dep't, 479 F.3d 377, 380 (5th Cir.2007) (applying Title VII of the Civil Rights Act).
[550] Restatement (Third) of Agency § 1.01, cmt. c.

represented, as in a master-servant situation, "has a right to control the ... agent."[551]

. . .

In summary, exactly what the relationship was between Bias and the School Board is unclear. It is plausible, though, that he was, as claimed, an agent (his counsel acknowledged Bias was not a contractor). Bias did not expressly contend that he was an employee. There is enough pleaded in the complaint to make it plausible, as required by *Twombly*, that Bias had the kind of relationship required by statute with the School Board.[552]

B. Retaliatory Acts

As for the alleged retaliatory acts, this court has not examined in any depth what constitutes retaliation under the FCA. The statute itself provides a list of non-exhaustive examples. . . . Other circuits, have expanded on that list, holding that "behavior ... constitute[s] retaliation [if] ... it would be sufficient to constitute an adverse employment action under Title VII."[553]

. . .

For purposes of deciding whether dismissal under Rule 12(b)(6) is appropriate, Bias's allegations about Stant "well might have dissuaded" Bias from reporting misappropriation of government funds. . . . Additionally, Bias pled enough facts to make it plausible that Stant was acting within the scope of his employment, or at the very least, with the apparent authority of the School Board. . . . Bias has sufficiently stated a claim against the School Board, based on Stant's alleged actions against him. . . . We reverse the district court's dismissal of his FCA retaliation claim as to that defendant.

. . .

We REVERSE the dismissal of Bias's FCA retaliation claim against the School Board, and REMAND. We otherwise AFFIRM.

---

[551] *Id.*
[552] 550 U.S. at 570, 127 S.Ct. 1955.
[553] Moore v. Cal. Inst. of Tech. Jet Propulsion Lab., 275 F.3d 838, 847-48 (9th Cir.2002).

United States ex rel. Booker et al. v. Pfizer, Inc.[554]

On August 31, 2009, the pharmaceutical company Pfizer, Inc. settled various claims that it had violated the False Claims Act ("FCA"),[555] with the U.S. Department of Justice ("DOJ"). As part of that settlement, Pfizer entered into a Corporate Integrity Agreement ("CIA") with the U.S. Department of Health and Human Services ("HHS").

Less than a year after that settlement, relators Alex Booker and Edmund Hebron, two former Pfizer sales representatives, brought this *qui tam* action against Pfizer in federal district court, alleging it was on behalf of the United States, more than two dozen individual states, and the District of Columbia, and asserting that despite the settlement, Pfizer had continued to engage in conduct prohibited by the FCA and state analogues. None of the sovereigns elected to intervene.

. . .

It is well settled that "[e]vidence of an actual false claim is 'the *sine qua non* of a False Claims Act violation.'"[556] That is, even when a relator can prove that a defendant engaged in "fraudulent conduct affecting the Government," FCA liability attaches only if that conduct resulted in the filing of a false claim for payment from the Government.[557] Because claims of fraud are involved, even at the pleading stage relators are required under Fed. R. Civ. P. 9(b) "to set forth with particularity [at least] the who, what, when, where, and how of" an actual false claim alleged to have been filed because of the defendant's actions.[558] And at the summary judgment stage, relators must produce competent evidence of an actual false claim made to the Government.

When FCA liability is predicated on a defendant's alleged off-label promotion of drugs to medical providers, that generally means the "specific medical provider[ ] who allegedly submitted [the] false claim[ ], the rough time period[ ], location[ ], and amount[ ] of the claim[ ], and the specific government program[ ] to which the claim[ ] [was] made."[559] This court has made clear that where relators offer only "aggregate expenditure data by the Government for" the drug at issue, "with[out] identify[ing] specific entities who submitted claims ... much less times,

---

[554] 847 F.3d 52 (1st Cir. 2017)
[555] 31 U.S.C. §§ 3729 et seq.
[556] United States *ex rel.* Karvelas v. Melrose–Wakefield Hosp., 360 F.3d 220, 225 (1st Cir. 2004) (citation omitted), abrogated on other grounds by *Allison Engine*, 553 U.S. 662, 128 S.Ct. 2123, 170 L.Ed.2d 1030.
[557] *Rost*, 507 F.3d at 727.
[558] Lawton *ex rel.* U.S. v. Takeda Pharm. Co., 842 F.3d 125, 130 (1st Cir. 2016) (citations omitted).
[559] *Id.* at 131 (citations omitted).

amounts, and circumstances," their claim falls "far short."⁵⁶⁰ Relators argue that this is an impossible standard for *qui tam* relators to meet and that we should change our law. We disagree.

After six years of litigation, relators' only proffered evidence of actual false claims was aggregate data reflecting the amount of money expended by Medicaid for pediatric Geodon prescriptions (an off-label use) between January 2008 and March 2012, according to the National Disease and Therapeutic Index's survey research. We have previously held comparable data insufficient on its own to support an FCA claim, even at the motion to dismiss stage.⁵⁶¹

Ultimately, "summary judgment ... is 'the put up or shut up moment in litigation,' " and a relator certainly must make a greater showing than is required in a pleading in order "to get in front of a jury."⁵⁶²

. . .

2. Booker's FCA Employment Retaliation Claim

Relators also contend that Pfizer terminated Booker's employment on January 6, 2010 in retaliation for two instances in which Booker complained to his superiors that the company was continuing to promote Geodon for off-label uses after the settlement.

Under the FCA's anti-retaliation provision, an employer is prohibited from retaliating against an employee for any "lawful acts done ... in furtherance of an [FCA] action ... or other efforts to stop ... violations of [the FCA]."⁵⁶³ We have defined the type of conduct protected under this provision as "limited to activities that 'reasonably could lead' to an FCA action; in other words, investigations,

---

560 United States *ex rel.* Ge v. Takeda Pharm. Co., Ltd., 737 F.3d 116, 121, 124 (1st Cir. 2013).
561 *See*, e.g., *Lawton*, 842 F.3d at 132; *Ge*, 737 F.3d at 124; cf. United States *ex rel.* Kelly v. Novartis Pharms. Corp., 827 F.3d 5, 13–14 (1st Cir. 2016) ("Merely alleging that a scheme was wide-ranging [and] that a [false] claim was presumably submitted ... will not suffice.").
562 Jakobiec v. Merrill Lynch Life Ins. Co., 711 F.3d 217, 226 (1st Cir. 2013) (quoting Goodman v. Nat'l Sec. Agency, Inc., 621 F.3d 651, 654 (7th Cir. 2010)); see also United States *ex rel.* Quinn v. Omnicare Inc., 382 F.3d 432, 440 (3d Cir. 2004) ("Without proof of an actual claim, there is no issue of material fact to be decided by a jury. [Relator's] theory that the claims 'must have been' submitted cannot survive a motion for summary judgment.").
563 31 U.S.C. § 3730(h)(1).

inquiries, testimonies or other activities that concern the employer's knowing submission of false or fraudulent claims for payment to the Government."[564]

. . .

As we stated in *Karvelas*, the FCA protects only conduct that concerns the "knowing submission of false ... claims" because only such conduct " 'reasonably could lead' to an FCA action."[565] Thus, we have rejected, at even the motion to dismiss stage, an FCA retaliation claim to the extent that it was based on an employee's allegations that he had reported "to his superiors" that his employer was "fail[ing] to meet regulatory standards ... required for reimbursement by Medicare and Medicaid."[566] We held that the employee had not alleged protected conduct because he had alleged only that he reported "regulatory failures but ... not [that he] investigat[ed] or report[ed] ... false ... claims knowingly submitted to the Government."[567] We reasoned that "[a]lthough '[c]orrecting regulatory problems may be a laudable goal,' " those problems were "not actionable under the FCA in the absence of actual fraudulent conduct," and so reporting them fell outside the purview of the FCA's anti-retaliation provision.[568] . . .

Relators do not assert that the disagreements between Booker and his supervisor concerned the submission of false claims. They thus have no trial-worthy claim of retaliation under the FCA.

. . .

II. CONCLUSION

The district court reached the proper outcome as to each of the merits issues before us on appeal, and we find no abuse of discretion in its management of discovery. We affirm the judgment in full. Costs are awarded to Pfizer.

---

[564] *Karvelas*, 360 F.3d at 237 (citation omitted).
[565] 360 F.3d at 237.
[566] *Karvelas*, 360 F.3d at 237.
[567] *Id.*
[568] *Id.*

United States ex rel. Bruno v. Schaeffer[569]

Before the Court are the **Motions to Dismiss (Doc. 35 and 39)** filed by Defendants . . . . For the following reasons, the **Motions to Dismiss (Doc. 35 and 39)** are **GRANTED IN PART** and **DENIED IN PART**.

I. BACKGROUND

Plaintiff-Relators, two former employees of a large medical laboratory called MedComp Laboratory Sciences, L.L.C. and MedComp Sciences, L.L.C ("MedComp") allege that Defendants conspired to defraud the United States out of millions of dollars arising from fraudulent Medicare and Medicaid claims. Relators allege that Defendants offered physicians ownership interests in labs called Physician Owned Labs ("POL"), which existed in name only, and they received payments from the labs in proportion to the number of urine specimens the physicians sent to a different lab called Quantum for urine testing covered by private insurance. Relators also allege that the scheme incentivized the same doctors to send their urine specimens covered by Medicare and Medicaid to another lab called MedComp.

. . .

Relators claim that Defendants violated the False Claims Act ("FCA"), 31 U.S.C. §§ 3729(a)(1)(A)-(C) by presenting false claims to the United States, making false records, and conspiring to violate the FCA. Relators also claim that Defendants violated the Anti-Kickback Statute, 42 U.S.C. § 1320a-7b, the Stark Law, 42 U.S.C. § 1395nn, and the Louisiana Anti-Kickback Statute, La. R.S. § 37:1745. *Id.* The United States declined to intervene.

. . .

Under the second element of an FCA claim, a relator must allege that a defendant made a false or fraudulent claim. 31 U.S.C. § 3729(a)(1)(A). Relators claim that Defendants made false and fraudulent claims by falsely certifying that their claims did not violate the Anti-Kickback Statute and the Stark Law. As the Court already discussed, falsely certifying compliance with the Stark Law or the Anti-Kickback Statute constitutes a "false claim" under the FCA.[570] The Court will therefore address in turn whether Relators sufficiently allege that Defendants violated the Stark Law or the Anti-Kickback Statute.

i. Stark Law

---

[569] 328 F.Supp.3d 550 (M.D. La., 2018).
[570] United States *ex rel.* Thompson, 125 F.3d at 902.

The Court concludes that Relators adequately allege an indirect compensation arrangement between physicians who invested in the POLs and MedComp, which submitted Medicare claims. The Stark Law implementing regulations are particularly helpful in defining indirect compensation arrangements. They provide that a financial relationship constitutes a prohibited "indirect compensation arrangement," if (1) "there exists an unbroken chain of any number ... of persons or entities that have financial relationships ... between them," (2) "[t]he referring physician ... receives aggregate compensation ... that varies with, or takes into account, the volume or value of referrals or other business generated by the referring physician for the entity furnishing" the designated health services, and (3) the entity has knowledge that the compensation so varies. 42 C.F.R. § 411.354(c)(2); *see also Drakeford*, 675 F.3d at 408.

First, there is an unbroken chain of persons with financial relationships because Relators allege that the POLs were formed by entities owned by Defendants Brad Schaeffer, Javid Janani, and Lisa Janani. Relators also allege that Brad Schaeffer owned MedComp, Javid Janani owned MedComp, and Lisa Janani owned Quantum. Second, Relators allege that the referring physicians received compensation based on the volume of referrals because physicians were paid in proportion to the number of urine specimens they sent to Quantum. Third, Relators allege that the entity furnishing the designated health services—Quantum—had knowledge of the compensation scheme. Relators allege that MedComp's sales directors told Bruno not to disclose that MedComp linked referred specimens to payouts because it was illegal. Relators have thus alleged a Stark Law violation.

ii. Anti-Kickback Statute

Here ... Relators allege fraud with particularity. First, Relators allege the content of the financial arrangement, the inducements, and the improper referrals with detail by alleging how the investments in the POLs operated, the cost of the investment, and the way that physicians were compensated in proportion to referrals. And although Relators do not allege the participating physicians by name, they sufficiently allege the identity of the physicians by claiming that about sixty-one physicians or physician groups from Louisiana, Tennessee, Mississippi, Illinois, Arizona, Alabama, and Georgia had an ownership interest in the POLs. Relators also allege the time-period of the alleged scheme by alleging that it began in early 2013, that the POLs were formed in 2013 and 2014, and that since April 2013 MedComp had been paid about $18 million for testing specimens covered by Medicare and Medicaid for specimens originating from physicians participating in the POLs. Relators complaint is far from conclusory, and it meets Rule 9(b)'s pleading standard for the Anti-Kickback Statute claim.

Defendants also argue that although Relators allege that physicians received payouts from the POLs based on their referrals to Quantum for private insurance patients, Relators fail to allege that Quantum provided physicians a financial incentive to refer Medicare and Medicaid specimens to MedComp. The Court disagrees. It is not dispositive that Quantum processed private insurance and MedComp processed Medicaid and Medicaid. Compensation for private insurance referrals may constitute a payment to induce referrals of federal health care program business if there is a nexus between the kickbacks for private insurance and Medicare or Medicaid business. Neither party cites any case that addresses this issue, nor is the Court aware of any. However, the Court is persuaded that carving-out referrals of federal health care programs can violate the Anti-Kickback Statute by disguising remuneration for federal health care program referrals.

. . .

Here, the Court finds that it is reasonable to infer that the POL scheme will likewise increase the chances that physicians refer urine specimens to MedComp, which takes Medicare and Medicaid even though physicians only receive payments proportionate to Quantum referrals for private insurance. MedComp and Quantum share similar owners with the POLs, and most importantly, Relators allege that Brad Schaeffer instructed MedComp's sales representatives to offer the POL model to physicians. As a result, it is plausible that physicians view MedComp and Quantum as related entities, and physicians will send urine specimens to MedComp because they receive remunerations for referrals to Quantum. The Anti-Kickback Statute "prohibits offering money or other things of value to entice another party to provide a good or service that would be paid for by a federal health care program."[571] The Court concludes that at this early stage, Relators have plead sufficient facts to conclude that the POL scheme enticed physicians to refer urine specimens to Quantum.

. . .

---

[571] United States *ex rel.* King, 871 F.3d at 331.

United States ex rel. Carson v. Manor Care, Inc., et al.[572]

. . .

In January 2009, Christine A. Ribik filed a *qui tam* suit under seal in the Eastern District of Virginia on behalf of the United States against Manor Care. . . .

In September 2011, Carson filed a *qui tam* suit under seal in the Eastern District of Virginia on behalf of the United States and several individual states against Manor Care under the FCA and the state-equivalent statutes. . . .

Carson also made a claim of retaliation under the FCA, alleging that his "employment with [Manor Care] was terminated in November of 2009 due to his repeated complaints about the fraudulent billing practices concerning patients associated with Government funded health programs including, but not limited to, Medicare and Medicaid."

. . .

Ribik and Carson's cases were consolidated in June 2012, and a third case was added in November 2014. The United States Government filed a notice of election to intervene in the consolidated case in December 2014, and its "Consolidated Complaint in Intervention" was filed in April 2015. . . .

Manor Care . . . filed a motion to dismiss Carson's amended complaint. Among other arguments, Manor Care contended that the FCA and Michigan *qui tam* claims were barred by the first-to-file rule, and the FCA and all the state-equivalent *qui tam* claims, save the Wisconsin claim, were barred because they were based on public disclosure. . . The district court granted the motion in December 2015 in a three-page order. . . .

. . .

It is clear that Carson's allegations are materially similar to those found in Ribik's complaint. . . Neither Carson's factual additions nor the fact that his experience took place in Pennsylvania, as opposed to Ribik's experience in Virginia, saves him from the first-to-file bar. Carson "has not managed to avoid § 3730(b)(5)'s first-to-file bar simply by alleging additional facts relating to how [Manor Care overbilled the Government], even though some of those specific allegations were not mentioned in [Ribik's] complaint."[573]

---

[572] 851 F.3d 293 (4th Cir. 2017).
[573] See *Grynberg*, 390 F.3d at 1280; see also *Branch Consultants*, 560 F.3d at 378 ("Any construction of § 3730(b)(5) that focused on the details of the later-filed action would

Alternatively, and even assuming Carson's complaint contains substantially the same claims as Ribik's, he argues that his complaint should not be dismissed because the district court consolidated his claims with Ribik's. Because the Government intervened in the consolidated action, Carson argues that his claims survive application of the first-to-file bar. While a novel argument, it has no merit. The FCA does not make an exception to the first-to-file rule for consolidated complaints. The first-to-file rule is "an absolute, unambiguous exception-free rule."[574] The statute is clear: "[w]hen a person brings an action under this subsection, *no person other than the Government* may intervene or bring a related action based on the facts underlying the pending action."[575] The statute does *not* read that "no person other than the Government may intervene or bring a related action based on the facts underlying the pending action *unless that person's case is consolidated with the earlier-filed case.*" Carson has not directed the Court to any authority supporting his unique position, which contravenes the plain language of the statute. . . Carson's alternative argument fails under the plain language of the FCA.

Accordingly, the district court properly determined that it lacked subject matter jurisdiction over Carson's *qui tam* action under the FCA.

While the foregoing resolves the jurisdictional issue as to the substantive FCA *qui tam* claims, Carson separately pleads a cause of action for retaliation in the termination of his employment. The FCA prohibits employers from retaliating against any employee "because of lawful acts done by the employee ... in furtherance of an action under this section or other efforts to stop 1 or more violations of this subchapter."[576] The district court dismissed Carson's retaliation claim on the same ground that it dismissed the FCA *qui tam* claims: the first-to-file rule. However, the first-to-file rule has no relation to a claim for retaliation.

. . .

We therefore affirm the district court's dismissal of Carson's *qui tam* action under the FCA for lack of subject matter jurisdiction, but vacate and remand that part of the judgment concerning Carson's retaliation and state fraud claims.

AFFIRMED IN PART AND VACATED AND REMANDED IN PART.

---

allow an infinite number of copycat *qui tam* actions to proceed so long as the relator in each case alleged one additional instance of the previously exposed fraud.").

[574] United States *ex rel.* Carter v. Halliburton Co., 710 F.3d 171, 181 (4th Cir. 2013), *aff'd in part, rev'd in part on other grounds sub nom.* Kellogg Brown & Root Servs., Inc. v. United States *ex rel.* Carter, ___ U.S. ___, 135 S. Ct. 1970, 191 L.Ed.2d 899 (2015).

[575] 31 U.S.C. § 3730(b)(5) (emphasis added).

[576] 31 U.S.C. § 3730(h)(1).

United States ex rel. Chase v. HPC Healthcare, Inc.[577]

In this *qui tam* action, relator Nancy Chase appeals from the District Court's dismissal of her complaint alleging that several health care providers violated the federal and Florida False Claims Acts. The District Court dismissed the complaint for failure to satisfy the heightened pleading requirements of Federal Rule of Civil Procedure 9(b) for claims alleging fraud. It also ruled that the complaint failed to state a claim with respect to Ms. Chase's conspiracy and retaliation claims. Ms. Chase now appeals both the dismissal of her complaint and the denial of her request to file an amended complaint. After careful review, we affirm.

. . .

The District Court concluded that Ms. Chase's complaint failed to meet Rule 9(b)'s heightened pleading standard for claims alleging fraud. The court acknowledged that Ms. Chase had "describe[d] a private scheme in detail" regarding "disturbing medical practices," but it ruled that she had failed to satisfy Rule 9(b) with her conclusory allegations that false claims were submitted as a result of that scheme. We conclude that the District Court properly dismissed these claims.

The submission of a false claim is "the *sine qua non* of a False Claims Act violation."[578] "Because it is the submission of a fraudulent claim that gives rise to liability under the False Claims Act, that submission must be pleaded with particularity and not inferred from the circumstances."[579] Therefore, unless a relator alleges with particularity that false claims were actually submitted to the Government, our precedent holds that dismissal is proper.[580]

The key inquiry is whether the complaint includes "some indicia of reliability" to support the allegation that an actual false claim was submitted.[581] One way to satisfy this requirement is by alleging the details of false claims by providing specific billing information—such as dates, times, and amounts of actual false claims or copies of bills.[582] In other circumstances, this Court has deemed indicia of reliability sufficient where the relator alleged direct knowledge of the

---

[577] --- F.App'x ----, 2018 WL 526039 (11th Cir. Jan. 24, 2018).
[578] United States *ex rel.* Clausen v. Laboratory Corporation of America, 290 F.3d 1301, 1311 (11th Cir. 2002).
[579] *Corsello*, 428 F.3d at 1013.
[580] *See Clausen*, 290 F.3d at 1311 (explaining that a plaintiff cannot "merely [ ] describe a private scheme in detail but then [ ] allege simply and without any stated reason for his belief that claims requesting illegal payments must have been submitted, were likely submitted or should have been submitted to the Government").
[581] *Id.*
[582] *See* Hopper v. Solvay Pharm., Inc., 588 F.3d 1318, 1326 (11th Cir. 2009); United States *ex rel.* Atkins v. McInteer, 470 F.3d 1350, 1358 (11th Cir. 2006).

defendants' submission of false claims based on her own experiences and on information she learned in the course of her employment.[583] However, the basis of this direct knowledge must be pleaded with particularity.[584]

. . .

Although Ms. Chase details a scheme, her complaint does not include specific examples of the conduct she describes or allege the submission of any specific fraudulent claim. Neither does Ms. Chase allege the basis of her knowledge of the defendants' fraudulent billing practices—a process she was far removed from as a social worker.[585] In light of all these deficiencies, we conclude that Ms. Chase failed to provide the required "indicia of reliability" to support her allegations of false claims for hospice services.

We also conclude that Ms. Chase did not adequately plead a False Claims Act violation predicated on illegal kickbacks under a false certification theory. The complaint alleged that the defendants falsely certified that they were in compliance with the Anti-Kickback statute and the Stark law. . . .

Ms. Chase alleged that the Referral Defendants engaged in separate kickback schemes with the Chapters Defendants, whereby Chapters conferred certain benefits on the Referral Defendants in exchange for patient referrals in violation of federal law. But her allegations fall far short of satisfying Rule 9(b). For example, she fails to identify a single individual from Sunrise, JSA, or Superior who made a referral to Chapters in exchange for a benefit, a single patient that was improperly referred, who at Chapters provided the bribes, or when those exchanges took place.[586] Ms. Chase also alleged that Chapters and Mobile Physicians Services (owned by LifePath's medical director) improperly referred ineligible patients to each other. But she again fails to allege any specific facts supporting this conclusory allegation. Without details to support her conclusory allegations of wrongdoing, Ms. Chase's complaint lacks the necessary "indicia of

---

583 *See* United States *ex rel.* Walker v. R&F Props. of Lake Cty., Inc., 433 F.3d 1349, 1360 (11th Cir. 2005) (holding that Rule 9(b) was satisfied where the relator was a nurse practitioner in the defendant's employ who was required to bill under a doctor's provider number and whose conversations about the defendant's billing practices with the office manager formed the basis for the relator's belief that fraudulent claims were actually submitted to the Government).

584 *See* United States *ex rel.* Sanchez v. Lymphatx, Inc., 596 F.3d 1300, 1302–03 & n.4 (11th Cir. 2010).

585 *See Id.* (affirming dismissal of complaint despite inclusion of specific examples of patients, dates, and services because relator lacked direct knowledge of defendants' submissions of false claims); cf. *Walker*, 433 F.3d at 1360.

586 *See* Clausen, 290 F.3d at 1310.

reliability" under Rule 9(b). We therefore affirm the dismissal of the substantive False Claims Act counts.

B. CONSPIRACY

Ms. Chase also alleged that the defendants violated the False Claims Act's conspiracy provision.

. . .

Ms. Chase's complaint alleged merely that "Defendants knowingly conspired with each other" to violate §§ 3729(a)(1)(A) and 3729(a)(1)(B) of the False Claims Act. On appeal, Ms. Chase argues that she sufficiently alleged an agreement between the Chapters Defendants and each of the Referral Defendants. But the complaint fails to identify the people from any of the Referral Defendants involved in the agreement or any specific facts that show an agreement to violate the False Claims Act. We therefore conclude that she falls far short of stating a conspiracy claim.

C. RETALIATION

. . .

The District Court correctly found that Ms. Chase's raising of ethical concerns about adherence to advance medical directives was not protected activity because this conduct is not related to a False Claims Act violation. We also agree that Ms. Chase's allegation that she was demoted "because she raised ethical issues concerning violations of the [False Claims] Acts" is a legal conclusion that fails to satisfy federal pleading requirements.[587] Finally, we reject Ms. Chase's argument that she sufficiently pleaded her retaliation claim by alleging—in a different section of her complaint unrelated to the retaliation claim—that she "objected to the default enrollment" of certain patients and noted specific Medicare and Medicaid requirements. Even assuming that this objection constituted protected activity, Ms. Chase failed to plead a causal link between that objection and any of the actions she alleged constituted retaliation (i.e., her demotion, her removal from committees, or her termination). And the complaint is devoid of any allegations that the decision-makers at LifePath were aware of this objection. . . We therefore conclude that the District Court properly dismissed the retaliation and discrimination claims.

. . .

---

[587] *See Iqbal*, 556 U.S. at 678, 129 S.Ct. at 1949 ("A pleading that offers labels and conclusions or a formulaic recitation of the elements of a cause of action will not do.") (quotation omitted).

United States ex rel. Christiansen and Ashton v. Everglades College, Inc.[588]

I. BACKGROUND

A. The Alleged FCA Violations

Keiser University is a non-profit college offering undergraduate and graduate programs across more than a dozen campuses. Many of Keiser's students receive federally sponsored financial aid under Title IV of the Higher Education Act of 1965, 20 U.S.C. §§ 1070–1099d. In order to receive Title IV funds, schools must enter into "program participation agreements" with the Department of Education that condition eligibility for financial aid funds on the institution's compliance with various enumerated requirements.[589] One of those requirements is known as the Incentive Compensation Ban (ICB), which prohibits a school from paying incentives to recruiters and admissions personnel based on the number of students they enroll.[590]

Relators, two former employees who worked in Keiser's admissions department, alleged that Keiser submitted more than 230,000 claims for a total of $1.2 billion in federal financial aid, all the while falsely certifying to the United States that Keiser was complying with the ICB. . . . Relying on the "implied false certification" theory, Relators asserted that Keiser was liable not only for its own express certifications, but also for the enormous volume of student-submitted claims.

B. The District Court's Merits Decision

. . . . After a bench trial, the district court handed Relators a victory that fell far short of their expectations.

. . .

Keiser was thus liable for only those two false claims, for which the district court awarded the minimum statutory penalty of $5,500 each—a total of $11,000. . . (T)he government was entitled only to the nominal statutory penalties for the two express certifications sent by Keiser.

C. The United States Intervenes to Settle the Case

Relators appealed the district court's decision to our Court. The United States, however, believed an appeal was risky because there was a chance the Eleventh Circuit would affirm the district court's narrow interpretation of FCA liability,

---

[588] 855 F.3d 1279 (11th Cir. 2017).
[589] 20 U.S.C. § 1094(a).
[590] *Id.* § 1094(a) (20); see also 34 C.F.R. § 668.14(b)(22).

thereby impairing FCA enforcement efforts throughout the circuit. Thus, after Relators' opening brief was filed in this Court, but before the United States moved to intervene in the *qui tam* action, the United States struck a tentative deal with Keiser. The tentative settlement agreement provided that Keiser would pay the United States $335,000—more than thirty times the amount recovered by Relators at trial—and the United States would in turn release Keiser from any further administrative or civil claims, and even more importantly, would also refrain from suspending or terminating Keiser's eligibility for future Title IV funds based on Keiser's challenged conduct in this case.

. . .

D. Attorneys' Fees and Costs

While these developments were unfolding, Relators also sought an award for attorneys' fees and costs. After the bench trial, but before the settlement, Relators asked for over $1 million in attorneys' fees and almost $76,000 in litigation costs. In light of Relators' limited success at trial, the district court reduced the fee award to $60,000 for their efforts at trial, and trimmed the award of costs to $27,000. After the eventual settlement, which Relators claimed was brought about by their appeal, they sought enhanced fees and costs based on the larger settlement figure that the United States had been able to procure with Keiser, as well as the additional fees and costs they incurred for their efforts on appeal. The district court denied that request on the ground that Relators objected to the settlement at every stage of the proceedings and should not reap the benefits of an outcome they so vigorously sought to prevent.

Relators now appeal all of these issues.

. . .

D. Attorneys' Fees and Costs

After trial, Relators sought over $1 million in attorneys' fees and almost $76,000 in litigation expenses. The district court determined, however, that Relators' limited trial victory warranted an across-the-board reduction in their total fee award to $60,000. Relators now object to that reduction. Reviewing the award for abuse of discretion,[591] we reject most of Relators' arguments for reversal as meritless. But one particular contention warrants further discussion. They argue that the amount of recovery is not an appropriate consideration—or at least not a significant consideration —in awarding attorneys' fees for *qui tam* FCA cases. We disagree.

---

[591] *See* Bivins v. Wrap It Up, Inc., 548 F.3d 1348, 1351 (11th Cir. 2008).

In spite of this direction from the Supreme Court, Relators ask us to limit *Hensley*[592] and *Farrar*[593] to claims for <u>private</u> damages—not FCA claims which involve a suit to recover from fraud on the public fisc. . . . And Relators say there is a good public-policy reason not to extend the *Hensley–Farrar* principle to FCA cases because that would deter potential whistleblowers and their attorneys from bringing *qui tam* cases that might result in only nominal or a small amount of damages.[594]

But Relators offer no authority that declines to apply *Hensley* and *Farrar* to FCA claims. In fact, although we are not bound by it, we have already held that the amount of recovery is relevant to the fee award in FCA cases.[595] We reject Relators' plea to carve out an exception to the *Hensley–Farrar* principle for FCA cases. Relators contend that *qui tam* FCA claims are different because such claims serve a substantial public interest, but it is not clear why that makes them different from civil-rights cases which also serve an important public need—or even why that alleged difference should matter for the award of attorneys' fees. Accordingly, we affirm the district court's reliance on the degree of success in awarding attorneys' fees in this case.

. . .

---

[592] Hensley v. Eckerhart, 461 U.S. 424, 434, 103 S.Ct. 1933, 76 L.Ed.2d 40 (1983).
[593] Farrar v. Hobby, 506 U.S. 103, 114, 113 S.Ct. 566, 121 L.Ed.2d 494 (1992).
[594] *See* S. Rep. 99–345, at 29 (1986), reprinted in 1986 U.S.C.C.A.N. 5266, 5294 (explaining the importance of attorneys' fees in FCA qui tam actions).
[595] *See* United States v. Patrol Servs., Inc., 202 F.App'x 357, 359 (11th Cir. 2006) (unpublished) ("The district court may adjust the amount depending on a number of factors, including the quality of the result and representation of the litigation.").

United States ex rel. Colquitt v. Abbott Laboratories[596]

. . .

These stents had been approved by the FDA to go into bile ducts, but Guidant was helping and encouraging doctors to use them in blood vessels. Two months before Colquitt left his job, Guidant was bought by Abbott Laboratories, which had a similar practice of promoting biliary stents for vascular use. Colquitt, who learned about the False Claims Act as a night law student, brought this *qui tam* action against Abbott because he thought that Guidant and Abbott had defrauded Medicare by seeking FDA approval for biliary stents but then encouraging and bribing providers to use them in vascular procedures for which the providers billed Medicare.

. . .

Abbott filed a combined motion to dismiss for failure to state a claim and for lack of subject matter jurisdiction due to public disclosure of the alleged fraudulent scheme. The court granted the motion to dismiss for failure to state a claim as to the Anti-Kickback allegations. It granted the motion to dismiss for want of jurisdiction as to the fraudulent inducement claim, holding that Colquitt's information had been publicly disclosed and that he was not an original source of that information. Colquitt's third theory—false presentment through encouraging doctors to present fraudulent claims to Medicare—survived this motion.

. . .

The district court dismissed Colquitt's Anti-Kickback allegations on the ground that he had failed to satisfy the heightened pleading requirements for fraud claims.[597] . . .

As the False Claims Act is about fraud, claims asserted under it must comply with Rule 9(b)'s heightened pleading standard.[598] "In alleging fraud or mistake, a party must state with particularity the circumstances constituting fraud or mistake."[599] This requires, at a minimum, that a plaintiff plead the "who, what, when, where, and how" of the alleged fraud.[600]

In dismissing Abbott's kickback allegations, the district court faulted Colquitt for not describing "any details of the actual claims made by the physicians or hospitals

---

[596] 858 F.3d 365 (5th Cir. 2017).
[597] *See* Fed. R. Civ. P. 9(b).
[598] *Id.* at 903.
[599] Fed R. Civ. P. 9(b).
[600] Williams v. WMX Tech., Inc., 112 F.3d 175, 179 (5th Cir. 1997).

that allegedly received kickbacks." It found that although Colquitt had identified some specific hospitals and doctors that allegedly received kickbacks, he did not plead that any of these hospitals or doctors signed up to be Medicare providers or submitted certified claims for reimbursement for procedures using Abbott's stents.

This may have been too rigid an application of Rule 9(b). The general rule is that a plaintiff must plead details such as the time and place of the false representations.[601] But *United States ex rel. Grubbs v. Kanneganti*[602] sounded a note of caution about its application in *qui tam* suits: "[T]he 'time, place, contents, and identity' standard is not a straitjacket for Rule 9(b). Rather, the rule is context specific and flexible and must remain so to achieve the remedial purpose of the False Claim Act."[603] The details of particular claims submitted to the Government may only be attainable for relators through discovery, which a dismissal on the pleadings forestalls altogether.[604] *Grubbs* thus concluded that "a relator's complaint, if it cannot allege the details of an actually submitted false claim, may nevertheless survive by alleging particular details of a scheme to submit false claims paired with reliable indicia that lead to a strong inference that claims were actually submitted."[605]

A strong inference that the named hospitals submitted claims to Medicare for vascular procedures using biliary stents could likely be drawn from Colquitt's allegations. Nearly every hospital in America participates in Medicare and would most likely have billed Medicare had they performed procedures using Abbott's stents on a person over age 65. The complaint makes extensive allegations about that off-label use being common. And Colquitt alleged that the claims carried a certification of compliance with the Anti-Kickback Statute.

But Colquitt's allegations fail at the first part of the *Grubbs* standard: it does not allege the details of the scheme with sufficient particularity. It devotes a single, vague paragraph to the alleged kickback scheme, mentioning defendants' programs that provide "significant volume discounts and rebates to hospitals that could not be attained based solely on biliary use, but required substantial vascular use of the stents in order to receive the discount or rebate." That, along with reference to "vascular specialists" who received dinners, training, and fellowships, is the extent of the details alleged about the scheme. No specifics about the discounts and rebates are provided. We are not told that a particular hospital (including the only two that are identified in the complaint, Valley Hospital Medical Center and Shady Grove Adventist Hospital) ever achieved these

---

[601] United States *ex rel.* Rafizadeh v. Cont'l Common, Inc., 553 F.3d 869, 873 (5th Cir. 2008).
[602] 565 F.3d 180 (5th Cir. 2009).
[603] *Id.* at 190.
[604] *See Id.* at 191.
[605] *Id.*

unspecified thresholds through off-label use of the stents. No particulars are alleged to show that the unidentified doctors who received the ill-defined benefits caused the hospital to use Abbott stents. In short, the complaint never links the alleged carrots to the purchase and use of the stents at either of the hospitals. Unlike details about the Medicare claims that ended up being submitted, much of this information would be known to a relator with original information about an unlawful kickback scheme. Rule 9(b) was not satisfied.

Colquitt's false inducement claim—that Medicare paying claims for stents used in vascular procedures was tainted by Abbott's making false statements about their intended use when obtaining FDA approval—was dismissed based on the public disclosure bar. . . .

. . .

Colquitt contends that even if the information supporting his fraudulent inducement claim was publicly disclosed, he was an original source of this information. To be an original source, a person must have direct and independent knowledge of the information on which the allegations are based.[606] If someone relies upon the public disclosures at issue, then his or her knowledge is not independent.[607] Colquitt attempts to show that his allegations derive from what he observed while working for Abbott and not just the 510(k) documents. What he observed, however, were efforts by Guidant to promote the biliary stents for vascular use. This is information bearing on his false presentment claim discussed below, not information about the alleged misrepresentations to the FDA in the approval process that form the basis of his fraudulent inducement claim. Colquitt had no involvement in, and thus no original information about, the FDA approval process.

The district court correctly dismissed the false inducement claim under the public disclosure bar.

. . .

The judgment of the district court is AFFIRMED.

---

[606] Little v. Shell Exploration & Production Co., 690 F.3d 282, 292 (5th Cir. 2012).
[607] United States *ex rel.* Fried v. West Indep. Sch. Dist., 527 F.3d 439, 442–43 (5th Cir. 2008).

United States ex rel. Crockett v. Complete Fitness Rehab., Inc.[608]

Carla Crockett worked for Complete Fitness Rehabilitation, Inc., a provider of physical rehabilitation services to Medicare patients. She was fired after repeatedly objecting to her supervisor's directives that she provide her patients with more extensive (and profitable) treatments. Crockett sued, claiming various breaches of the False Claims Act (FCA), but the district court dismissed her entire complaint as not meeting Rule 9(b)'s particularity requirements. The court below was correct in dismissing Crockett's claims of FCA violations, given that Rule 9(b) required her to identify fraudulent claims that were actually submitted to the Government, and that Crockett did not do so here. However, the district court improperly dismissed Crockett's claim of FCA retaliation—that she was fired for resisting what she believed was a FCA violation—because an FCA retaliation claim does not require a plaintiff to meet the particularity standards of Rule 9(b), and Crockett did allege sufficient facts to suggest that she reasonably believed her objections would stop an FCA violation. Crockett is therefore entitled to proceed to discovery on her FCA retaliation claim.

. . .

The district court correctly dismissed Crockett's FCA fraud claims because Crockett failed to allege with the particularity required by Rule 9(b) that a specific false claim was submitted to the United States. Crockett identified various improprieties that, if credited, could demonstrate that Complete Rehab provided patients with more treatments than medical need justified. Crockett did not, however, show—especially not with any particularity—that the United States was charged for this purported over-treatment, or that there was a claim on the Government. Indeed, in her complaint, Crockett expressly conceded she "never had access to Complete Rehab's billing or to the specific claims submitted to the Government for reimbursement." Crockett's inability to identify any particular false claim means the court below was correct in finding that her FCA fraud claims fail.

. . .

Although Crockett's three FCA claims about Complete Rehab's billing were subject to dismissal, she is entitled to proceed on her FCA retaliation claim, because such claims are not subject to Rule 9(b)'s heightened standards, and Crockett otherwise sufficiently pleaded that she was fired because of her efforts to stop what Crockett reasonably believed was fraud on the Government. . . . .

It is true that Crockett has still not pleaded a specific FCA violation, in that she does not identify claims actually submitted to the Government because of the misfeasance she identifies. But, as the Ninth Circuit has explained, "unlike a FCA

---

[608] 721 F.App'x 451 (6th Cir. 2018).

violation claim, a FCA retaliation claim 'does not require a showing of fraud and therefore need not meet the heightened pleading requirements of Rule 9(b).'"[609] Thus, as we have held, a plaintiff "need not establish that [the employer] actually violated the FCA," so long as she "show[s] that her allegations of fraud grew out of a reasonable belief in such fraud."[610] Crockett's allegations meet that lower standard required to survive a motion to dismiss on a FCA retaliation claim, in that she sufficiently alleges that she acted in furtherance of efforts to stop FCA violations.

. . .

The judgment of the district court is affirmed with respect to the FCA fraud claims and Michigan public policy discharge claim; reversed with respect to the FCA retaliation claim; and remanded for further proceedings consistent with this opinion.

---

[609] Mendiondo v. Centinela Hosp. Med. Ctr., 521 F.3d 1097, 1103 (9th Cir. 2008) (quoting United States *ex rel.* Karvelas v. Melrose-Wakefield Hosp., 360 F.3d 220, 238 n. 23 (1st Cir. 2004)).

[610] Jones-McNamara v. Holzer Health Systems, 630 F.App'x 394, 400 (6th Cir. 2015); see also Graham Cty. Soil & Water Conservation Dist. v. United States *ex rel.* Wilson, 545 U.S. 409, 416 n.1, 125 S.Ct. 2444, 162 L.Ed.2d 390 (2005).

United States ex rel. Escobar v. Universal Health Services, Inc.[611]

. . .

The language that the Supreme Court used in *Escobar II* makes clear that courts are to conduct a holistic approach to determining materiality in connection with a payment decision, with no one factor being necessarily dispositive.

. . .

Applying the holistic approach to determining materiality laid out by the Supreme Court, we have little difficulty in concluding that Relators have sufficiently alleged that UHS's misrepresentations were material. We reach this conclusion for three reasons. First, Relators have alleged in their Second Amended Complaint that regulatory compliance was a condition of payment—itself a "relevant" though "not dispositive" factor in determining materiality. Second, the centrality of the licensing and supervision requirements in the MassHealth regulatory program, which go to the "very essence of the bargain," of MassHealth's contractual relationships with various healthcare providers under the Medicaid program, is strong evidence that a failure to comply with the regulations would be "sufficiently important to influence the behavior" of the Government in deciding whether to pay the claims. And third, while the Supreme Court observed that "if the Government pays a particular claim in full despite its actual knowledge that certain requirements were violated, that is very strong evidence that those requirements are not material," the Court did not state that such knowledge is dispositive. In any case, . . . there is no evidence in the record that MassHealth paid those claims to UHS despite knowing of the violations.

. . .

We therefore REVERSE the district court's grant of UHS's Motion to Dismiss the Second Amended Complaint and REMAND to the district court for further proceedings.

---

[611] 842 F.3d 103 (1st Cir. 2016).

United States ex rel. Grabcheski v. American International Group, Inc.[612]

Plaintiff-Appellant Alex Grabcheski ("Grabcheski") appeals from the judgment of the United States District Court for the Southern District of New York, denying his motion for leave to file a third amended complaint and dismissing his False Claims Act ("FCA"),[613] case against Defendant-Appellee American International Group, Inc. ("AIG") with prejudice. We assume the parties' familiarity with the underlying facts, the procedural history of the case, and the issues on appeal.

. . .

Failure to State a Claim

On the merits, we find that Grabcheski has failed adequately to allege an FCA claim. Under the FCA, any person who "knowingly makes, uses, or causes to be made or used, a false record or statement material to an obligation to pay or transmit money or property to the Government" is liable for a civil penalty.[614] We affirm because, even assuming arguendo that Grabcheski has sufficiently alleged knowing "false ... statement [s]" . . . he has not plausibly pleaded that they were material.

The FCA defines materiality as "having a natural tendency to influence, or be capable of influencing, the payment or receipt of money or property."[615] Therefore, in assessing materiality, we "look to the effect on the likely or actual behavior of the recipient of the alleged misrepresentation."[616] Materiality must be pleaded with particularity under Rule 9(b).[617]

The district court correctly concluded that Grabcheski failed adequately to allege that the Agreements would have been different absent the alleged misrepresentation. Grabcheski claims that ALICO and AIA were worth "at least $100 million less" than they appeared given their domestic insurance business. Yet, as Grabcheski also alleged, FRBNY entered the Agreements here as part of an effort "to avoid a total financial panic and collapse." It is therefore unsurprising that the Agreements were tilted towards AIG; in exchange for a $25 billion reduction in AIG's debt, FRBNY accepted equity interests in ALICO and AIA purportedly worth only $24.4 billion, or 2.4% less than the corresponding debt reduction. Given this posture, and even assuming that Grabcheski's $100

---

[612] 687 F.App'x 84 (7th Cir. 2017).
[613] 31 U.S.C. § 3729 *et seq.*
[614] 31 U.S.C. § 3729(a)(1)(G).
[615] 31 U.S.C. § 3729(b)(4).
[616] *Universal Health Servs.*, 136 S.Ct. at 2002 (alterations omitted) (quoting 26 Richard A. Lord, Williston on Contracts § 69:12 (4th ed. 2003)).
[617] *See, e.g., id.* at 2004 n.6; Minzer v. Keegan, 218 F.3d 144, 151 (2d Cir. 2000).

million figure is backed by sufficient allegations, he has failed to allege with particularity facts that demonstrate how that difference in value—only 0.4%—was likely to have had any effect on the Agreements.... Grabcheski has therefore not plausibly pleaded materiality.

Denial of Leave to Amend

While Federal Rule of Civil Procedure 15(a)(2) requires district courts to freely grant leave to amend "when justice so requires," a district court may nonetheless decline to grant such leave "for good reason, including futility, bad faith, undue delay, or undue prejudice to the opposing party."[618] Given the Third Amended Complaint failed to state a claim under the FCA, the district court did not abuse its discretion in denying as futile Grabcheski's motion for leave to file that complaint....

The district court also did not abuse its discretion in dismissing the case with prejudice. Even if materiality was not explicitly challenged by AIG until after it filed its motion to dismiss, ignorance is no excuse for a repeated failure to plead a plausible FCA claim with particularity. It was thus not an abuse of discretion to deny Grabcheski a fifth bite at the apple....

We have considered Grabcheski's remaining arguments and find them to be without merit. Accordingly, we AFFIRM the judgment of the district court.

---

[618] *TechnoMarine*, 758 F.3d at 505 (quoting McCarthy v. Dun & Bradstreet Corp., 482 F.3d 184, 200 (2d Cir. 2007)).

United States ex rel. Hafter, et al. v. Spectrum Emergency Care, Inc., et al.[619]

.... The primary issue in this case is whether the *qui tam* plaintiffs or relators, Dr. Lance Hafter and Dr. George Schwartz, qualify as "original sources" under § 3730(e)(4)(B).

Drs. Hafter and Schwartz claim Appellees Spectrum Emergency Care, Inc. and other affiliated organizations ("Spectrum") obtained payment from the United States for false and fraudulent Medicare, Medicaid and/or Champus reimbursement claims. The district court granted Spectrum's motion to dismiss on the ground it lacked subject matter jurisdiction to hear the case. The court concluded Appellants based their suit on information previously disclosed in a state court civil suit and that Appellants were not original sources of that information. We exercise jurisdiction pursuant to 28 U.S.C. § 1291 and affirm.

. . .

Soon after Dr. Hafter's employment at the Medical Center ended, he received a call from an attorney researching a medical malpractice case. The attorney, Mr. Cameron Spradling, contacted Dr. Hafter in hopes of obtaining information about the treatment his client received in the Medical Center emergency room in 1991. . . . Mr. Spradling enlisted Dr. Hafter to serve as a fact witness in the case. Dr. Schwartz, the other relator in this case, served as an expert witness. . . .

Approximately one year after the filing of the Mallory suit, Dr. Hafter filed the instant *qui tam* suit alleging Spectrum submitted false and fraudulent Medicare, Medicaid and/or Champus reimbursement claims to the Government. As required under the False Claims Act, Dr. Hafter provided the Government with a copy of his complaint and a disclosure statement.[620] After an investigation, the Government declined to intervene and the district court ordered the Complaint unsealed and served on Spectrum. Subsequently, Spectrum moved to dismiss for lack of subject matter jurisdiction or, in the alternative, for failure to plead fraud with particularity, to which Dr. Hafter filed a response. Before the court ruled on that motion, it consolidated Drs. Hafter and Schwartz's separate cases into one cause of action. The district court then granted Spectrum's renewed motion to dismiss Drs. Hafter and Schwartz's combined Second Amended Complaint.

In its order, the court first determined the information underlying the complaint had been publicly disclosed in the Mallory suit and, as such, jurisdiction was proper only if the Appellants qualified as original sources of the information. To qualify as original sources, the court required Appellants to show: (1) they possessed direct and independent knowledge of all the essential elements of the

---

[619] 190 F.3d 1156 (10th Cir. 1999).
[620] *See* 31 U.S.C. § 3730(b)(2).

fraud allegations, and (2) they provided the Government with the information prior to the public disclosure. Because Appellants failed to meet either requirement, the court concluded it lacked jurisdiction and dismissed the suit. Drs. Hafter and Schwartz appeal, arguing the district court erred by (1) concluding they lacked direct and independent knowledge of the information underlying their Complaint and (2) requiring them to provide government notice prior to any public disclosure in order to qualify as original sources.

. . .

At the summary judgment stage, application of this statutory language involves a four-part inquiry: (1) whether the alleged "public disclosure" contains allegations or transactions from one of the listed sources; (2) whether the alleged disclosure has been made "public" within the meaning of the False Claims Act; (3) whether the relator's complaint is "based upon" this public disclosure; and, if so, (4) whether the relator qualifies as an "original source."[621] A court should address the first three public disclosure issues first.[622] Consideration of the fourth, "original source" issue is necessary only if the court answers the first three questions in the affirmative.[623]

Here, Drs. Hafter and Schwartz concede the answer to the first three questions is "yes" because their complaint is based upon allegations disclosed in the Mallory civil suit. Accordingly, our inquiry focuses on the fourth issue, whether Drs. Hafter and Schwartz qualify as "original sources" of the information underlying the allegations of their complaint. To qualify as original sources, Appellants must demonstrate: (1) they have "direct and independent knowledge of the information on which the allegations are based," and (2) they "voluntarily provided such information to the Government prior to filing suit."[624] Because we find Appellants' inability to demonstrate the first element of this test to be determinative, we proceed directly to that issue.

. . .

We agree with the district court's ultimate conclusion that Appellants failed to make the required showing of direct and independent knowledge. As stated above, Drs. Hafter and Schwartz bear the burden of alleging the facts essential to show jurisdiction.[625] Because Spectrum has challenged jurisdiction, Appellants must show it by a preponderance of the evidence.[626] They may not rely on mere conclusory allegations of jurisdiction but must support the facts showing

---

[621] *MK–Ferguson*, 99 F.3d at 1544.
[622] *Id.*
[623] *Id.*
[624] *Precision*, 971 F.2d at 553.
[625] *See Precision Co.*, 971 F.2d at 551.
[626] *See Celli*, 40 F.3d at 327.

jurisdiction by competent proof.[627] For purposes of this case, the facts essential to show jurisdiction are that Appellants possessed knowledge that was both "direct and independent" and "of the information on which the allegations are based."[628] Direct and independent knowledge is knowledge "marked by the absence of an intervening agency ... [and] unmediated by anything but the relator's own labor."[629] The "information on which the allegations are based" means the information underlying or supporting the fraud allegations contained in the plaintiff's *qui tam* complaint.[630] Thus, Drs. Hafter and Schwartz must demonstrate they discovered the information on which the allegations of their Second Amended Complaint are based through their own efforts and not by the labors of others, and that their information was not derivative of the information of others.[631] Our review of the record leads us to conclude that Appellants failed to make this showing.

The Second Amended Complaint merely states "Dr. Hafter and Dr. Schwartz ... have direct and independent knowledge of the information upon which this suit is based." This unsupported, conclusory allegation is insufficient to establish jurisdiction.[632] The memorandum in support of Dr. Hafter's response to Spectrum's motion to dismiss is similarly deficient because it presents only generalized and conclusory arguments that Dr. Hafter obtained knowledge of "Spectrum's fraud" through his "employment relationship" and his "involvement in Spectrum's business operations." To establish original source status knowledge, a *qui tam* plaintiff must allege specific facts—as opposed to mere conclusions—showing exactly how and when he or she obtained direct and independent knowledge of the fraudulent acts alleged in the complaint and support those allegations with competent proof. Only in this way will the district court be able to adequately identify legitimate *qui tam* actions and weed out parasitic plaintiffs who offer only secondhand information, speculation, background information or collateral research. . . . Thus, Dr. Hafter's equivocal statements that his position gave him "access to information" and "allowed him to understand" Spectrum's business operations, along with Dr. Schwartz's assertion that he entered into contract negotiations with Spectrum and served as a litigation consultant, do not amount to "competent proof" of Appellants' direct and independent knowledge and fail to persuade us jurisdiction under § 3730(e)(4) is appropriate.

---

[627] *See Precision Co.*, 971 F.2d at 551; see also *Trentacosta*, 813 F.2d at 1559 (treating Rule 12(b)(1) motion as one for summary judgment and requiring plaintiff to set forth facts showing a genuine issue of material fact exists).
[628] 31 U.S.C. § 3730(e)(4)(B).
[629] *MK–Ferguson Co.*, 99 F.3d at 1547 (quotation marks and citation omitted).
[630] *See* John T. Boese, Civil False Claims & *Qui tam* Actions, 4–65 (1999 Supp.).
[631] *See* United States *ex rel.* Fine v. Advanced Sciences, Inc., 99 F.3d 1000, 1006–07 (10th Cir.1996); *MK–Ferguson Co.*, 99 F.3d at 1548.
[632] *See Penteco Corp.*, 929 F.2d at 1521.

. . .

Furthermore, Mr. Spradling's affidavit is lacking in specific, particularized fact allegations showing which fraudulent activities Dr. Hafter witnessed, how he witnessed them and when. Instead, much of the information contained in the affidavit attests to Dr. Hafter's possession of background knowledge and his opinions about Spectrum's management techniques. These statements do not satisfy Appellants' burden of establishing direct and independent knowledge of the information underlying the allegations. . . . Thus, Mr. Spradling's affidavit fails to persuade us Dr. Hafter possessed direct and independent knowledge sufficient to support the core basis of the allegations contained in the Second Amended Complaint. . . .

. . .

In sum, we conclude Drs. Hafter and Schwartz failed to sufficiently allege facts demonstrating direct and independent knowledge of the information on which the allegations of the Second Amended Complaint are based. The district court therefore lacked jurisdiction to hear the case and summary judgment was appropriate. The judgment of the district court is **AFFIRMED**.

United States ex rel. Hanlon v. Columbine Management Services, Inc.[633]

Relators Anthony Hanlon and Linda Dollar appeal the district court's dismissal of their *qui tam* complaint alleging the defendants violated the Anti-Kickback statute ("AKS"),[634] the False Claims Act ("FCA"),[635] and Colorado state law, as well as its refusal to allow them to amend their complaint. Exercising jurisdiction under 28 U.S.C. § 1291, we affirm.

. . .

2. FCA Claim

The relators argue that their original complaint states a claim for violation of the FCA. We conclude their allegations raise no more than speculative right to relief. The allegations that the defendants referred patients to their own facilities in "vastly disproportionate number[s]," and charged more for services than other facilities in the area do not amount to a showing that the relators are entitled to relief. A false certification claim under the FCA requires a showing that the Government might not have made a payment had the alleged violation been known.[636] But the relators do not point to a single claim by the defendants which the Government would not have paid had it known of any alleged falsity.

The relators have made no showing that the "funneling" they accuse the defendants of was illegal or that any disclosures they made to patients were inadequate. Their reliance on a special advisory bulletin issued by the Office of Inspector General ("OIG") is misplaced. A release by the OIG explains that "[t]he bulletin offers several examples of suspect contractual arrangements that could provide the basis for law enforcement action" and lists "[c]haracteristics of potentially problematic arrangements." However, "a sheer possibility that a defendant has acted unlawfully" is insufficient to withstand a motion to dismiss for failure to state a claim.[637] . . . The relators' allegations do not rise to the level of a plausible claim for relief; as a result, they have not stated a claim for relief under the FCA.

. . .

---

[633] 676 F.App'x 787 (10th Cir. 2017).
[634] 42 U.S.C. § 1320a-7b.
[635] 31 U.S.C. § 3729.
[636] United States *ex rel.* Lemmon v. Envirocare of Utah, Inc., 614 F.3d 1163, 1170 (10th Cir. 2010).
[637] *Iqbal*, 556 U.S. at 678, 129 S.Ct. 1937

United States ex rel. Hartpence v. Kinetic Concepts, Inc., et al.[638]

If a whistleblower informs the Government that it has been bilked by a provider of goods and services, and that scheme is unmasked to the public, under what conditions can that same whistleblower recover part of what the guilty provider is forced to reimburse the Government? We hold today that there are two, and only two, requirements in order for a whistleblower to be an "original source" who may recover under the False Claims Act: (1) Before filing his action, the whistleblower must voluntarily inform the Government of the facts which underlie the allegations of his complaint; and (2) he must have direct and independent knowledge of the allegations underlying his complaint. Abrogating our earlier precedent, we conclude that it does not matter whether he also played a role in the public disclosure of the allegations that are part of his suit.

. . .

In these consolidated *qui* tam cases, Steven Hartpence and Geraldine Godecke ("Relators") allege their former employer fraudulently claimed reimbursements from Medicare. After these allegations of Medicare fraud were publicly disclosed, Relators each informed the Government of the alleged fraud and then filed separate complaints in district court. Under the public disclosure bar, the district court lacked jurisdiction over these actions unless Relators qualified as "original sources" under the FCA.[639] Relying on our existing precedent, the district court held that neither Relator qualified as an original source, because neither had a "hand in the public disclosure" of the fraud, a requirement we announced in *Wang ex rel. United States v. FMC Corp.*[640] The district court further held that Godecke's complaint was also barred by the first-to-file bar, because her complaint alleged the same material elements of fraud as the complaint Hartpence had filed six months earlier. After a careful review of the statutory text, we overrule *Wang* as wrongly decided, and we remand for the district court to consider whether Relators qualify as original sources under the two-part test we announce today. Second, we hold that the district court erred in finding Godecke's action barred by the first-to-file bar, because some of Godecke's claims are materially distinct from Hartpence's claims.

. . .

We previously interpreted the requirements of the original source exception in *Wang*.[641] There, we affirmed the dismissal of a suit brought by an engineer against his former employer under the FCA. Because the relator's suit was based on allegations already in the public domain, which triggered the public disclosure bar

---

[638] 792 F.3d 1121 (9th Cir. 2015).
[639] 31 U.S.C. § 3730(e)(4).
[640] 975 F.2d 1412, 1418 (9th Cir.1992).
[641] 975 F.2d 1412.

in 31 U.S.C. § 3730(e)(4)(A), jurisdiction turned on whether the relator was an "original source." In *Wang*, we adopted a three-part test to determine whether a plaintiff is an original source: (1) he must have direct and independent knowledge of the information on which his allegations are based; (2) he must have voluntarily provided that information to the Government before filing his lawsuit; and (3) he must have "had a hand in the public disclosure of allegations that are a part of [his] suit."[642] Although the first two requirements parallel the statutory language, we inferred the third requirement from the FCA's legislative history, which suggested to us that the "information" referenced in the phrase "original source of the information,"[643] meant the information underlying the publicly disclosed allegations that triggered the public disclosure bar, rather than the information which underlay the plaintiff's complaint.[644] We were also persuaded by the Second Circuit's similar interpretation of the original source exception in *United States ex rel. Dick v. Long Island Lighting Co.*[645] In *Dick*, the Second Circuit concluded that, to qualify as an original source, a relator "must have directly or indirectly been a source to the entity that publicly disclosed the allegations on which a suit is based." Id. at 16. We then found that Wang did not qualify as an original source, because he did not have "a hand in the public disclosure of [the] allegations" of fraud.[646]

Wang has been the law of this circuit for 23 years. As an *en banc* court, however, we have the authority—and, indeed, the obligation—to review whether *Wang* was correctly decided. . . . We note that many of our sister circuits have declined to adopt *Wang*'s third prong—the hand-in-the-public-disclosure requirement—finding that it impermissibly grafts onto the statute a requirement nowhere to be found in the statute's text. Today, we join our sister circuits; after reviewing the statutory text, we conclude that *Wang*'s hand-in-the-public-disclosure requirement has no textual basis, and we give it a respectful burial.

.   .   .

---

[642] 975 F.2d at 1417–18.
[643] 31 U.S.C. § 3730(e)(4)(A).
[644] *Id.* at 1418–20.
[645] 912 F.2d 13 (2d Cir.1990).
[646] *Wang*, 975 F.2d at 1418.

United States ex rel. Hirt v. Walgreen Co.[647]

Andrew Hirt, owner of Andy's Pharmacies, alleges that Walgreen Company distributed kickbacks to Medicare and Medicaid recipients when they transferred their prescriptions to Walgreens. By sending these fraudulent insurance claims to the Government, Hirt maintains that Walgreens violated the False Claims Act, and he filed this *qui tam* claim as a result. The district court rejected Hirt's claim as a matter of law. Because Hirt failed to state his claim with particularity, as Civil Rule 9(b) requires, we affirm.

. . .

In addition to satisfying the False Claims Act's requirements, *qui tam* plaintiffs must meet the heightened pleading standards of Civil Rule 9(b).[648] In all averments of "fraud or mistake," the plaintiff must state with "particularity the circumstances constituting fraud or mistake."[649] The identification of at least one false claim with specificity is "an indispensable element of a complaint that alleges a [False Claims Act] violation in compliance with Rule 9(b)."[650] Adherence to this requirement not only respects Civil Rule 9(b), but it also helps in determining whether the public-disclosure bar applies.

Hirt has not met this standard. His complaint does not identify a single false claim. He describes the unlawful distribution of gift cards in general but not the submission of any claims obtained with those gift cards. All that Hirt says is that "his [Medicaid and Medicare] customers accepted the $25.00 gift cards to move their business to (Willow) Walgreens in Cookeville during the period November 19, 2012 through August 25, 2014," and that Walgreens "induce[d] ... false or fraudulent claims to the United States Government for the payment of pharmaceuticals." But he does not identify any false claim arising from any of those (allegedly) induced customers. He does not tell us the names of any such customers or their initials. He does not tell us the dates on which they filled prescriptions at Walgreens. He does not tell us the dates on which Walgreens filed the reimbursement claims with the Government. He does not, indeed, even say that these unnamed customers filled any prescriptions at Walgreens at all, let alone that Walgreens processed them and filed reimbursement claims with the Government. We are left to infer these essential elements from the fact that Hirt's customers moved their business from his pharmacies. But inferences and implications are not what Civil Rule 9(b) requires. It demands specifics—at least if the claimant wishes to raise allegations of fraud against someone.

---

[647] 846 F.3d 879 (6th Cir. 2017).
[648] United States *ex rel.* Bledsoe v. Cmty. Health Sys., Inc., 501 F.3d 493, 503 (6th Cir. 2007).
[649] Fed. R. Civ. P. 9(b).
[650] *Bledsoe*, 501 F.3d at 504.

Relying on an unpublished decision from the Eleventh Circuit, we raised the possibility in 2007 of "relaxing" the requirement that a plaintiff identify at least one false claim with particularity if that plaintiff, through no fault of his own, "cannot allege the specifics of actual false claims that in all likelihood exist."[651] But we did not resolve the point, ultimately "express[ing] no opinion as to the contours or existence of any such exception."[652] In two later decisions, we repeated the "relax" language.[653] The Eleventh Circuit's use of the word "relax," and our repetition of it in later cases, runs the risk of misleading lawyers and their clients. We have no more authority to "relax" the pleading standard established by Civil Rule 9(b) than we do to increase it. Only by following the highly reticulated procedures laid out in the Rules Enabling Act can anyone modify the Civil Rules, whether in the direction of relaxing them or tightening them.[654] To the extent the words of Civil Rule 9(b) need elaboration, and it's not obvious that they do, the most that can be said is that "particular" allegations of fraud may demand different things in different contexts.

In practice, we have applied the "relax[ed]" standard just once, and that application has no purchasing power here.[655] Prather's allegations satisfied the particularity requirement because she had sufficient personal knowledge of the defendant's claims submission and billing processes. Her job required her to review the company's Medicare claims documentation to ensure compliance with state and federal insurance guidelines.[656] This review took place, according to Prather, for the sole purpose of submitting the claims to Medicare. After her review, Prather would deliver the claims documents to the billing department, whose job it was to submit the claims for payment. In context, that set of pleading statements sufficed to establish with particularity that the defendant "submitted a claim for payment,"—as it described when, where, and how the defendant submitted the claim.[657]

Hirt offers no equivalent basis for satisfying the particularity requirement here. The reason is straightforward. Unlike Prather, Hirt failed to provide the factual predicates necessary to convince us that "actual false claims" "in all likelihood exist."[658] He does not allege personal knowledge of Walgreen's claim submission procedures.[659] And he does not otherwise allege facts "from which it is highly

---

[651] *Bledsoe*, 501 F.3d at 504 n.12.
[652] *Id.*
[653] Chesbrough v. VPA, P.C., 655 F.3d 461, 471 (6th Cir. 2011); United States *ex rel.* Prather v. Brookdale Senior Living Comtys., Inc., 838 F.3d 750, 769 (6th Cir. 2016).
[654] *See* 28 U.S.C. §§ 2071–2077.
[655] *See Prather*, 838 F.3d at 769.
[656] *Id.* at 770.
[657] See United States *ex rel.* Marlar v. BWXT Y-12, LLC, 525 F.3d 439, 445 (6th Cir. 2008); *Chesbrough*, 655 F.3d at 470.
[658] *Bledsoe*, 501 F.3d at 504 n.12.
[659] *Prather*, 838 F.3d at 770.

likely that a claim was submitted to the Government."⁶⁶⁰ At the least, Hirt could have described a prescription filled by one of his previous customers at the Willow Walgreens. In the same way that Hirt discovered that his former customers had accepted the gift cards, he could have determined whether they used those gift cards when filling a prescription at Walgreens. And if that is somehow not the case, how could he know that Walgreens violated the False Claims Act—the first requirement for filing an action?

Hirt's general allegations that Walgreens offered gift cards and some Medicare and Medicaid recipients accepted them do not meet the particularity requirement. "To conclude that a claim was presented" in this setting "requires a series of assumptions," leaving only a "possibility" of fraudulent submissions rather than an establishment of them.⁶⁶¹ Hirt failed to describe even one unlawful prescription purchase—that customer X of his pharmacy filled prescription Y with Willow Walgreens on date Z after receiving a gift card from Walgreens. If Hirt lacked the information to do even this, he was not the right plaintiff to bring this *qui tam* claim—and almost certainly not the right one to do so in a way that would allow a court to decide whether the public-disclosure bar applies to the allegation. We have no basis for excluding a lack of personal knowledge when it comes to the essential—the primary—illegal conduct at issue.⁶⁶² The point of Civil Rule 9(b) is to prevent, not facilitate, casual allegations of fraud.

The privacy concerns reflected in the Health Insurance Portability and Accountability Act (HIPAA) do not permit us to overlook this problem. Hirt could have used customer initials, dates, or other non-identifying descriptions. Exposing a false claim with particularity does not require risking the personal privacy of the claimant.

For these reasons, we affirm.

---

660 *Chesbrough*, 655 F.3d at 472.
661 *Id.*
662 *Id.*

United States ex rel. Hunt v. Cochise Consultancy, Inc.[663]

Relator Billy Joe Hunt filed a *qui tam* action alleging that his employer The Parsons Corporation and another entity, Cochise Consultancy, Inc., violated the False Claims Act ("FCA"),[664] by submitting to the United States false or fraudulent claims for payment. Hunt filed his action more than six years after the alleged fraud occurred but within three years of when he disclosed the fraud to the Government. In this appeal, we are called upon to decide whether Hunt's FCA claim is time barred. To answer this question, we must construe the FCA's statutory provision that requires a civil action alleging an FCA violation to be brought within the later of:

- "6 years after the date on which the violation ... is committed," 31 U.S.C. § 3731(b)(1), or

- "3 years after the date when facts material to the right of action are known or reasonably should have been known by the official of the United States charged with responsibility to act in the circumstances, but in no event more than 10 years after the date on which the violation is committed," id. § 3731(b)(2).

The question we answer today, which is one of first impression, is whether § 3731(b)(2)'s three year limitations period applies to a relator's FCA claim when the United States declines to intervene in the *qui tam* action.

The district court concluded that the limitations period in § 3731(b)(2) is inapplicable in such cases and thus Hunt's claim is time barred. After careful consideration of the statutory scheme, we hold that § 3731(b)(2)'s three year limitations period applies to an FCA claim brought by a relator even when the United States declines to intervene. Further, because the FCA provides that this period begins to run when the relevant federal government official learns of the facts giving rise to the claim, when the relator learned of the fraud is immaterial for statute of limitations purposes. Here, it is not apparent from the face of Hunt's complaint that his claim is untimely because his allegations show that he filed suit within three years of the date when he disclosed facts material to the right of action to United States officials and within ten years of when the fraud occurred. The district court therefore erred in dismissing his complaint. We reverse and remand to the district court for further proceedings.

• • •

---

[663] 887 F.3d 1081 (11th Cir. 2018).
[664] 31 U.S.C. §§ 3729-33.

After the United States declined to intervene, Hunt's complaint was unsealed. The contractors moved to dismiss, arguing that the claim was time barred under the six year limitations period in 31 U.S.C. § 3731(b)(1), and Hunt had waited more than seven years after the fraud occurred to file suit. Hunt responded that his claim was timely under the limitations period in § 3731(b)(2) because he had filed suit within three years of when the Government learned of the fraud at his FBI interview and ten years of when the fraud occurred. The district court disagreed, concluding that § 3731(b)(2)'s limitations period was either (1) unavailable to Hunt because the United States had declined to intervene or (2) expired because it began to run when Hunt learned of the fraud. The district court then granted the motions to dismiss, finding Hunt's claim untimely under § 3731(b)(1)'s limitation period because it was apparent from the face of Hunt's complaint that he failed to file suit within six years of when the fraud occurred. This is Hunt's appeal.

. . .

This appeal concerns the second mechanism, a *qui tam* action brought by a relator under § 3730(b). In a *qui tam* action, the relator "pursues the Government's claim against the defendant, and asserts the injury in fact suffered by the Government."[665] In bringing a *qui tam* action, the relator "in effect, su[es] as a partial assignee of the United States."[666]

. . .

Although the United States is not a party to a non-intervened case, it nevertheless retains a significant role in the litigation. The Government may request to be served with copies of all pleadings and deposition transcripts, seek to stay discovery if it "would interfere with the Government's investigation or prosecution of a criminal or civil matter arising out of the same facts," and veto a relator's decision to voluntarily dismiss the action.[667] Additionally, the court may permit the Government to intervene later "upon a showing of good cause."[668]

. . .

The primary question before us is whether Congress intended to allow relators in non-intervened cases to rely on § 3731(b)(2)'s limitations period. We must begin "where courts should always begin the process of legislative interpretation, and where they often should end it as well, which is with the words of the statutory

---

[665] Stalley *ex rel.* United States v. Orlando Reg'l Healthcare Sys., Inc., 524 F.3d 1229, 1233 (11th Cir. 2008).
[666] Vt. Agency of Nat. Res. v. United States *ex rel.* Stevens, 529 U.S. 765, 773 n.4, 120 S.Ct. 1858, 146 L.Ed.2d 836 (2000) (emphasis omitted).
[667] *Id.* § 3730(b)(1), (c)(3), (c)(4).
[668] *Id.* § 3730(c)(3).

provision."⁶⁶⁹ In considering the text, we bear in mind that "[a] provision that may seem ambiguous in isolation is often clarified by the remainder of the statutory scheme."⁶⁷⁰ We look to "the whole statutory text, considering the purpose and context of the statute, and consulting any precedents or authorities that inform the analysis."⁶⁷¹ As part of this inquiry, we also consider the canons of statutory construction.⁶⁷² Legislative history may prove helpful when the statutory language remains ambiguous after considering "the language itself, the specific context in which that language is used, and the broader context of the statute as a whole."⁶⁷³

We conclude that the phrase "civil action under section 3730" in § 3731(b) refers to civil actions brought under § 3730 that have as an element a violation of § 3729, which includes § 3730(b) *qui tam* actions when the Government declines to intervene. Section § 3731(b) begins by providing that its limitations periods apply to "[a] civil action under section 3730."⁶⁷⁴ A non-intervened cases is a type of civil action under § 3730.⁶⁷⁵ And nothing in § 3731(b)(2) says that its limitations period is unavailable to relators when the Government declines to intervene. In the absence of such language, we conclude that the text supports allowing relators in non-intervened cases to rely on § 3731(b)(2)'s limitations period.

To ascertain its meaning, we must, of course, view § 3731(b)(2) in the broader statutory context. Looking to the statutory context, the Supreme Court has recognized that the phrase "[a] civil action under section 3730" did not refer to all types of § 3730 civil actions because it excluded retaliation actions brought under § 3730(h).⁶⁷⁶ In Graham County, the Supreme Court considered whether § 3731(b)(1)'s six year limitations period—which begins to run when the defendant submits a false claim—applied to an employee's § 3730(h) retaliation claim alleging that her employer forced her to resign after she assisted federal officials investigating her employer for submitting false claims to the United States. On its face, § 3731(b) appeared to apply to § 3730(h) retaliation actions, which were a type of civil action under § 3730.⁶⁷⁷ Relying on statutory context, the Court

---

669 Harris v. Garner, 216 F.3d 970, 972 (11th Cir. 2000) (*en banc*).
670 Koons Buick Pontiac GMC, Inc. v. Nigh, 543 U.S. 50, 60, 125 S.Ct. 460, 160 L.Ed.2d 389 (2004) (internal quotation marks omitted).
671 Dolan v. U.S. Postal Serv., 546 U.S. 481, 486, 126 S.Ct. 1252, 163 L.Ed.2d 1079 (2006).
672 CBS Inc. v. PrimeTime 24 Joint Venture, 245 F.3d 1217, 1225 (11th Cir. 2001).
673 Robinson v. Shell Oil Co., 519 U.S. 337, 341, 117 S.Ct. 843, 136 L.Ed.2d 808 (1997).
674 31 U.S.C. § 3731(b).
675 *See Id.* § 3730(b)(1) (permitting any person to bring a civil action alleging a violation of § 3729); id. § 3730(c)(3) (allowing a relator to continue to conduct a qui tam action after the United States declines to intervene).
676 Graham Cty. Soil & Water Conservation Dist. v. United States *ex rel.* Wilson, 545 U.S. 409, 415, 125 S.Ct. 2444, 162 L.Ed.2d 390 (2005).
677 *Id.* at 415, 125 S.Ct. 2444.

nonetheless concluded that § 3731(b)'s literal text was ambiguous as to whether the phrase "[a] civil action under section 3730" included § 3730(h) retaliation actions.[678] The Court observed that § 3731(b)(1)'s limitations period was triggered by the defendant's submission of a false claim.[679] But a plaintiff bringing a retaliation claim under § 3730(h) did not need to allege or prove that the defendant actually submitted a false claim because an employer can be liable for retaliating against an employee who assists with an investigation or civil action even if the employer is innocent.[680] This tension in applying § 3731(b)(1)'s limitation period to retaliation actions led the Court to find the statute ambiguous as to whether "action under section 3730" referred to "all actions under § 3730, or only §§ 3730(a) and (b) actions."[681]

The Supreme Court resolved this ambiguity by concluding that § 3731(b)(1)'s limitations period did not apply to retaliation claims under § 3730(h). The Court recognized that Congress generally drafted statutes of limitations to begin to run when a cause of action accrues.[682] Applying § 3731(b)(1)'s limitations period to an FCA retaliation action would violate this general rule because the limitations period would begin to run when the employer committed the actual or suspected FCA violation, not when it retaliated against the employee. This interpretation could lead to the odd result that a plaintiff's retaliation claim was time barred before the employer took any retaliatory action.[683] To "avoid[ ] these counterintuitive results," the Court construed "civil action under section 3730" to "mean[ ] only those civil actions under § 3730 that have as an element a violation of section 3729, that is, §§ 3730(a) and (b) actions."[684] Graham County thus made clear that to determine whether § 3731(b)(2) includes *qui tam* actions where the United States declines to intervene, we must consider the text of § 3731(b)(2) in the relevant statutory context. But nothing in Graham County directly addressed whether the statutory context shows that § 3731(b)(2)'s limitations period is available only when the Government is a party.

Here, the contractors raise several arguments contending that the statutory context and the canons of statutory construction show that Congress intended for § 3731(b)(2) to be unavailable to relators in non-intervened cases. They claim that allowing a relator in a non-intervened action to rely on a limitations period that is triggered by a government official's knowledge would lead to absurd results and render a portion of § 3731(b) superfluous. We reject each of these arguments. The text of § 3731(b)(2), when viewed in context, shows that § 3731(b)(2) is available to relators when the Government declines to intervene. But even if we

---

[678] *Id.* at 417, 125 S.Ct. 2444.
[679] *Id.* at 415, 125 S.Ct. 2444.
[680] *Id.* at 416, 125 S.Ct. 2444.
[681] *Id.*
[682] *Id.* at 418, 125 S.Ct. 2444.
[683] *Id.* at 420-21, 125 S.Ct. 2444.
[684] *Id.* at 421-22, 125 S.Ct. 2444 (internal quotation marks omitted).

were to conclude that § 3731(b)(2) is ambiguous making it appropriate to consider legislative history, as the contractors urge us to do, we still would conclude that § 3731(b)(2) is available to relators when the Government declines to intervene.

1. We Reject that Allowing a Relator in a Non-Intervened Case to Rely on § 3731(b)(2)'s Limitations Period Is Absurd.

The contractors' primary argument is that the statutory context shows that § 3731(b)(2) is available only when the United States is a party to the case because the limitations period is triggered by a federal official's knowledge. They argue that Congress must have intended such a limitations period to be available only when the Government is a party to the case because to apply a limitations period triggered by a federal official's knowledge when the United States is not a party would create a "bizarre scenario." Put differently, they argue that reading § 3731(b)(2) to apply to non-intervened actions would lead to an absurd result. Of course, we should refrain from interpreting a statute in a way that "produces a result that is not just unwise but is clearly absurd."[685] But we have cautioned that the absurdity doctrine is "rarely applied" to avoid having "clearly expressed legislative decisions ... be subject to the policy predilections of judges."[686]

This case presents no such rare instance when the absurdity doctrine applies. Certainly, it is generally the case that a discovery-based limitations period begins to run when a party—the plaintiff—knew or should have known about the fraud or claim.[687] We cannot say that in the unique context of an FCA *qui tam* action, however, it would be absurd to peg a limitations period to a federal official's knowledge unless the United States brings the action or chooses to intervene. We reject the contractors' absurdity argument because even though the United States is not a party to a non-intervened *qui tam* action, the United States remains the real party in interest and retains significant control over the case.

. . .

The contractors argue that allowing a relator in a non-intervened case to rely on § 3731(b)(2)'s limitations period conflicts with the Supreme Court's decision in *Eisenstein*. In *Eisenstein*, the relators in a non-intervened case filed a notice of appeal 54 days after the district court entered a final judgment dismissing their claims.[688] Although parties normally have 30 days to file a notice of appeal, the

---

[685] *CBS*, 245 F.3d at 1228 (internal quotation marks omitted).
[686] *Id.* (internal quotation marks omitted).
[687] *See, e.g.*, Merck & Co. v. Reynolds, 559 U.S. 633, 637, 130 S.Ct. 1784, 176 L.Ed.2d 582 (2010) (recognizing that a securities fraud claim accrued when the plaintiff knew or should have known the facts constituting the violation); see also Restatement (Second) of Torts § 899(e) (statute of limitations begins to run when "the injured person has knowledge or reason to know of the facts").
[688] 556 U.S. at 930, 129 S.Ct. 2230.

relators argued that they could avail themselves of the 60 day deadline that applies when the United States is a party to the action.[689] The Supreme Court rejected this argument and affirmed the dismissal of the appeal, holding that the United States is not a party to a *qui tam* action when it declines to intervene.[690] But our decision today in no way relies on the United States being a party to the non-intervened case, and nothing in Eisenstein addressed whether the United States' non-party status means that the limitations period in § 3731(b)(2) is unavailable to relators in non-intervened cases.

We recognize that our decision to reject the absurdity doctrine is at odds with the published decisions of two other circuits.[691]

These cases do not persuade us. They reflexively applied the general rule that a limitations period is triggered by the knowledge of a party. They failed to consider the unique role that the United States plays even in a non-intervened *qui tam* case. In light of this role, we cannot say that it would be absurd or "bizarre" to peg the limitations period to the knowledge of a government official when the Government declines to intervene. We disagree that Congress, by specifying that § 3731(b)(2)'s limitations period is triggered by the knowledge of a United States official, necessarily intended that this limitations period be available only in § 3730 civil actions where the United States is a party and not in non-intervened *qui tam* actions.10 We thus cannot say that the statutory context shows that § 3731(b)(2)'s limitations period is unavailable to relators in non-intervened *qui tam* actions.

2. Our Interpretation Does Not Render a Portion of § 3731(b) Superfluous.

The contractors, relying on a canon of construction, next argue that to give meaning to the entirety of § 3731(b), we must construe § 3731(b)(2) to exclude non-intervened cases. Certainly, "a statute ought, upon the whole, to be so construed that, if it can be prevented, no clause, sentence, or word shall be superfluous, void, or insignificant."[692] But this canon does not apply when a

---

[689] *Id.* at 930-31, 129 S.Ct. 2230.
[690] *Id.* at 937, 129 S.Ct. 2230.
[691] *See Sanders*, 546 F.3d at 293 ("Congress intended Section 3731(b)(2) to extend the FCA's default six-year period only in cases in which the Government is a party, rather than to produce the bizarre scenario in which the limitations period in a relator's action depends on the knowledge of a nonparty to the action."); United States *ex rel.* Sikkenga v. Regence Bluecross Blueshield of Utah, 472 F.3d 702, 726 (10th Cir. 2006) ("Surely, Congress could not have intended to base a statute of limitations on the knowledge of a non-party.").
[692] TRW Inc. v. Andrews, 534 U.S. 19, 31, 122 S.Ct. 441, 151 L.Ed.2d 339 (2001) (internal quotation marks omitted).

statutory provision would remain operative under the interpretation in question in at least some situations.[693]

The contractors assert that if relators have three years from the date when the Government learned of the fraud to file suit under § 3731(b)(2), relators will always delay telling the Government about the fraud to increase the damages in the case. Therefore, they say, the limitations period in § 3731(b)(1), which expires six years after the date when the violation occurred, will never apply, rendering the provision meaningless. We disagree. The contractors overlook that other provisions of the FCA create strong incentives to ensure that relators promptly report fraud.

A relator who waits to report a fraud risks recovering nothing or having his relator's share decreased. The relator's claim may be barred if another relator beats him to the courthouse with an FCA claim based on the same facts, 31 U.S.C. § 3730(b)(5), or if the allegations or transactions are publicly disclosed either in a federal hearing where the Government was a party or in a news report, unless the relator was the original source of the information.[694] And because § 3731(b)(2)'s limitations period begins to run when the relevant government officials learns about the fraud from any source, a relator who delays reporting the fraud to the Government also runs the risk that the Government will learn about the fraud from another source and thus that § 3731(b)(2)'s three year period will expire before the relator files suit. But even if there were no risk that the Government could learn of the fraud from another source, a relator still would have an incentive to report fraud promptly because the court in setting the relator's share may consider whether he "substantially delayed in reporting the fraud or filing the complaint."[695]

Looking at the FCA as a whole, we conclude that relators who can rely on the limitations period in § 3731(b)(2) will still have sufficient incentive to report fraud promptly. Because relators will continue to report fraud promptly and under § 3731(b)(2) suit must be filed within three years of the fraud being reported, there will be cases in which § 3731(b)(1)'s six year limitations period will expire later. We thus reject the contractors' argument that our reading of the FCA would render superfluous one of its provisions.

3. To the Extent that Legislative History is Relevant, It Bolsters Our Conclusion.

The contractors argue that the legislative history shows that § 3731(b)(2)'s limitations period is unavailable to a relator when the United States declines to

---

[693] *See* Black Warrior Riverkeeper, Inc. v. Black Warrior Minerals, Inc., 734 F.3d 1297, 1304 (11th Cir. 2013).
[694] *Id.* § 3730(e)(4).
[695] United States *ex rel.* Shea v. Verizon Commc'ns, Inc., 844 F.Supp.2d 78, 89 (D.D.C. 2012).

intervene. Assuming that the statutory language, after viewing it in light of the statutory context and the canons of construction, remains ambiguous such that a resort to legislative history is appropriate,[696] we cannot agree that the relevant Congressional records undermine our interpretation of § 3731(b)(2).

Congress added the limitations period in § 3731(b)(2) to the FCA in 1986. False Claims Amendments Act of 1986 ("1986 FCA Amendments"), Pub. L. No. 99-562, 100 Stat. 3153 (1986). The legislative history reveals that one of the broad purposes of the 1986 FCA Amendments was to "encourage more private enforcement suits."[697] This purpose is consistent with Congress's historical use of *qui tam* rights of action to create incentives for private individuals to help root out fraud against the Government.[698] Allowing relators to continue to pursue FCA claims even after the Government declines to intervene is consistent with the broad underlying purpose of the FCA because it creates the potential for "more fraud [to] be discovered, more litigation [to] be maintained, and more funds [to] flow back into the Treasury."[699]

The contractors argue that we should not infer Congressional intent to extend the limitations period for non-intervened cases because in the legislative history for the 1986 FCA Amendments Congress indicated that *qui tam* actions must be brought shortly after the fraud occurred. To support their position, the contractors point to the following portion of the Senate Committee Report, which quotes from the reasoning in a Supreme Court decision:

> [The FCA] is intended to protect the Treasury against the hungry and unscrupulous host that encompasses it on every side, and should be construed accordingly. It was passed upon the theory, based on experience as old as modern civilization, that one of the least expensive and most effective means of preventing frauds on the Treasury is to make the perpetrators of them liable to actions by private persons acting, if you please, under the strong stimulus of personal ill will or the hope of gain. Prosecutions conducted by such means compare with the ordinary methods as the enterprising privateer does to the slow-going public vessel.[700]

The contractors argue this language shows that Congress allowed relators to bring *qui tam* actions under the FCA because relators are able to expose fraud more

---

[696] *See* United States v. Alabama, 778 F.3d 926, 939 (11th Cir. 2015).
[697] S. Rep. No. 99-345 at 23-24 (1986).
[698] *See* United States *ex rel.* Williams v. NEC Corp., 931 F.2d 1493, 1497 (11th Cir. 1991).
[699] *Milam*, 961 F.2d at 49.
[700] S. Rep. No. 99-345, at 11 (quoting United States *ex rel.* Marcus v. Hess, 317 U.S. 537, 541 n.5, 63 S.Ct. 379, 87 L.Ed. 443 (1943)).

rapidly than the United States can discover it, from which they infer that Congress intended for a shorter limitations period to apply when the United States was not a party to the case. But nothing in this statement addresses the length of time that a relator should have to bring a *qui tam* action or whether the limitations period should depend on the Government's decision to intervene. And so we fail to see how this legislative history supports the contractors' position that a shorter limitations period should apply when the Government declines to intervene.

All told, there is little legislative history for § 3731(b)(2). And the few references there are do not directly address the question before us. The contractors point to a floor statement from Senator Charles Grassley and testimony from Assistant Attorney General Richard K. Willard before a House subcommittee. But neither piece of legislative history is particularly helpful.

. . .

To wrap up, we conclude that Congress intended for § 3731(b)(2)'s limitations period to be available to relators even when the United States declines to intervene. The statutory text reflects that this limitations period applies to "[a] civil action under section 3730," and nothing in § 3731(b)(2) makes the limitations period unavailable in *qui tam* actions under § 3730 simply because the United States decides not to intervene. The contractors argue that because § 3731(b)(2)'s limitations period is triggered by government knowledge, Congress must have intended for it to apply only when the United States is a party to avoid absurd results. But in the unique context of a non-intervened *qui tam* action, we cannot say that it is absurd to apply a limitations period triggered by government knowledge. And even if the contractors are correct that we may consider legislative history, the legislative history provides no convincing support for their position.

B. The Statute of Limitations in § 3731(b)(2) Depends on the Government's Knowledge, Not the Relator's Knowledge.

Having concluded that the statute of limitations in § 3731(b)(2) is available to a relator in a non-intervened case, we must now address whether that limitations period is triggered by the knowledge of a government official or of the relator. We hold that it is the knowledge of a government official, not the relator, that triggers the limitations period.

Section 3731(b)(2) is clear that the time period begins to run when "the official of the United States charged with responsibility to act in the circumstances" knew or reasonably should have known the material facts about the fraud.[701] Nothing in the statutory text or broader context suggests that the limitations period is triggered by the relator's knowledge. Given that the language is plain, we cannot

---

[701] 31 U.S.C. § 3731(b)(2).

rewrite the statute to say that the limitations period is triggered when the relator knew or should have known about the facts material to the fraud.

The Ninth Circuit nonetheless adopted such an approach, concluding that the statute of limitations is triggered by the relator's knowledge.[702] The Ninth Circuit created a new legal fiction that because the relator "sue[d] on behalf of the Government," the relator became a government agent and the Government official charged with responsibility to act.[703] Again, we find nothing in the text of § 3731(b)(2) or the statutory context to support this legal fiction. Because the text unambiguously identifies a particular official of the United States as the relevant person whose knowledge causes the limitations period to begin to run, we must reject the Ninth Circuit's interpretation as inconsistent with that text.

Applying our conclusions that § 3731(b)(2) applies in non-intervened cases and is triggered by the knowledge of a government official, not of the relator, we hold that it is not apparent from the face of Hunt's complaint that his FCA claim is untimely. Hunt alleged that the relevant government official learned the material facts on November 30, 2010 when he disclosed the fraudulent scheme to FBI agents, and he filed suit within three years of this disclosure. The district court therefore erred in dismissing his complaint on statute of limitations grounds.

V. CONCLUSION

For the reasons set forth above, we reverse the district court's order dismissing Hunt's FCA claim as time barred and remand the case for further proceedings consistent with this opinion.

REVERSED AND REMANDED.

---

[702] *See* United States *ex rel.* Hyatt v. Northrop Corp., 91 F.3d 1211, 1217 (9th Cir. 1996).
[703] *Id.* at 1217 n.8.

United States ex rel. Ibanez v. Bristol-Myers Squibb Company[704]

Relators Joseph Ibanez and Jennifer Edwards, former employees of Bristol-Myers Squibb Co. (BMS), bring this *qui tam* action alleging that BMS, together with Otsuka America Pharmaceutical, Inc. (Otsuka), engaged in a complex, nationwide scheme to improperly promote the antipsychotic drug Abilify. Relators assert that this scheme caused claims for reimbursement for the drug to be submitted to the Government, in violation of the False Claims Act (FCA),[705] and several state-law analogues. The district court dismissed the complaint in part and subsequently denied relators' motion to amend. Because neither the second amended complaint nor the proposed third amended complaint satisfies Rule 9(b)'s pleading requirements, we affirm the district court's orders.

. . .

Relators' FCA complaint boils down to two separate theories. First, relators allege that defendant pharmaceutical companies engaged in a scheme to encourage providers to prescribe Abilify for unapproved ("off-label") uses and that some of those off-label prescriptions were paid for by government programs. Second, relators assert that defendants improperly induced providers to prescribe Abilify through remunerations and benefits in violation of the Anti-Kickback Statute. Relators assert that requests for government reimbursement for off-label prescriptions and prescriptions induced by kickbacks constitute false claims under the FCA.

. . .

In order to survive defendants' motion, relators must provide a representative claim that describes each step with particularity: a prescription reimbursement submitted to the Government for a tainted prescription of Abilify.[706] Relators do not adequately identify a representative false claim. Relators allege knowledge of a complex scheme related to the promotion of Abilify, but they do not provide any representative claim that was actually submitted to the Government for payment. Lacking a specific claim, relators encourage the court to apply a "relaxed" Rule 9(b) pleading standard that, despite having been suggested by prior opinions, had not been applied by this court until very recently.[707] The *Prather* standard is an exception to our usual rule, and applies only if "a relator alleges specific personal knowledge that relates directly to billing practices," supporting a "strong inference that a [false] claim was submitted."[708]

---

[704] 874 F.3d 905 (6th Cir. 2017).
[705] 31 U.S.C. § 3729 et seq.
[706] *See Prather*, 838 F.3d at 768.
[707] *See Id.*
[708] *Id.* (citing *Chesbrough*, 655 F.3d at 471).

Prather's personal knowledge exception applies in limited circumstances.⁷⁰⁹ In *Chesbrough*, an independent radiology consultant—alleging the radiology billings he reviewed were fraudulent—had insufficient personal knowledge to support the necessary inference that false claims were submitted because he had no involvement with billing procedures.⁷¹⁰ Likewise, in *Eberhard*, relators failed to adequately plead knowledge because they could not show they had "personal knowledge of billing practices or contracts with the Government."⁷¹¹ In fact, the only time this court has ever applied a personal knowledge exception to FCA pleading requirements was in *Prather* itself.⁷¹² There, the exception applied under circumstances where the relator was specifically employed to review medical treatment documentation allegedly submitted to Medicare—i.e., she reviewed allegedly false claims themselves.⁷¹³ It was only this "detailed knowledge of the billing and treatment documentation related to the submission of requests for final payment, combined with her specific allegations regarding requests for anticipated payments" that satisfied a relaxed 9(b) standard.⁷¹⁴

Here, relators do not allege this type of personal knowledge. Relators were sales representatives of BMS and, unlike the relator in Prather, did not directly engage with claims whatsoever. In order for the Prather exception to apply, it is not enough to allege personal knowledge of an allegedly fraudulent scheme; a relator must allege adequate personal knowledge of billing practices themselves. Id. at 768. Relators fail to do so. Thus, absent a representative false claim derived from the alleged promotional scheme, the second amended complaint fails to adequately plead a violation of 31 U.S.C. § 3729(a)(1)(A).

Accordingly, relators have failed to adequately allege a violation of 31 U.S.C. § 3729(a)(1)(A) in their second amended complaint.

. . .

Section 3719(a)(1)(B) requires a relator to "plead a connection between the alleged fraud and an actual claim made to the Government."⁷¹⁵ The alleged connection must be evident.⁷¹⁶ Otherwise, "a cause of action under the FCA for fraud directed at private entities would threaten to transform the FCA into an all-purpose antifraud statute."⁷¹⁷ Thus, although relators allege defendants made

---

⁷⁰⁹ *See* United States *ex rel.* Hirt v. Walgreen Co., 846 F.3d 879, 881 (6th Cir. 2017).
⁷¹⁰ *Chesbrough*, 655 F.3d at 471.
⁷¹¹ *Eberhard*, 642 F.App'x at 552 (6th Cir. 2016) (citing *Chesbrough*, 655 F.3d at 471–72).
⁷¹² *See Prather*, 838 F.3d at 770.
⁷¹³ *Id.* at 768.
⁷¹⁴ *Id.* at 770.
⁷¹⁵ *Chesbrough*, 655 F.3d at 473.
⁷¹⁶ *See* Allison Engine Co. v. United States *ex rel.* Sanders, 553 U.S. 662, 671–72, 128 S.Ct. 2123, 170 L.Ed.2d 1030 (2008).
⁷¹⁷ *Id.* at 672, 128 S.Ct. 2123.

false or fraudulent statements in order to increase the number of Abilify prescriptions, there are no allegations connecting these statements to any claim made to the Government. Such statements, even if false, rely on a "link between the false statement and the Government's decision to pay or approve a false claim [that] is too attenuated to establish liability."[718] Thus, relators fail to adequately plead a 31 U.S.C. § 3729(a)(1)(B) claim because they rely on a too-attenuated chain connecting alleged false statements to the submission of claims.[719]

. . .

We therefore affirm the district court's order dismissing in part relators' second amended complaint.

. . .

To decide whether a claim has been publicly disclosed, courts look at the essential elements of alleged fraud to determine if enough information exists in the public domain to expose the fraudulent transaction.[720] Thus, the public disclosure bar is not implicated—even if one or more of a claim's essential elements are in the public domain—unless the exposed elements, taken together, provide adequate notice that there has been a fraudulent transaction.[721]

. . .

Here, defendants assert that the Government's previous FCA actions and resultant Corporate Integrity Agreements constitute disclosure of defendants' improper promotion of Abilify. The district court agreed, finding that relators' alleged scheme "closely track[s]" the pre-agreement promotion scheme. However, it was error for the court to hold that this resemblance alone called for dismissal under the public disclosure bar.

If a fraudulent off-label promotion scheme was publicly disclosed and then resolved, allegations of improper promotion that took place before the agreements putatively ended the scheme would necessarily implicate the public disclosure bar. But allegations that the scheme either continued despite the agreements or was restarted after the agreements are different. It cannot be assumed that the Government is aware a fraudulent scheme continues (or was restarted) simply because it had uncovered, and then resolved, a similar scheme before. Indeed, the most logical inference to draw from defendants' agreements

---

[718] *Id.*
[719] *See Chesbrough*, 655 F.3d at 473.
[720] *See* Dingle v. Bioport Corp., 388 F.3d 209, 212 (6th Cir. 2004); *Antoon*, 788 F.3d at 614–15.
[721] *See Dingle*, 388 F.3d at 212; United States *ex rel.* Poteet v. Medtronic, Inc., 552 F.3d 503, 512–13 (6th Cir. 2009).

to cease improper promotion of Abilify is that they had done so. Thus, to the extent that relators are able to describe with particularity post-agreement, improper promotion of Abilify, the mere resemblance of those allegations to a scheme resolved years earlier is not by itself enough to trigger the public disclosure bar.

Here, other than the fact that the alleged scheme resembled that described in the prior enforcement action, defendants do not otherwise show the alleged improper promotion was publicly disclosed. Thus, there was not enough information in the public domain to expose the alleged fraudulent transactions, meaning the public disclosure bar does not implicate fraud connected to post-agreement improper promotion of Abilify.

. . .

The amended reverse false claims allegations rely on the Corporate Integrity Agreements, attached to the third amended complaint. Relators assert these documents created an obligation to pay the Government under the FCA. However, section 3729(a)(1)(G)'s "obligation" does not include "those contingent obligations that arise only because the Government has prohibited an act, or arising after the exercise of government discretion."[722] The district court found the Corporate Integrity Agreements to be "contingent obligations" and failed to trigger a reverse false claim.

We agree. Both defendants were subject to nearly identical Corporate Integrity Agreements, the breach of which "may" have led to obligations to pay stipulated penalties. Yet even an alleged breach of these agreements did not, by itself, constitute an obligation to pay the Government. This is because the penalties for a breach of the agreements were subject to discretionary enforcement by the Office of the Inspector General, who was to determine whether the penalties were "appropriate" before triggering an administrative review process to collect those penalties. This is the type of non-obligation that fails to satisfy 31 U.S.C. § 3729(a)(1)(G).[723] Accordingly, relators fail to adequately plead a reverse false claim in their third amended complaint.

In sum, even considering the newly pleaded facts, amending the complaint would be futile as it would not survive a motion to dismiss. Accordingly, we affirm the district court's denial of relators' motion to amend.

Because relators have failed to plead a violation of the FCA with adequate particularity, we AFFIRM the orders certified for appeal by the district court and REMAND for further proceedings consistent with this opinion.

---

[722] *Am. Textile Mfrs. Inst.*, 190 F.3d at 741.
[723] *Id.* at 738.

United States ex rel. King v. Solvay Pharmaceuticals, Inc.[724]

John King and Tammy Drummond (collectively, "Relators") appeal the district court's grant of summary judgment to Solvay Pharmaceuticals, Inc., on their False Claims Act ("FCA") claims and a subsequent ruling that partly granted court costs to Solvay. For the reasons explained below, we AFFIRM.

i. Background

Relators are both former Solvay sales and marketing employees. They brought this FCA suit against Solvay claiming that Solvay induced false Medicaid claims through a nationwide off-label marketing and kickback scheme to promote three drugs: Luvox, Aceon, and AndroGel.[725] They allege that this scheme proximately caused physicians to prescribe these drugs for off-label uses to Medicaid patients, the cost of which was reimbursed by the federal government. Relators also claim they were retaliated against for their internal complaints about Solvay's off-label marketing. The district court granted summary judgment to Solvay on all of Relators' claims.

After final judgment, Solvay sought an award of $961,380.51 in taxable costs against Relators under 28 U.S.C. § 1920. Relators objected to almost all of those costs, claiming that Solvay was entitled to just $5,808.17. The district court awarded Solvay $232,809.92. Relators appealed both the final order granting summary judgment on all of Relators' claims and the order granting taxable costs to Solvay.

. . .

B. Taxable Costs

A district court may award certain taxable costs to a prevailing party.[726] "Taxable costs are limited to relatively minor, incidental expenses" amounting to "a fraction of the nontaxable expenses borne by litigants for attorneys, experts, consultants, and investigators."[727] Taxable costs may include, among other things, "[f]ees for printed or electronically recorded transcripts necessarily obtained for use in the case" and "[f]ees for exemplification and the costs of making copies of any materials where the copies are necessarily obtained for use in the case."[728]

---

[724] 871 F.3d 318 (5th Cir. 2017).
[725] *See* 31 U.S.C. § 3729(a)(1)(A)–(B).
[726] *See* 28 U.S.C. § 1920; FED. R. CIV. P. 54(d)(1).
[727] Taniguchi v. Kan Pac. Saipan, Ltd., 566 U.S. 560, 132 S.Ct. 1997, 2006, 182 L.Ed.2d 903 (2012).
[728] § 1920(2), (4).

Solvay sought taxable costs on both of these grounds, which the district court granted in part. Relators argue on appeal that Solvay failed to show that its costs were "necessarily obtained for use in the case." Relators also contend that the district court erred in overruling some of its specific objections to costs related to deposition transcripts, photocopying, and e-discovery.

1. Materials Necessarily Obtained for Use in the Case

Relators claim that a document is only "necessarily obtained for use in the case" if it "was actually used at trial or as a summary judgment exhibit." But we have interpreted "necessarily obtained for use in the case" to include documents "reasonably expected to be used for trial or trial preparation" at the time it was obtained.[729] "Whether a deposition or copy was necessarily obtained for use in the case is a factual determination within the district court's discretion, and 'we accord the district court great latitude in this determination.'"[730]

. . .

Relators also claim that "[t]he vehicle for recovering the costs of complying with discovery obligations is a protective order under Rule 26(e)," and "section 1920 [and] Rule 54 ... are not intended to govern the taxing of discovery costs." However, we have repeatedly said that "the authority of the trial court to assess 'necessary and reasonable' costs incurred during discovery 'can hardly be doubted.'"[731] Discovery costs are recoverable under Rule 54 "if the party making the copies has a reasonable belief that the documents will be used 'during trial or for trial preparation.'"[732]

After reviewing Solvay's declaration in support of its bill of costs, the district court exercised its considerable discretion and determined that Solvay adequately explained the necessity of its costs. Relators have failed to show that the district court abused its discretion in making this determination.

. . .

IV. Conclusion

For the foregoing reasons, the district court's grant of both summary judgment and taxable costs to Solvay is AFFIRMED.

---

[729] United States *ex rel.* Long v. GSDMIdea City, LLC, 807 F.3d 125, 130 (5th Cir. 2015).
[730] *Id.*
[731] Rundus v. City of Dallas, 634 F.3d 309, 316 (5th Cir. 2011) (quoting Harrington v. Texaco, Inc., 339 F.2d 814, 822 (5th Cir. 1964)).
[732] *Id.* (quoting *Fogleman*, 920 F.2d at 285).

United States ex rel. Lager v. CSL Behring, LLC, et al.[733]

Relator Shane Lager brought this *qui tam* action . . . alleging that drug manufacturer CSL Behring, LLC, and its parent corporation CSL Behring Limited conspired with pharmacies to submit false claims to the United States for reimbursement for prescription drugs. The Government declined to intervene. CSL Behring, Accredo, and Coram (collectively, "defendants") moved to dismiss the complaint based on, among other things, the FCA's public disclosure bar.[734] The district court granted the motion. Lager appeals this dismissal, and we affirm.

. . .

Pharmacies that dispense drugs to beneficiaries of government health care programs submit claims for reimbursement to the federal government. Since Congress's enactment in 2003 of the Medicare Prescription Drug, Improvement, and Modernization Act (MMA),[735] most drugs that Medicare and other government health programs cover are reimbursed based on the average sales price (ASP).[736] However, the MMA excluded DME infusion drugs, such as Vivaglobin and Hizentra; instead, reimbursements for these drugs are based on 95 percent of the average wholesale price (AWP). While the ASP is based on actual sales data, the AWP is based on figures that the drug manufacturer reports to third-party publishers, such as Red Book.[737] And, while the ASP is defined by law, the AWP is not.[738] The ASP is "substantially lower" than the AWP. Id. at 8. For example, in 2004, "[f]or 2,077 national drug codes with ASP and AWP data, ASP [was] 49 percent lower than AWP at the median."[739]

. . .

Lager brought this *qui tam* action pursuant to the FCA against CSL Behring, Accredo, and Coram, alleging that they agreed to and engaged in a joint action to defraud the Government over the course of several years. Specifically, Lager alleges that CSL Behring reported inflated AWPs for Vivaglobin and Hizentra to third-party publishers when, in actuality, the "true selling price" at which CSL sold the drugs was "substantially less than their falsely reported amounts." Lager

---

[733] 855 F.3d 935 (8th Cir. 2017).
[734] 31 U.S.C. § 3730(e)(4)(A).
[735] 42 U.S.C. §§ 1395w-21-1395w-28.
[736] *See* 42 U.S.C. §§ 1395u(o), 1395w-3, 1395w-3a, 1395w-3b.
[737] Office of Inspector Gen., U.S. Dep't of Health & Human Servs., OEI-12-12-00310, Part B Payments for Drugs Infused Through Durable Medical Equipment at 2-3 (2013) ("2013 OIG Report").
[738] *See* Office of Inspector Gen., U.S. Dep't of Health & Human Servs., OEI-03-05-00200, Medicaid Drug Price Comparison: Average Sales Price to Average Wholesale Price (2005) ("2005 OIG Report").
[739] *Id.*

Appendix G: Cases

alleges that CSL Behring used the "spread" between the actual cost and the reported AWPs to induce their customers, including Accredo and Coram, to buy its products. Lager alleges that Accredo and Coram then sought out patients covered by government health programs to take advantage of the spread. As a result of the defendants' conduct, Lager claims that the federal government has overpaid in excess of $100 million for Vivaglobin and in excess of $180 million for Hizentra.

After the United States declined to intervene in Lager's suit, the defendants moved to dismiss the complaint . . . . The district court dismissed Lager's complaint pursuant to the FCA's public disclosure bar, which bars an action or claim "if substantially the same allegations or transactions as alleged in the action or claim were publicly disclosed" in qualifying sources.[740]

. . .

We will first address Lager's contention that the public disclosures that the district court relied on do not identify the defendants. According to Lager, the public disclosure bar is inapplicable when the disclosures fail to specifically identify the defendants named in the *qui tam* action with the specific fraud at issue. He asserts that 15 of the 17 disclosures that the district court relied on make no mention of the defendants or of transactions involving Vivaglobin and Hizentra. According to Lager, only two disclosures "specifically discuss the Defendants and Specified Drugs at issue in this litigation" without tying them to the specific fraud. He additionally maintains that only in "very limited circumstances" have courts "applied the public disclosure bar in cases where the defendants named in the *qui tam* action were identifiable, though not specifically named in the disclosures." He urges that these cases are inapplicable to the present case because they concern "defendants operating in very narrow industries, and where the public disclosures were of industry-wide fraud."

. . .

Lager asserts that *Cooper*[741] articulates the appropriate standard for identifying defendants for purposes of the public disclosure bar. . . . The defendant moved to dismiss, arguing that the allegations were publicly disclosed by several sources that mentioned similar activities to the ones that the relator alleged.[742] Some of these source materials mentioned the defendant by name, while others made general allegations of fraud against the healthcare industry.[743]

---

[740] 31 U.S.C. § 3730(e)(4)(A).
[741] United States *ex rel.* Cooper v. Blue Cross & Blue Shield of Fla., Inc., 19 F.3d 562, 566 (11th Cir. 1994).
[742] *Id.* at 565.
[743] *Id.* at 566-67.

The Eleventh Circuit "consider[ed] it to be crucial whether [the defendant] was mentioned by name or otherwise specifically identified in public disclosures" and "consider[ed] separately those sources in which it was identified and those in which it was not."[744] The court held that "[t]he allegations of widespread ... fraud made in sources in which [the defendant] was *not specifically named or otherwise directly identified* are insufficient to trigger the jurisdictional bar."[745] (emphasis added).

"*Cooper*'s holding has its limits," as evidenced in *Fine*,[746] where the Tenth Circuit distinguished *Cooper*. *United States ex rel. Kester v. Novartis Pharm. Corp.*[747] In *Fine*, a former government auditor filed a *qui tam* action under the FCA, asserting that a laboratory under the Department of Energy's (DOE) control had "misappropriated nuclear waste funds in violation of the Nuclear Waste Policy Act."[748] The relator conceded that a General Accounting Office (GAO) report and a congressional hearing were types of disclosures that invoke the public disclosure bar.[749] Nonetheless, he argued that those disclosures "merely described the national laboratories' practice of 'taxing' Nuclear Waste Funds for discretionary ... projects"; by contrast, his complaint alleged that the defendant "in particular 'taxed' nuclear waste funds" in certain fiscal years.[750] The Tenth Circuit held that the GAO report and congressional hearing "sufficiently alerted the Government to the likelihood that [the defendant] would ... 'tax' nuclear waste funds in the future" "[b]ecause these disclosures detailed the mechanics of the practice, revealed that at least two of [the defendant's] eight sister laboratories were engaged in it, and indicated the DOE's acquiescence."[751] The court distinguished *Cooper*, stating, "When attempting to identify individual actors, little similarity exists between combing through the private insurance industry in search of fraud and examining the operating procedures of nine, easily identifiable, DOE-controlled, and government-owned laboratories."[752]

Similarly, in *Gear*,[753] the Seventh Circuit was "unpersuaded by an argument that for there to be public disclosure, the specific defendants named in the lawsuit must have been identified in the public records."[754] . . . It concluded that prior nationwide news reports, an investigation, and audits of how teaching hospitals

---

[744] *Id.* at 566.
[745] *Id.*
[746] United States *ex rel.* Fine v. Sandia Corp., 70 F.3d 568, 571-72 (10th Cir. 1995).
[747] No. 11 CIV. 8196 CM, 2015 WL 109934, at *14 (S.D.N.Y. Jan. 6, 2015) (citing *Fine*, 70 F.3d at 569-72).
[748] 70 F.3d at 569.
[749] *Id.* at 571.
[750] *Id.*
[751] *Id.*
[752] *Id.* at 572.
[753] United States *ex rel.* Gear v. Emergency Med. Assocs. of Ill., Inc., 436 F.3d 726 (7th Cir. 2006).
[754] 436 F.3d at 729.

billed Medicare for services that residents performed already exposed "allegations that Medicare was being billed for services provided by residents as if attending physicians had actually performed the services."⁷⁵⁵ According to the court, these public "disclosures ... were of industry-wide abuses and investigations. Defendants were implicated. Industry-wide public disclosures bar *qui tam* actions against any defendant who is *directly identifiable* from the public disclosures."⁷⁵⁶ . . .

. . .

Based on our review of the caselaw, we conclude that "[i]n order to bar claims against a particular defendant, the public disclosures relating to the fraud must either explicitly identify that defendant as a participant in the alleged scheme, or provide enough information about the participants in the scheme such that the defendant is identifiable."⁷⁵⁷ This means that "the public disclosures must 'set the Government squarely on the trail' of a specific and identifiable defendant's participation in the fraud."⁷⁵⁸ In applying this standard, we consider "public disclosures contained in different sources" as a whole to determine whether they collectively "provide information that leads to a conclusion of fraud."⁷⁵⁹

. . .

We conclude that all elements critical to Lager's complaint theory were already in the public domain before Lager brought suit. Lager's allegations of purported fraud on the part of the defendants are substantially the same as those revealed in the public disclosures, both pre- and post-2006.⁷⁶⁰

. . .

Accordingly, we affirm the judgment of the district court.

---

755   *Id.* at 728.
756   *Id.* at 729 (emphases added).
757   *Kester*, 2015 WL 109934, at *8.
758   *Id.* (quoting *In re Nat. Gas Royalties*, 562 F.3d 1032, 1041 (10th Cir. 2009)).
759   United States *ex rel.* Gilligan v. Medtronic, Inc., 403 F.3d 386, 390 (6th Cir. 2005).
760   Cf. United States *ex rel.* Morgan v. Express Scripts, Inc., 602 Fed.Appx. 880, 881, 883 (3d Cir. 2015) (affirming district court's dismissal of relator's FCA claim that pharmaceutical companies profited from "artificially inflated ... AWPs ... for brand-name drugs" because the prior disclosure "of a specific, industry-wide markup shift provided [the relator] with all the 'essential elements' needed to arrive at a 4.16% price differential").

United States ex rel. Lutz v. Berkeley Heartlab, Inc.[761]

. . .

The Government seeks penalties on each claim for payment Defendants presented or caused to be presented to Medicare and TRICARE, as well as treble damages under the FCA. (*See* Dkt. No. 75 at 43–46). Further, the Government's common law claims effectively seek to recover overpayments from Defendants for "certain sums of money to which they were not entitled." (*Id.* at 46–47).

. . .

[C]ourts have held that "a party that violates the FCA incurs a debt to the Government as soon as the Government pays the fraudulent claim. Thus by alleging that the defendants submitted false claims and made false statements under the FCA, the Government sufficiently alleges the existence of a debt under the FDCPA."[762] In short, the Government's claims are for a debt that is presently owing.

. . .

In addition to directly attacking the probable validity of the claim, § 3101(d)(2)(A) permits parties challenging prejudgment remedies to address any defenses that may be available. Defendants assert an advice-of-counsel defense.

To establish an advice-of-counsel defense, Defendants "must show the (a) full disclosure of all pertinent facts to counsel, and (b) good faith reliance on counsel's advice."[763] Unwritten but understood is the assumption that counsel's advice will have in some way related to the underlying actions or activities at issue. Here, Defendant's attorney provided no such advice.

. . .

Sellers simply did not provide any advice regarding the legality of the agreements vis-à-vis the healthcare laws. Furthermore, the Ruggio legal opinion was written

---

[761] 225 F.Supp.3d 460 (D.S.C. 2016).

[762] United States v. First Choice Armor & Equip., Inc., 808 F.Supp.2d 68, 79 (D.D.C. 2011) (internal citation omitted); *see also* U.S. *ex rel* Doe v. DeGregorio, 510 F.Supp.2d 877, 884 (M.D. Fla. 2007) ("Treble damages under the False Claims Act likewise constitutes 'debt.'"); cf. United States v. Lighthouse Disaster Relief, No. 06–161–D–M2, 2006 U.S. Dist. LEXIS 96195, at *9 (discussing FDCPA in context of FEMA contract, court held that "there is no need for the 'debt' to be liquidated or otherwise preexisting").

[763] U.S. *ex rel.* Drakeford v. Tuomey, 792 F.3d 364, 381 (4th Cir. 2015) (internal quotation marks and alterations omitted).

two years after BlueWave, Dent, and Johnson entered into the agreements with HDL and Singulex, so it could not have formed the basis for Sellers' advice. Finally, the compliance audit Defendants participated in and their cooperation with the Government's investigation are irrelevant with respect to the advice-of-counsel defense. For these reasons, Defendants' attempted assertion of the advice-of-counsel defense does not place the validity of the Government's claim for debt in dispute.

. . .

V. Conclusion

For the abovementioned reasons, the Court **DENIES** Defendants BlueWave, Dent, and Johnson's Motion to Quash FDCPA Prejudgment Remedies; the Johnson-related Entities' Motion to Quash; and the Dent-related Entities' Motion to Dissolve Prejudgment Attachments. The Court **GRANTS** Government's motion to amend/correct writ issued.

AND IT IS SO ORDERED.

United States ex rel. Marcus v. Hess[764]

Respondents, electrical contractors, were employed to work on P.W.A. projects in the Pittsburgh area. Their contracts were made with local governmental units rather than with the United States government, but a substantial portion of their pay came from the United States. Charging the respondents with defrauding the United States through the device of collusive bidding on these projects, the petitioner, in the name of the United States and on his own behalf brought this action under [the False Claims Act].

. . .

Second. Previous to the filing of this action these respondents were indicted for defrauding the Government and on a plea of *nolo contendere* were fined $54,000. They and the Government, which has filed a brief amicus curiae at our request, assert that the petitioner received his information not by his own investigation, but from the previous indictment; and both argue that [the *qui tam* section of the FCA] should not under such circumstances be construed as permitting suit by the petitioner. The petitioner denies that he relied upon the information contained in the indictment, asserts that he spent money in conducting an investigation of his own, and claims that he presented more evidence than the Government had discovered.

Even if, as the Government suggests, the petitioner has contributed nothing to the discovery of this crime, he has contributed much to accomplishing one of the purposes for which the Act was passed. The suit results in a net recovery to the Government of $150,000, three times as much as the fines imposed in the criminal proceedings; and this recovery was obtained at the risk of a considerable loss to the petitioner since [the FCA] explicitly provides that the informer must bear the risk of having to pay the full cost of the litigation.

Neither the language of the statute nor its history lends support to the contention made by respondents and the Government. "Suits may be brought and carried on by any person," says the Act, and there are no words of exception or qualification such as we are asked to find. The Senate sponsor of the bill explicitly pointed out that he was not offering a plan aimed solely at rewarding the conspirator who betrays his fellows, but that even a district attorney, who would presumably gain all knowledge of a fraud from his official position, might sue as the informer.

. . .

The Government presses upon us strong arguments of policy against the statutory plan, but the entire force of these considerations is directed solely at

---

[764] 317 U.S. 537 (1943).

what the Government thinks Congress should have done rather than at what it did. It is said that effective law enforcement requires that control of litigation be left to the Attorney General; that divided control is against the public interest; that the Attorney General might believe that war interests would be injured by filing suits such as this; that permission to outsiders to sue might bring unseemly races for the opportunity of profiting from the Government's investigations; and finally that conditions have changed since the Act was passed in 1863. But the trouble with these arguments is that they are addressed to the wrong forum. Conditions may have changed, but the statute has not.

Furthermore, one of the chief purposes of the Act, which was itself first passed in war time, was to stimulate action to protect the Government against war frauds. To that end, prosecuting attorneys were enjoined to be diligent in enforcement of the Act's provisions, and large rewards were offered to stimulate actions by private parties should the prosecuting officers be tardy in bringing the suits.

The very fact that Congress passed this statute shows that it concluded that other considerations of policy outweighed those now emphasized by the Government; for most of the arguments made here militate against any informer action at all.

. . .

Reversed.

United States ex rel. Nargol v. DePuy Orthopaedics, Inc.[765]

In this action brought by two private individuals under the False Claims Act ("FCA"),[766] and various state analogues, we review de novo the dismissal of a complaint under Federal Rules of Civil Procedure 9(b) and 12(b)(6). Applying and extending our holding in *United States ex rel. D'Agostino v. ev3, Inc.*,[767] we affirm the dismissal of the complaint to the extent it relies on the alleged falsity of statements made by the product manufacturer in securing approval from the U.S. Food and Drug Administration ("FDA") to market a hip-replacement device. At the same time, we reverse the district court's dismissal of the complaint to the extent it rests on allegations that the manufacturer palmed off latently defective versions of its FDA-approved product on unsuspecting doctors who sought government reimbursement for the defective products.

. . .

Relators allege two types of fraud in DePuy's marketing of the Pinnacle MoM device. First, Relators allege that DePuy made a series of false statements to the FDA and doctors, but for which the FDA would not have approved the Pinnacle MoM device for hip replacements or would have withdrawn that approval, and doctors would not have certified the devices for government reimbursement. Second, Relators allege that DePuy falsely palmed off devices that, due to latent manufacturing defects, materially deviated from the design specification of the FDA-approved Pinnacle MoM device.

. . .

Relators allege that DePuy made direct claims to the federal government and various state governments seeking payment for some of the defectively manufactured Pinnacle MoM devices. They also allege that DePuy was indirectly responsible for the claims for payment that healthcare providers submitted to the federal and state governments for reimbursement for defectively manufactured Pinnacle MoM devices that the healthcare providers had purchased from DePuy.

. . .

Rather than initially separating Relators' allegations into those involving "direct" false claims for government payment and those involving "indirect" false claims, we focus first on all of Relators' claims, whether direct or indirect, that rest on the allegation that DePuy misrepresented the safety and effectiveness of the product's design in order to secure or maintain FDA approval for the Pinnacle MoM device. We recently dealt with an analogous claim in *D'Agostino*, in which

---

[765] 865 F.3d 29 (1st Cir. 2017).
[766] 31 U.S.C. § 3729.
[767] 845 F.3d 1 (1st Cir. 2016).

we held that "the FDA's failure actually to withdraw its approval of [the device at issue] in the face of [the relator's] allegations precludes [the relator] from resting his claims on a contention that the FDA's approval was fraudulently obtained."⁷⁶⁸ The claim in this case is not quite on all fours with the claim we confronted in *D'Agostino* because the FDA does not independently assess the safety and effectiveness of a medical device that qualifies for approval under section 510(k).⁷⁶⁹ Rather, the process under section 510(k) allows a device manufacturer to piggyback on the full-scale review and approval of another device by demonstrating that the new device is "'substantially equivalent' to a predicate device" which itself may be marketed pending the completion of a full premarket approval process.⁷⁷⁰

Nevertheless, the process constitutes the Government's method of determining whether a device is safe and effective as claimed. That determination is what makes the product marketable, and Relators offer no suggestion that government reimbursement rules require government health insurance programs to rely less on section 510(k) approval than they do other forms of FDA approval. The FDA, in turn, possesses a full array of tools for "detecting, deterring, and punishing false statements made during ... approval processes."⁷⁷¹ Its decision not to employ these tools in the wake of Relators' allegations so as to withdraw or even suspend its approval of the Pinnacle MoM device leaves Relators with a break in the causal chain between the alleged misstatements and the payment of any false claim.⁷⁷² It also renders a claim of materiality implausible.⁷⁷³ The FCA's "materiality standard is demanding."⁷⁷⁴ Even in an ordinary situation not involving a misrepresentation of regulatory compliance made directly to the agency paying a claim, when "the Government pays a particular claim in full despite its actual knowledge that certain requirements were violated, that is very strong evidence that those requirements are not material."⁷⁷⁵ Such very strong evidence becomes compelling when an agency armed with robust investigatory powers to protect public health and safety is told what Relators have to say, yet sees no reason to change its position. In such a case, it is not plausible that the conduct of the manufacturer in securing FDA approval constituted a material falsehood capable of proximately causing the payment of a claim by the Government. Ruling otherwise would "turn the FCA into a tool with which a jury of six people could retroactively eliminate

---

768   845 F.3d at 8.
769   *See* Medtronic, Inc. v. Lohr, 518 U.S. 470, 493, 116 S.Ct. 2240, 135 L.Ed.2d 700 (1996).
770   Buckman Co. v. Plaintiffs' Legal Comm., 531 U.S. 341, 345, 121 S.Ct. 1012, 148 L.Ed.2d 854 (2001) (quoting 21 U.S.C. § 360e(b)(1)(B)).
771   *Id.* at 349, 121 S.Ct. 1012.
772   *D'Agostino*, 845 F.3d at 8.
773   *See Id.* at 7.
774   Universal Health Servs., Inc. v. United States, ─── U.S. ───, 136 S.Ct. 1989, 2003, 195 L.Ed.2d 348 (2016).
775   *Id.*

the value of FDA approval and effectively require that a product largely be withdrawn from the market even when the FDA itself sees no reason to do so."[776]

Here, as in *D'Agostino*, there is no allegation that the FDA withdrew or even suspended product approval upon learning of the alleged misrepresentations. To the contrary, the complaint alleges that Relators told the FDA about every aspect of the design of the Pinnacle MoM device that they felt was substandard, yet the FDA allowed the device to remain on the market until DePuy, on its own volition, discontinued the device in 2013. There are allegations that an FDA official sent a letter in 2005 that "imposed an affirmative obligation on DePuy to provide the FDA with updated information if ... data indicated that DePuy's 'change or modification to the device or its labeling could significantly affect the device's safety or effectiveness and thus require submission of a new 510(k),'" and that a 2011 FDA Establishment Inspection Report concerning a DePuy plant in Indiana determined that DePuy was not adequately reporting adverse events or investigating complaints of device failure. Such evidence does show that the FDA was paying attention. But the lack of any further action also shows that the FDA viewed the information, including that furnished by Relators, differently than Relators do.

. . .

We now arrive at Relators' principal theory of fraud raised on this appeal: that DePuy often sold to health care providers a defectively manufactured product that materially differed from the device the FDA approved. . . . The key question is whether this theory has been pleaded with the requisite particularity.

The complaint in this case contains a description of just one actual sale of a defectively manufactured product to a provider that sought government reimbursement.

. . .

The question remains, however, whether identifying this single exemplar false claim is sufficient to clear the hurdle imposed by Federal Rule of Civil Procedure 9(b). Rule 9(b) applies because FCA actions sound in fraud.[777] FCA complaints must therefore "state with particularity the circumstances constituting fraud." Fed. R. Civ. P. 9(b).

---

[776] *D'Agostino*, 845 F.3d at 8.
[777] *See* United States *ex rel.* Karvelas v. Melrose-Wakefield Hosp., 360 F.3d 220, 228 (1st Cir. 2004), abrogated on other grounds by Allison Engine Co. v. United States *ex rel.* Sanders, 553 U.S. 662, 128 S.Ct. 2123, 170 L.Ed.2d 1030 (2008); see generally John T. Boese, *Civil False Claims and Qui Tam Actions* § 5.04[C] (4th ed. 2016) (collecting cases).

The circuits have varied, though, in their statements of exactly what Rule 9(b) requires in a *qui tam* action. Of most relevance here, a consensus has yet to develop on whether, when, and to what extent a relator must state the particulars of specific examples of the type of false claims alleged. . . .

Following the lead of the Eleventh Circuit, our circuit staked out its general position in *Karvelas*, which concerned allegations that a hospital subverted government standards but claimed it was in full compliance when it billed Medicare and Medicaid for services rendered.[778] As we explained:

> In a case such as this, details concerning the dates of the claims, the content of the forms or bills submitted, their identification numbers, the amount of money charged to the Government, the particular goods or services for which the Government was billed, the individuals involved in the billing, and the length of time between the alleged fraudulent practices and the submission of claims based on those practices are the types of information that may help a relator to state his or her claims with particularity. These details do not constitute a checklist of mandatory requirements that must be satisfied by each allegation included in a complaint. However, like the Eleventh Circuit, we believe that "some of this information for at least some of the claims must be pleaded in order to satisfy Rule 9(b)."[779]

In applying this general rule over time, we have nevertheless recognized at least one exception to the expectation that a relator should be able to allege the essential particulars of at least some actual false claims that were in fact submitted to the Government for payment. "[W]e have ... recognized a difference between *qui tam* actions alleging that the defendant made false claims to the Government and those alleging that the defendant induced third-parties to file false claims with the Government."[780] We apply a "more flexible" standard in actions of the latter, indirect type: where the defendant allegedly "induced third parties to file false claims with the Government ... a relator could satisfy Rule 9(b) by providing 'factual or statistical evidence to strengthen the inference of fraud beyond

---

[778] 360 F.3d at 223.
[779] *Id.* at 233 (quoting United States *ex rel.* Clausen v. Lab. Corp. of Am., 290 F.3d 1301, 1312 n.21 (11th Cir. 2002)); see United States *ex rel.* Ge v. Takeda Pharm. Co., 737 F.3d 116, 123–25 (1st Cir. 2013).
[780] Lawton *ex rel.* United States v. Takeda Pharm. Co., 842 F.3d 125, 130 (1st Cir. 2016) (citing *Duxbury*, 579 F.3d at 29).

possibility' without necessarily providing details as to each false claim."[781] Such evidence must pair the details of the scheme with "reliable indicia that lead to a strong inference that claims were actually submitted."[782]

. . .

To summarize, Relators allege that, over a five-year period, several thousand Medicare and Medicaid recipients received what their doctors understood to be Pinnacle MoM device implants; that more than half of those implants fell outside the specifications approved by the FDA; and that the latency of the defect was such that doctors would have had no reason not to submit claims for reimbursement for noncompliant devices. In this context, where the complaint essentially alleges facts showing that it is statistically certain that DePuy caused third parties to submit many false claims to the Government, we see little reason for Rule 9(b) to require Relators to plead false claims with more particularity than they have done here in order to fit within *Duxbury's*[783] "more flexible" approach to evaluating the sufficiency of fraud pleadings in connection with indirect false claims for government payment. In short, we have in this case a complaint that alleges the details of a fraudulent scheme with "reliable indicia that lead to a strong inference that claims were actually submitted,"[784] for government reimbursement from the United States and from the state of New York.

. . .

We vacate the dismissal of Relators' claims that DePuy caused physicians to submit claims to the United States and New York for payment for Pinnacle MoM devices that did not materially comport with the specifications of the FDA approval for those devices in violation of the FCA . . . and its New York state analogue. . . . We affirm the dismissal of all other claims, and of the denial of further requests to amend the complaint. We remand the case solely for resolution of the surviving claims. All parties shall bear their own costs on this appeal.

---

[781] *Duxbury*, 579 F.3d at 29 (quoting United States *ex rel.* Rost v. Pfizer, Inc., 507 F.3d 720, 733 (1st Cir. 2007)); see *Ge*, 737 F.3d at 123–24.
[782] *Id.* (quoting United States *ex rel.* Grubbs v. Kanneganti, 565 F.3d 180, 190 (5th Cir. 2009)).
[783] U.S. Duxbury v. Ortho Biotech Pro, 579 F.3d 13 (1st Cir. 2009)
[784] *Duxbury*, 579 F.3d at 29 (quoting *Grubbs*, 565 F.3d at 190)

United States ex rel. Petratos v. Genentech, et al.[785]

This appeal arising under the False Claims Act involves a multi-billion dollar cancer drug, Avastin, which was developed by Appellee Genentech. Relator Gerasimos Petratos, who was head of healthcare data analytics for Genentech, filed a *qui tam* action soon after leaving the company. He alleged that Genentech suppressed data that caused doctors to certify incorrectly that Avastin was "reasonable and necessary" for certain at-risk Medicare patients. The District Court dismissed Petratos's suit for failure to state a claim. Although we disagree with the District Court's grounds for dismissal, we will affirm because Petratos failed to satisfy the False Claims Act's materiality requirement.

. . .

Petratos alleged that Genentech concealed information about Avastin's health risks. Specifically, he claimed the company ignored and suppressed data that would have shown that Avastin's side effects for certain patients were more common and severe than reported. . . .

As a consequence of Genentech's data-suppression strategy, Petratos claimed the company caused physicians to submit Medicare claims that were not "reasonable and necessary." In the opinion of one oncologist, if Genentech had properly disclosed Avastin's side-effects for certain at-risk patients, "the standard of care would have been to prescribe a lower dose of Avastin, a lower frequency of doses, or no dose at all."

. . .

Petratos's claims implicate three interlocking federal schemes: the False Claims Act, Medicare reimbursement, and FDA approval. We begin by briefly outlining each scheme.

. . .

First, CMS guidance makes clear that the "reasonable and necessary" determination does not end with FDA approval. The claim at issue must also be "reasonable and necessary for [the] *individual patient*" based on "accepted standards of medical practice and the medical circumstances of the *individual case*."[786] The Manual provides examples of when a drug treatment could be approved by the FDA and used for a medically accepted indication, but still not be "reasonable and necessary." For example, a drug treatment is not " 'reasonable and necessary' for Medicare Part B if standard medical practice indicates that oral administration (as opposed to injection) 'is effective and is an accepted or

---

[785] 855 F.3d 481 (3d Cir. 2017).
[786] Medicare Benefit Policy Manual, ch. 15, § 50.4.3 (emphases added).

preferred method of administration,' or if the administration of injections 'exceed[s] the frequency or duration of injections indicated by accepted standards of medical practice.' "[787]

Second, other Medicare provisions and regulations underscore the critical role of the physician in Medicare's payment and reimbursement scheme. The regulations provide that "[t]he physician has a major role in determining utilization of health services furnished by providers. The physician decides upon admissions, orders tests, drugs, and treatments, and determines the length of stay."[788] Under Medicare Parts A and B, it usually is "a condition for Medicare payment that a physician certify the necessity of the services and, in some instances, recertify the continued need for those services."[789] Indeed, physicians prescribing Avastin often must submit CMS Form 1500 along with a claim for reimbursement, wherein the doctor certifies that the drug was "medically necessary and personally furnished by me or ... my employee under my direct supervision."[790] In addition, the Medicare statute contains a separate section that outlines the obligations of physicians when providing services to plan beneficiaries, including the obligation to provide services "economically and only when, and to the extent, medically necessary."[791]

Third, principles of statutory construction show that "medically accepted" and "reasonable and necessary" are not coterminous. "[T]he use of different words or terms within a statute demonstrates that Congress intended to convey a different meaning for those words."[792] And once this erroneous premise is removed from the District Court's decision, its analysis falters. . . .

The cases cited by the District Court do not hold that the "reasonable and necessary" decision is decided exclusively by federal agencies. Rather, these cases show that federal agencies retain ultimate control over the decision and that Government approval is a necessary component of the determination.[793] And none of the cited cases purports to eliminate the treating physician from the process. Indeed, other Courts of Appeals have recognized that "Congress intends

---

[787] Medicare Benefit Policy Manual, ch. 15, § 50.4.3.
[788] 42 C.F.R. § 424.10(a).
[789] *Id.*
[790] CMS Form 1500.
[791] 42 U.S.C. § 1320c-5(a).
[792] Race Tires Am., Inc. v. Hoosier Racing Tire Corp., 674 F.3d 158, 165 (3d Cir. 2012) (citation omitted).
[793] *See,* e.g., United States *ex rel.* Bodnar v. Secretary of Health & Human Servs., 903 F.2d 122, 125 (2d Cir. 1990).

the physician to be a key figure in determining what services are needed and consequently reimbursable."[794]

. . .

Although we disagree with the District Court's reasoning, we may affirm its judgment on any ground supported by the record.[795] Our review of the record leads us to conclude that Petratos cannot establish materiality, which the False Claims Act defines as "having a natural tendency to influence, or be capable of influencing, the payment or receipt of money."[796]

. . .

The Supreme Court ... explained that a misrepresentation is not material "merely because the Government designates compliance with a particular statutory, regulatory, or contractual requirement as a condition of payment ... [or because] the Government would have the option to decline to pay if it knew of the defendant's noncompliance."[797] Materiality may be found where "the Government consistently refuses to pay claims in the mine run of cases based on noncompliance with the particular statutory, regulatory, or contractual requirement."[798] On the other hand, it is "very strong evidence" that a requirement is not material "if the Government pays a particular claim in full despite its actual knowledge that certain requirements were violated."[799] Finally, materiality "cannot be found where noncompliance is minor or insubstantial."[800]

Petratos's allegations do not meet this high standard. As the District Court noted: "there are no factual allegations showing that CMS would not have reimbursed these claims had these [alleged reporting] deficiencies been cured." Petratos does not dispute this finding, which dooms his case. Simply put, a misrepresentation is not "material to the Government's *payment decision*," when the relator concedes that the Government would have paid the claims with full knowledge of the alleged noncompliance.[801] Similarly, we think that where a relator does not plead that knowledge of the violation could influence the Government's decision to pay, the misrepresentation likely does not "have[ ] a natural tendency to influence ... payment," as required by the statute. . . .

---

[794] Goodman v. Sullivan, 891 F.2d 449, 450 (2d Cir. 1989) (citing *Rush v. Parham*, 625 F.2d 1150, 1157 (5th Cir. 1980)).
[795] *See*, e.g., Guthrie v. Lady Jane Collieries, Inc., 722 F.2d 1141, 1145 n.1 (3d Cir. 1983).
[796] 31 U.S.C. § 3729(b)(4).
[797] *Escobar*, 136 S.Ct. at 1995.
[798] *Id.*
[799] *Id.*
[800] *Id.*
[801] *See Universal Health Servs.*, 136 S.Ct. at 1996 (emphasis added).

The Supreme Court's guidance in *Universal Health Services* also militates against a finding of materiality. The mere fact that § 1395y is a condition of payment, without more, does not establish materiality.[802] In addition, Petratos not only fails to plead that CMS "consistently refuses to pay" claims like those alleged, *see id.*, but essentially concedes that CMS would *consistently reimburse* these claims with full knowledge of the purported noncompliance. Nor has he cited to a single successful claim under § 1395y involving drugs prescribed for their on-label uses or a court decision upholding such a theory.

. . .

In fact, Petratos admits that he disclosed "material, non-public evidence of Genentech's campaign of misinformation" to the FDA and Department of Justice in 2010 and 2011. Since that time, the FDA has not merely continued its approval of Avastin for the at-risk populations that Petratos claims are adversely affected by the undisclosed data, but has *added* three more approved indications for the drug. Nor did the FDA initiate proceedings to enforce its adverse-event reporting rules or require Genentech to change Avastin's FDA label, as Petratos claims may occur. And in those six years, the Department of Justice has taken no action against Genentech and declined to intervene in this suit.

. . .

In holding that Petratos did not sufficiently plead materiality, we now join the many other federal courts that have recognized the heightened materiality standard after *Universal Health Services*. . . . .

. . .

Petratos's allegations may be true and his concerns may be well founded—but a False Claims Act suit is not the appropriate way to address them. He concedes that Genentech followed all pertinent statutes and regulations. If those laws and regulations are inadequate to protect patients, it falls to the other branches of government to reform them. We will affirm the judgment of the District Court.

---

[802] *Id.*

United States ex rel. Roycroft v. Geo Group, Inc., et al.[803]

J. Lynn Roycroft, a former clinical supervisor at a drug and alcohol residential treatment center operated by the defendants (collectively, "Geo Group"), alleges that Geo Group presented false claims for payment to Ohio Medicaid. As part of the fraudulent billing scheme, Geo Group allegedly submitted claims billing for services that were not provided and making implied false certifications of compliance with statutory and regulatory requirements. Roycroft, as a relator in this action, maintains that this conduct violated the False Claims Act, 31 U.S.C. § 3729 *et seq*. The district court dismissed Roycroft's complaint with prejudice for failure to plead with particularity the submission of at least one representative false claim, as required by Federal Rule of Civil Procedure 9(b). We affirm.

. . .

Roycroft argues that Geo Group presented false claims to Ohio Medicaid, in violation of § 3729(a)(1)(A). Section 3729(a)(1)(A) imposes civil liability on "any person who ... knowingly presents, or causes to be presented, a false or fraudulent claim for payment or approval." A claim under § 3729(a)(1)(A), commonly referred to as a presentment claim, requires proof that the false claim was in fact "presented" to the Government.[804] At the pleadings stage, this requirement is satisfied so long as the relator pleads the presentment of at least one representative false claim with particularity in compliance with Rule 9(b).[805]

Roycroft sufficiently alleges many of the required particulars. In the complaint, she details a fraudulent billing scheme, whereby Geo Group submitted claims to Ohio Medicaid that (1) improperly billed for group counseling services and (2) impliedly made false certifications of compliance with various statutory and regulatory requirements. And Roycroft identifies seven claims allegedly representative of that scheme. The allegations pertaining to the seven claims sufficiently identify who provided the services, to whom those services were provided, and when the bills were submitted.

Presentment of those representative claims to Ohio Medicaid is not disputed. The actual invoices for the claims referenced in the complaint were attached to Geo Group's reply in support of its motion to dismiss. Although we do not ordinarily consider such integral documents when attached to a reply, as opposed to a motion to dismiss, doing so here would not result in unfairness to Roycroft who herself presses for their consideration on appeal.[806] Those invoices reveal—and Geo Group does not dispute—that six of the seven claims were billed to

---

[803] --- Fed.Appx. ----, 2018 WL 266782 (6th Cir. Jan. 3, 2018).
[804] United States *ex rel.* Marlar v. BWXT Y-12, LLC, 525 F.3d 439, 445 (6th Cir. 2008).
[805] *Bledsoe*, 501 F.3d at 510–11.
[806] See Brown v. Daniels, 128 F.App'x 910, 913 (3d Cir. 2005); see also Bassett v. Nat'l Collegiate Athletic Ass'n, 528 F.3d 426, 430 (6th Cir. 2008).

Medicaid. Notwithstanding the parties' arguments to the contrary, this court's decision relaxing the pleading requirements for showing that a claim was submitted under certain limited circumstances is therefore inapposite.[807]

But the allegations are flawed in their failure to identify what is false in the representative claims, so as to connect the claims to the broader scheme.[808] Roycroft does not allege that each and every claim was false in the same respect, as may otherwise be sufficient.[809] Instead, she alleges a laundry list of prohibited conduct, "at least one or more" of which rendered false or fraudulent the claims involved in the scheme. In such circumstances, a relator must specify what is purportedly false in a representative claim.

. . .

Accordingly, Roycroft fails to plead a presentment claim with the requisite particularity under Rule 9(b).

. . .

B. Leave to Amend

. . .

While a district court "should freely give leave [to amend] when justice so requires,"[810] the district court must have before it the substance of the proposed amendment to determine whether "justice so requires."[811] In applying this rule, we have held that a district court does not abuse its discretion where, as here, the plaintiff never sought leave to amend.[812] And we have applied this holding in affirming a district court's failure to sua sponte grant leave to amend a complaint that, like here, was dismissed for failure to comply with Rule 9(b).[813]

. . .

---

[807] *See* United States *ex rel.* Prather v. Brookdale Senior Living Cmtys., Inc., 838 F.3d 750, 769 (6th Cir. 2016).

[808] *See Bledsoe*, 501 F.3d at 510.

[809] *See*, e.g., United States *ex rel.* McDonough v. Symphony Diagnostic Servs., Inc., 2012 WL 628515, at *9 (S.D. Ohio Feb. 27, 2012).

[810] Fed. R. Civ. P. 15(A)(2).

[811] Beydoun v. Sessions, 871 F.3d 459, 469 (6th Cir. 2017).

[812] Islamic Ctr. of Nashville v. Tennessee, 872 F.3d 377, 387 (6th Cir. 2017); Sinay v. Lamson & Sessions Co., 948 F.2d 1037, 1041 (6th Cir. 1991).

[813] *See* CNH Am. LLC v. Int'l Union, United Auto., Aerospace & Agr. Implement Workers of Am. *(UAW)*, 645 F.3d 785, 795 (6th Cir. 2011).

United States ex rel. Sant v. Biotronik, Inc.[814]

Mychal Wilson appeals the district court's order granting in part and denying in part his motion for attorneys' fees pursuant to the False Claims Act.[815] Because the district court did not abuse its discretion in determining the reasonable attorneys' fees to which Wilson was entitled, we affirm.

Wilson's client, Brian Sant, brought a *qui tam* action under the FCA against his employer, Biotronik, Inc., on behalf of the United States. The United States later intervened in Sant's suit and reached a settlement agreement with Sant, Biotronik, and certain states. The settlement provided that Biotronik would pay the attorneys' fees to which Sant was "statutorily entitled." Subsequently, Wilson filed his motion for attorneys' fees in the district court.

. . .

1. The district court did not err by reducing Wilson's requested hours for work performed on the underlying litigation or for work performed on the fee petition. The district court reduced Wilson's requested hours for work performed on the underlying litigation by 20 percent because it found that Sant had achieved only limited success in the underlying litigation. The district court reduced Wilson's request for work performed on the underlying litigation by an additional 5 percent due to Wilson's vague billing entries, unnecessary tasks, block billing, and work which should have been delegated to a non-attorney. Wilson contends both reductions were in error.

A district court may reduce a request for attorneys' fees when the applicant achieved only limited success in the underlying litigation.[816] District courts also have the discretion to reduce attorneys' fee awards for deficiencies in the billing records submitted by the fee applicant.[817] Here, the record adequately supports the district court's decision to reduce Wilson's fee request for work performed on the underlying litigation.

Similarly, we find no error in the district court's decision to reduce Wilson's requested hours for work performed on the fee petition by 30 percent based on a lack of success and inefficient litigation practices. A district court can reduce a fees-on-fees request in proportion to the applicant's success on the underlying

---

[814] 876 F.3d 1011 (9th Cir. 2017).
[815] 31 U.S.C. § 3729, et seq.
[816] Hensley v. Eckerhart, 461 U.S. 424, 440, 103 S.Ct. 1933, 76 L.Ed.2d 40 (1983) ("A reduced fee award is appropriate if the relief, however significant, is limited in comparison to the scope of the litigation as a whole.").
[817] *See* Welch v. Metro. Life Ins. Co., 480 F.3d 942, 948 (9th Cir. 2007) (allowing a reduction for block billing).

petition.[818] Because the district court denied more than 70 percent of the fees Wilson requested for work performed on the underlying litigation, it could have reduced Wilson's request for fees-on-fees by the same amount. Consequently, we find no error with the court's decision to reduce Wilson's request for hours spent on the fee petition by 30 percent.

. . .

Finally, the district court did not err when it refused to apply a two-times multiplier to the lodestar amount based on exceptional results and/or the fact that the nature of Wilson's solo practice required him to forego work in order to prosecute Sant's case. The district court rejected a multiplier because it had already considered both the quality of Sant's results and the nature of Wilson's practice in setting the lodestar amount, and Supreme Court precedent prohibits a district court from "double counting" these factors for purposes of a multiplier.[819] We find no error in the district court's decision to reject Wilson's request for a lodestar multiplier.

---

[818] Thompson v. Gomez, 45 F.3d 1365, 1368 (9th Cir. 1995).
[819] Blum v. Stenson, 465 U.S. 886, 898–901, 104 S.Ct. 1541, 79 L.Ed.2d 891 (1984).

United States ex rel. Takemoto v. Nationwide Mutual Insurance Co., et al.[820]

Relator Kent Takemoto, a doctor who owns a Medicare Secondary Payer compliance company, appeals the dismissal of his complaint, brought pursuant to the False Claims Act ("FCA"),[821] which accuses various insurance industry participants, self-insured corporations, and third-party administrators ("defendants") of failing to comply with repayment obligations under the Medicare Secondary Payer Act ("MSPA").[822] Takemoto further appeals the denial of leave to amend his complaint.

.   .   .

1. Adequacy of the Complaint

The district court adopted the magistrate judge's recommendation to dismiss Takemoto's complaint insofar as it grouped defendants together and failed to plead facts as to each defendant's obligation to repay the Government, an essential element of his FCA claims. Takemoto faults the district court for failing to assume the veracity of facts alleged in the complaint, viewing allegations in isolation rather than in their totality, and incorrectly finding group pleading impermissible given defendants' participation in the same relevant conduct. We are not persuaded.

Even when we review the complaint's allegations as a whole and assume the truthfulness of pleaded facts, Takemoto fails to plead plausible claims for relief because he does not allege facts admitting an inference of a reimbursement obligation on the part of any defendant. The FCA defines "obligation" as "an established duty, whether or not fixed, arising from an express or implied contractual, grantor-grantee, or licensor-licensee relationship, from a fee-based or similar relationship, from statute or regulation, or from the retention of any overpayment."[823] As an initial matter, this statutory language contemplates individualized pleading for each defendant of the source of the obligation. . . .

.   .   .

To the extent Takemoto seeks to avoid this conclusion by arguing that defendants' obligation was to adopt adequate MSPA compliance procedures, he points to no authority supporting such an obligation, much less the proposition that such a claim is actionable under the FCA. The language of the statutory section under which Takemoto's claims are brought, in fact, indicates otherwise

---

[820] 674 F.App'x 92 (2d Cir. 2017).
[821] 31 U.S.C. § 3729 et seq.
[822] 42 U.S.C. § 1395y(b).
[823] 31 U.S.C. § 3729(b)(3).

insofar as it locates liability in the avoidance of an "obligation to pay or transmit money ... to the Government."[824] A compliance program is not an obligation to pay money.

.   .   .

2. Denial of Leave to Amend

Because Takemoto's request to amend gave "no clue as to how the complaint's defects would be cured," denial of amendment was not an abuse of discretion. . . . Thus, vacatur is not warranted on this ground.

3. Conclusion

We have considered all of Takemoto's remaining arguments and conclude that they are without merit. Accordingly, the dismissal of his complaint for failure to state a claim is AFFIRMED.

---

[824] 31 U.S.C. § 3729(a)(1)(G).

United States ex rel. Taxpayers Against Fraud, et al. v. General Electric Co.[825]

The General Electric Company ("GE") appeals from an award of attorneys' fees to a "whistleblower" who brought a *qui tam* action against the company. For the reasons set forth below, we affirm the constitutionality of the federal *qui tam* laws; we reverse the district court's decision to deny GE access to portions of a deposition that was taken *in camera;* and, while generally affirming the award of attorneys' fees, we remand the matter to the district court with instructions to reduce certain components of the award and to conduct further factfinding proceedings.

. . .

In November 1990, Relators–Plaintiffs–Appellees Walsh and Taxpayers Against Fraud ("TAF") filed a *qui tam* action against GE under 31 U.S.C. § 3730, alleging that GE Aircraft had billed the United States Treasury for millions of dollars in false claims. The United States intervened in August 1991 and took the lead role in the prosecution. A settlement was reached before trial, in which GE agreed to pay $59.5 million in civil damages and $9.5 million in criminal fines, as well as $6,158,301 in restitution, for a total payment of more than $75 million to the United States Treasury.

. . .

2. The Attorneys' Fees Litigation

After the Relators'–Share Litigation ended, the relators moved in federal district court, pursuant to 31 U.S.C. § 3730(d)(1), to recoup from GE their reasonable attorneys' fees and costs, as well as their reasonable and necessarily incurred legal expenses. GE sharply challenged the relators' claims on a number of grounds. However, the district judge ordered GE to pay $2,329,228.50 in attorneys' fees and $226,875.17 in costs and expenses. The law firm of Hall & Phillips provided approximately 80% of Walsh's, and nearly all of TAF's, legal services. Therefore, that firm's share of the relators' attorneys' fees exceeded $1.8 million. Hereinafter, we shall refer to this litigation, which pitted GE against the relators and their attorneys, as "the Attorneys' Fees Litigation."

3. The Contingency Fee Agreement

In a separately negotiated arrangement, Walsh had promised to pay his legal counsel 25% of whatever bounty he ultimately collected from the *qui tam* action. Since Walsh received approximately $11,300,000 from the Relators'–Share Litigation, his contingency-payment agreement called for him to pay his attorneys

---

[825] 41 F.3d 1032 (6th Cir. 1994).

approximately $2,825,000. Therefore, Hall & Phillips's 80% portion of the contingency fee came to approximately $2,260,000. Thus, having won more than $1.8 million as its share of the fees that were awarded during the Attorneys' Fees Litigation, Hall & Phillips's total fees for its part in this *qui tam* action amounted to more than $4 million, approximately half payable by the relators from their $11.3 million bounty and half payable by GE from its corporate funds. Usually, a statutory fee would be awarded to the plaintiff rather than to the lawyers.[826] The plaintiff could then use the statutory fee to satisfy the contingency fee. In this case, though, Walsh's contract with Hall & Phillips calls for him to pay the statutory fee to Hall & Phillips *in addition to* any contingency fees.

. . .

2. The "Attorneys' Fees" Litigation

The losing defendant in an FCA *qui tam* action must pay the reasonable attorneys' fees and court costs of the victorious relators, as well as all reasonable and necessarily incurred expenses.[827] . . .

Hall & Phillips prepared a breakdown of the billable hours that their attorneys had worked on the case, and the firm submitted its rate schedule for legal services. GE stipulated to the reasonableness of the rates and most of the hours. However, GE raised a number of policy-based objections, which the court rejected and which comprise the crux of this appeal. As noted above, the court ordered GE to pay a total of $2,329,228.50 in attorneys' fees, as well as $226,875.17 in costs and expenses. Hall & Phillips's share of that award exceeded $1.8 million. Consequently, when combined with the $2.26 million that it received in contingency fees, Hall & Phillips emerged from this FCA action with combined fees of more than $4 million.

General Electric appeals from the award of attorneys' fees, expenses, and costs.

. . .

In addition, the judge should broaden his inquiry into the role that TAF played in this litigation. First, the judge should determine whether TAF had standing to act as a co-plaintiff with Walsh.[828] If TAF had no standing, then the statutory fee award must be reduced by the amount of the award attributable to TAF's legal fees. Second, the judge should investigate whether Hall & Phillips's relationship

---

[826] Evans v. Jeff D., 475 U.S. 717, 730, 106 S.Ct. 1531, 1538–39, 89 L.Ed.2d 747 (1986).
[827] 31 U.S.C. § 3730(d)(1).
[828] *See* 31 U.S.C. § 3730(e)(4)(A), (B); United States v. Rockwell Int'l Corp., 730 F.Supp. 1031 (D. Colo.1990) (holding TAF had no standing in similar case).

with TAF violated ethical canons.[829] The judge should determine whether TAF's involvement as a co-plaintiff is tantamount to participation by Hall & Phillips as a plaintiff in the case. If TAF is in fact a front for Hall & Phillips as well as a co-plaintiff in the case, then the ethical mandates of Rule 1.8(j) have been implicated. Third, the judge should determine the validity of the contracts involving Walsh, TAF, and Hall & Phillips. If the contracts fail for lack of consideration or other reasons, the judge should make appropriate findings modifying the division of the bounty and the contingency fees among the parties.

GE also contends that the district judge should not have ordered it to pay the approximately $1 million in attorneys' fees, legal expenses, and costs that Walsh incurred while conducting his separate Relators'-Share Litigation against the Government. GE notes that the Relators'-Share Litigation had nothing to do with the company; rather, those proceedings involved an internal dispute among the victorious plaintiffs. Indeed, the district court barred GE counsel from attending the *in camera* hearing and from submitting deposition questions to Agent Kosky.

. . .

In this case, GE chose to minimize its losses by settling its case before the matter even came to trial. As in *Bigby,* the defendant here should not be required to pay the costs incurred by the prevailing plaintiffs in the course of their collateral litigation.[830]

Therefore, we reverse the award of Relators'-Share Litigation attorneys' fees, legal expenses, and costs to Walsh.

. . .

The problem we face in this case is whether the aggregated bonanza, which comes to more than $4,000,000, exceeds the boundaries of professional propriety. The question here is further complicated by GE's argument that, if the attorneys have been overpaid, we should hold that GE, the guilty defendant that Congress expressly designated to pay the relators' fees,[831] should be excused from some or all of its statutory obligation. Thus, we are being asked to make an equitable ruling for a party with "unclean hands." Yet, if we agree with the principle that underlies GE's appeal from the fees, our other alternative would be to reduce or strike down the independently negotiated agreement between Walsh and his attorneys. We again note that the district court has broad equity powers to do just that if it determines that the overall compensation exceeds the bounds of professional

---

[829] *See* Model Rules of Professional Conduct Rule 1.8(j) (prohibiting lawyer from acquiring proprietary interest in subject matter of litigation).
[830] Accord Reeves v. Harrell, 791 F.2d 1481 (11th Cir.1986), *cert. denied,* 479 U.S. 1033, 107 S.Ct. 880, 93 L.Ed.2d 834 (1987).
[831] 31 U.S.C. § 3730(d)(1).

propriety. The curiosity here is compounded by Walsh's apparent satisfaction with his negotiated arrangement; he has not asked us to reduce his fees to Hall & Phillips.

We need not resolve this troubling ethical question today because our instructions to the district court on remand will modify the attorneys' fees award under the statutory scheme, perhaps reducing the award substantially. Normally, a district court's award of attorneys' fees should be based on the lodestar. The uniform application of lodestar equations is preferred over an unpredictable system in which different trial judges devise their own subjective, spontaneous formulas.[832] However, the district judge may make modifications to account for unreasonable and excessive hours or when unique circumstances justify adjustments to hourly rates.[833] The judge's discretion is not diminished even when parties have stipulated to the reasonableness of the number of hours and the hourly rate. Moreover, in this case, we observe that § 3730(d)(1) calls for the award of *reasonable* attorneys' fees. On remand, in the course of setting relators' attorneys' fees in a manner that is consistent with the rest of this opinion, the district court should make findings of fact for the appellate record that will enable us to review the reasonableness of the § 3730(d)(1) award, in light of the standards set by the *Model Rules of Professional Conduct*, the Supreme Court's opinion in *Venegas,* and our court's holding in *United Slate.*

. . .

---

[832] *See*, e.g., Northcross v. Board of Educ., 611 F.2d 624, 636 (6th Cir.1979), *cert. denied*, 447 U.S. 911, 100 S.Ct. 2999, 3000, 64 L.Ed.2d 862 (1980).
[833] *Id.* at 636–38.

United States ex rel. Troxler v. Warren Clinic, Inc., et al.[834]

Mark Troxler brought this suit under the False Claims Act ("FCA"),[835] alleging that defendants Warren Clinic, Inc. and Saint Francis Health System, Inc. (collectively "clinic") were fraudulently billing the Government for services provided by non-physicians. The district court dismissed the suit under Federal Rule of Civil Procedure 12(b)(6), and exercising jurisdiction under 28 U.S.C. § 1291, we affirm.

. . .

We review the district court's dismissal de novo . . . and agree that Dr. Troxler failed to plead a plausible FCA claim. The complaint fails to state a factually false claim because there are no allegations that the clinic submitted anything false to the Government or that the services were not actually provided. Dr. Troxler suggests the reimbursement requests were false because only physicians can certify whether services are medically necessary, . . . but there are no allegations that the services were unnecessary. Rather, the complaint alleges that HPI information was collected by unqualified personnel. But as the district court recognized, absent allegations that the clinic was required to identify who collected HPI information, the complaint fails to state a factually false claim.

Likewise, the complaint fails to state a legally false claim. There are no allegations to support an express false certification theory because the complaint does not identify any expressly false certification or statement. Nor does the complaint identify a statute, regulation, or contract requiring that only physicians collect HPI information as a prerequisite to payment. . . . Although Dr. Troxler alludes to the 1997 Documentation Guidelines for Evaluation and Management Services, . . . he does not allege—and we find no indication—that these guidelines legally mandate and condition payment of services on a health-care provider's certification that HPI information was collected exclusively by physicians. . . . Under these circumstances, the district court correctly dismissed the complaint.

Accordingly, having reviewed the parties' appellate materials, the relevant legal authorities, and the record on appeal, we affirm the district court's judgment for substantially the same reasons stated by the district court in its decision dated November 5, 2014.

---

[834] 630 Fed.Appx. 822 (10th Cir. 2015).
[835] 31 U.S.C. §§ 3729, 3730.

United States ex rel. Uhlig v. Fluor Corp., et al.[836]

Eric Uhlig brought False Claims Act and retaliation claims against his former employer, Fluor Corporation, and related entities (collectively, "Fluor"). Fluor contracted with the United States Army to provide, among other services, electrical engineering work in Afghanistan.

Uhlig says Fluor violated the False Claims Act when it knowingly breached the terms of its Army contract by using unlicensed electricians as journeymen and billing the Government for the services. Uhlig also contends Fluor wrongfully terminated Uhlig as a whistleblower in violation of 31 U.S.C. § 3730(h).

The district court granted summary judgment for Fluor. We affirm.

. . .

Fluor moved for summary judgment, and the district court granted Fluor's motion on August 6, 2014. In dismissing the False Claims Act claim, the district court held that Fluor's contract with the Army did not require that journeyman electricians be licensed and therefore that Fluor had not breached the contract. The court dismissed Uhlig's retaliation claim because Uhlig had no objective basis for asserting that Fluor had defrauded the Government, thus his complaint was not "protected activity" under the False Claims Act. This appeal followed.

. . .

Uhlig's retaliation claim cannot proceed because he did not show that, at the time he sent the December 4, 2010 email, a reasonable employee in Uhlig's position would have believed Fluor was defrauding the Government. As a result, his conduct was not protected activity that could give rise to a retaliation claim.

. . .

Even if Uhlig subjectively believed Fluor was breaching its contract, he lacked a sufficient basis on which to satisfy the objective component of the protected-activity test. Uhlig's emails attempting to blow the whistle on Fluor's alleged noncompliance were therefore not protected activity. As a result, even if the December 2010 email was the reason for Uhlig's termination, it cannot be the basis for a retaliation claim.

III. Conclusion

For the foregoing reasons, we AFFIRM the judgment of the district court.

---

[836] 839 F.3d 628 (7th Cir. 2016).

United States ex rel. Vatan v. QTC Medical Services, Inc., et al.[837]

David Vatan appeals the district court's dismissal of two of the three claims in his second amended complaint and its denial of leave to amend that complaint. In these two claims, Vatan alleges that defendants presented false or fraudulent claims for payment, in violation of 31 U.S.C. § 3729(a)(1)(A), and made, used, or caused to be made or used false records material to false or fraudulent claims, in violation of § 3729(a)(1)(B). The district court dismissed for failure to state a claim under Fed. R. Civ. P. 8(a) and 9(b). We reverse the dismissal and accordingly do not reach the denial of leave to amend.

1. Neither Rule 8(a) nor Rule 9(b) requires that Vatan plead the specific terms of QTC's contract with the VA. Vatan's second amended complaint pleads the contents of that contract pursuant to information and belief and adduces the factual basis for that belief. Where, as here, the relevant information is within the defendant's exclusive possession and control, such pleading is sufficient to satisfy Rule 9(b)'s particularity requirement.[838] The district court's requirement to the contrary would vitiate the False Claims Act, by excluding many whistleblowers who—as here—allege insider knowledge of wrongdoing that few others would be positioned to reveal and solely lack access to the corporate documents outlining the precise nature of the company's obligations.[839]

. . .

2. Vatan's complaint otherwise meets Rule 9(b)'s heightened pleading standard. Vatan has "allege[d] the who, what, when, where, and how of the misconduct charged, including what is false or misleading ... and why it is false."[840] The allegations are "specific enough to give defendants notice of the particular [alleged] misconduct ... so that they can defend against the charge."[841]

---

[837] 721 Fed.Appx. 662 (9th Cir. 2018).

[838] Moore v. Kayport Package Exp., Inc., 885 F.2d 531, 540 (9th Cir. 1989) (affirming that Rule 9(b)'s particularity requirements "may be relaxed as to matters within the opposing party's knowledge"); Concha v. London, 62 F.3d 1493, 1503 (9th Cir. 1995) ("Rule 9(b) ... requires that plaintiffs specifically plead those facts surrounding alleged acts of fraud to which they can reasonably be expected to have access" (emphasis added)); Sanford v. MemberWorks, Inc., 625 F.3d 550, 558-59 (9th Cir. 2010) (requiring particularity only where "it is not unreasonable to expect ... personal knowledge of the relevant facts").

[839] *See* United States *ex rel.* Presser v. Acacia Mental Health Clinic, LLC, 836 F.3d 770, 778 (7th Cir. 2016).

[840] United States v. United Healthcare Ins. Co., 848 F.3d 1161, 1180 (9th Cir. 2016) (citation and internal quotation marks omitted).

[841] *Id.* (quoting *Bly-Magee v. Cal.*, 236 F.3d 1014, 1019 (9th Cir. 2001)).

QTC's argument that Vatan has failed to adequately plead "who" was responsible for the misconduct is incorrect. Vatan has proffered the names of individuals allegedly involved in perpetuating the purported fraud. He has also alleged "with specificity how the company itself institutionalized and enforced its fraudulent scheme."[842] We have previously found that such allegations sufficiently identify "who" was involved, such that the defendant has the requisite notice to "defend against the charge."[843] The same is true here.

3. Vatan's claims satisfy Rule 8(a). Vatan has alleged the requisite elements of False Claims Act claims under theories of both factually false and implied false certification.[844] Regarding factually false certification, he alleges that QTC instructed analysts to always answer yes to question six on the VA checklist, "was the entire claims folder reviewed," irrespective of whether that answer was true. He provides specific examples of VA review in which the answer was, allegedly, not true. He therefore successfully alleges that QTC "misrepresent[ed] what goods or services ... it provided to the Government."[845]

As to implied false certification, Vatan alleges, in essence, that QTC charged the Government for worthless services and concealed the worthlessness of those services. That concealment allegedly took the form of misrepresentations on the checklists that the files had been reviewed, while "omitting critical information" regarding the extraordinarily cursory—in some cases, as alleged by Vatan, nearly non-existent—nature of that review.[846] The claims that Vatan alleges that QTC made here, like the claims in Universal Health Services, "fall squarely within the rule that half-truths—representations that state the truth only so far as it goes, while omitting critical qualifying information—can be actionable misrepresentations."[847]

We REVERSE and REMAND for further proceedings consistent with this disposition.

REVERSED and REMANDED.

---

[842] United States *ex rel.* Heath v. AT&T, Inc., 791 F.3d 112, 125 (D.C. Cir. 2015).
[843] *United Healthcare*, 848 F.3d at 1180-81 (finding similar allegations sufficient under Rule 9(b)).
[844] Universal Health Servs., Inc. v. United States *ex rel.* Escobar, —— U.S. ——, 136 S.Ct. 1989, 1999, 195 L.Ed.2d 348 (2016); United States *ex rel.* Campie v. Gilead Sciences, Inc., 862 F.3d 890, 898-99 (9th Cir. 2017).
[845] *Campie*, 862 F.3d at 900.
[846] See *Campie*, 862 F.3d at 903.
[847] 136 S.Ct. at 2000.

United States ex rel. Wall v. Circle C. Construction, LLC[848]

This case is before us for a third time. The defendant, Circle C Construction, is a family-owned general contractor that built 42 warehouses for the United States Army in Kentucky and Tennessee. In the course of building all those warehouses, over a period of seven years, a subcontractor, Phase Tech, paid two of its electricians about $9,900 less than the wages mandated by the Davis-Bacon Act. That underpayment rendered false a number of "compliance statements" that Circle C submitted to the Government along with its invoices. As a result, the Government thereafter pursued Circle C for nearly a decade of litigation, demanding not merely $9,900 — Phase Tech itself had paid $15,000 up front to settle that underpayment — but rather $1.66 million, of which $554,000 was purportedly "actual damages" for the $9,900 underpayment. The Government's theory in support of that demand was that all of Phase Tech's electrical work, in all of the warehouses, was "tainted" by the $9,900 underpayment — and therefore worthless. "The problem with that theory," we wrote in the last appeal, was that, "in all of these warehouses, the Government turns on the lights every day."[849] We therefore reversed a $763,000 judgment in favor of the Government and remanded for entry of an award of $14,748 — less than 1% of the Government's demand.

Over the past decade, Circle C paid its attorneys an estimated $468,704 to defend against the Government's claim. In Circle C's view, Congress has contemplated situations like this one: a 1996 amendment to the Equal Access to Justice Act provides that, if a court awards damages to the federal government, but the Government's original demand for damages was both "substantially in excess of the judgment finally obtained" and "unreasonable when compared with such judgment," then (subject to two exceptions) the court must "award to the [defendant] the fees and other expenses related to defending against the excessive demand."[850]

Accordingly, on remand after the last appeal, Circle C moved under § 2412(d)(1)(D) for recovery of its attorneys' fees in this litigation. But the district court denied the motion. . . .

We review the district court's denial of Circle C's motion for an abuse of discretion. . . . The relevant statutory scheme is straightforward. Title 31 U.S.C. § 3730(g) provides, "[i]n civil actions brought under this section by the United States, the provisions of section 2412(d) of title 28 shall apply." This case is undisputedly an action brought under § 3730 by the United States — which

---

[848] 868 F.3d 466 (6th Cir. 2017).
[849] United States *ex rel.* Wall v. Circle C Constr., *LLC*, 813 F.3d 616, 617 (6th Cir. 2016).
[850] 28 U.S.C. § 2412(d)(1)(D).

means that § 2412(d)(1)(D) (the fee-shifting section cited in Circle C's motion) "shall apply" here.

Yet the Government ventures to argue that § 2412(d)(1)(D) does not apply. Section 3730(g) is entitled, "Fees and expenses to prevailing defendant." Circle C technically was not a prevailing defendant, because on remand the district court entered a judgment in favor of the Government (albeit in an amount that was less than 1% of the amount the Government initially sought).

. . .

Thus we turn to § 2412(d)(1)(D), which provides in relevant part:

> If, in a civil action brought by the United States ... the demand by the United States is substantially in excess of the judgment finally obtained by the United States and is unreasonable when compared with such judgment, under the facts and circumstances of the case, the court shall award to the party the fees and other expenses related to defending against the excessive demand, unless the party has committed a willful violation of law or otherwise acted in bad faith, or special circumstances make an award unjust.

Under this subsection, the party seeking fees bears the burden of proving (i) that the Government's demand was substantially in excess of the award obtained by the judgment and (ii) that the Government's demand was unreasonable compared to that judgment. . . . Here, the Government demanded $553,807.71 in purported actual damages, trebled to about $1.66 million. . . . And "the judgment finally obtained by the United States" was $14,748. To say that the Government's demand was substantially in excess of the judgment, therefore, only understates matters.

That leaves the question whether the Government's demand was "unreasonable" as that term is used in § 2412(d)(1)(D). Neither this circuit nor, so far as we can tell, any other has specifically interpreted the term "unreasonable" as used in that provision. But that term is hardly abstruse. As a matter of ordinary usage, "unreasonable" means "not governed by reason" or "exceeding reasonable limits; immoderate[.]"[851] And meanwhile there is a well-developed body of law concerning a similar inquiry under a related provision: namely, whether the Government's position was "substantially justified" under § 2412(d)(1)(A). . . . We therefore look to the caselaw interpreting "substantially justified" under § 2412(d)(1)(A) to determine whether the Government's demand was "unreasonable" under § 2412(d)(1)(D).

---

[851] The American Heritage Dictionary 1957 (3d ed. 1994).

. . .

The question, then, is whether the Government's demand for $1.66 million as compensation for Phase Tech's $9,900 underpayment of its electricians, in a project spanning seven years, was justified to that degree. The short answer to that question, as we said in the last appeal, is that the damages the Government sought to recover in this case were "fairyland rather than actual."[852]

A longer answer begins with the observation that actual damages are a simple concept, familiar to any first-year student in law school. In the context of this case, actual damages are simply "the difference in value between what the Government bargained for and what the Government received."[853] And here those damages were easy to calculate. "[T]he government bargained for two things: the buildings, and the payment of Davis-Bacon wages. It got the buildings but not quite all of the wages. The shortfall was $9,916. That amount [was] the Government's actual damages."[854]

. . .

That means Circle C was entitled to a fee award unless it "committed a willful violation of law or otherwise acted in bad faith, or special circumstances make an award unjust."[855] The district court did not reach this issue because it mistakenly thought that the Government's demand was reasonable. Yet we choose to reach the issue because the parties have briefed it, the merits are clear, and this litigation has already persisted for nearly ten years. . . .

. . .

[T]he government contends that, "[b]y definition, a defendant who has been found liable under the False Claims Act has 'knowingly' made or caused 'false or fraudulent claims' on public money." Under the False Claims Act, however, "knowingly" is itself a term of art, which refers to three mental states: "actual knowledge," "deliberate ignorance," or "reckless disregard."[856] The district court found that Circle C was reckless — the least culpable of these states — as to whether its compliance reports were accurate regarding the wages paid to Phase Tech's electricians (actually, on this record, just two of them). But "recklessness is a less stringent standard than bad faith[.]"[857] . . . . And on this record we see no reason to depart from that rule.

---

[852] *Wall*, 813 F.3d at 618.
[853] *Id.* at 617.
[854] *Id.*
[855] 28 U.S.C. § 2412(d)(1)(D).
[856] 31 U.S.C. § 3729(b)(1)(A).
[857] United States v. Wallace, 964 F.2d 1214, 1219 (D.C. Cir. 1992).

Second — and finally — the Government warns that a fee award in this case would have a "chilling effect" on its efforts "to vigorously enforce" the False Claims Act. One should hope so. In this case the Government made a demand for damages a hundredfold greater than what it was entitled to, and then pressed that demand over nearly a decade of litigation, all based on a theory that as applied here was nearly frivolous. The consequences for Circle C included nearly a half-million dollars in attorneys' fees. Section 2412(d)(1)(D) makes clear that the Government must bear its share of those consequences as well.

The district court abused its discretion when it denied Circle C's motion. We reverse the district court's June 17, 2016 Order and remand the case for an award to Circle C of "the fees and other expenses related to defending against the [government's] excessive demand,"[858] including, to the extent appropriate, fees incurred during this appeal and on remand.

---

[858] 28 U.S.C. § 2412(d)(1)(D).

Universal Health Services, Inc. v. United States ex rel. Escobar et al.[859]

JUSTICE THOMAS delivered the opinion of the Court.

The False Claims Act, 31 U. S. C. §3729 et seq., imposes significant penalties on those who defraud the Government. This case concerns a theory of False Claims Act liability commonly referred to as "implied false certification." According to this theory, when a defendant submits a claim, it impliedly certifies compliance with all conditions of payment. But if that claim fails to disclose the defendant's violation of a material statutory, regulatory, or contractual requirement, so the theory goes, the defendant has made a misrepresentation that renders the claim "false or fraudulent" under §3729(a)(1)(A). This case requires us to consider this theory of liability and to clarify some of the circumstances in which the False Claims Act imposes liability.

We first hold that, at least in certain circumstances, the implied false certification theory can be a basis for liability. Specifically, liability can attach when the defendant submits a claim for payment that makes specific representations about the goods or services provided, but knowingly fails to disclose the defendant's noncompliance with a statutory, regulatory, or contractual requirement. In these circumstances, liability may attach if the omission renders those representations misleading.

We further hold that False Claims Act liability for failing to disclose violations of legal requirements does not turn upon whether those requirements were expressly designated as conditions of payment. Defendants can be liable for violating requirements even if they were not expressly designated as conditions of payment. Conversely, even when a requirement is expressly designated a condition of payment, not every violation of such a requirement gives rise to liability. What matters is not the label the Government attaches to a requirement, but whether the defendant knowingly violated a requirement that the defendant knows is material to the Government's payment decision.

A misrepresentation about compliance with a statutory, regulatory, or contractual requirement must be material to the Government's payment decision in order to be actionable under the False Claims Act. We clarify below how that rigorous materiality requirement should be enforced.

Because the courts below interpreted §3729(a)(1)(A) differently, we vacate the judgment and remand so that those courts may apply the approach set out in this opinion.

. . .

---

[859] 136 S. Ct. 1989 (2016).

In 2011, respondents filed a *qui tam* suit in federal court,[860] alleging that Universal Health had violated the False Claims Act under an implied false certification theory of liability. The operative complaint asserts that Universal Health (acting through Arbour) submitted reimbursement claims that made representations about the specific services provided by specific types of professionals, but that failed to disclose serious violations of regulations pertaining to staff qualifications and licensing requirements for these services.

. . .

The District Court granted Universal Health's motion to dismiss the complaint. Circuit precedent had previously embraced the implied false certification theory of liability. But the District Court held that respondents had failed to state a claim under that theory because, with one exception not relevant here, none of the regulations that Arbour violated was a condition of payment.

. . .

The United States Court of Appeals for the First Circuit reversed in relevant part and remanded.

. . .

We granted certiorari to resolve the disagreement among the Courts of Appeals over the validity and scope of the implied false certification theory of liability. The Seventh Circuit has rejected this theory, reasoning that only express (or affirmative) falsehoods can render a claim "false or fraudulent" under 31 U. S. C. §3729(a)(1)(A). Other courts have accepted the theory, but limit its application to cases where defendants fail to disclose violations of expressly designated conditions of payment. Yet others hold that conditions of payment need not be expressly designated as such to be a basis for False Claims Act liability.

. . .

We first hold that the implied false certification theory can, at least in some circumstances, provide a basis for liability. By punishing defendants who submit "false or fraudulent claims," the False Claims Act encompasses claims that make fraudulent misrepresentations, which include certain misleading omissions. When, as here, a defendant makes representations in submitting a claim but omits its violations of statutory, regulatory, or contractual requirements, those omissions can be a basis for liability if they render the defendant's representations misleading with respect to the goods or services provided . . . . Congress did not define what makes a claim "false" or "fraudulent." But "[i]t is a settled principle of interpretation that, absent other indication, Congress intends to incorporate the well-settled meaning of the common-law terms it uses." And the term

---

[860] *See* 31 U. S. C. §3730.

"fraudulent" is a paradigmatic example of a statutory term that incorporates the common-law meaning of fraud.

. . .

We need not resolve whether all claims for payment implicitly represent that the billing party is legally entitled to payment. The claims in this case do more than merely demand payment. They fall squarely within the rule that half-truths—representations that state the truth only so far as it goes, while omitting critical qualifying information—can be actionable misrepresentations.

. . .

Accordingly, we hold that the implied certification theory can be a basis for liability, at least where two conditions are satisfied: first, the claim does not merely request payment, but also makes specific representations about the goods or services provided; and second, the defendant's failure to disclose noncompliance with material statutory, regulatory, or contractual requirements makes those representations misleading half-truths.

III

The second question presented is whether, as Universal Health urges, a defendant should face False Claims Act liability only if it fails to disclose the violation of a contractual, statutory, or regulatory provision that the Government expressly designated a condition of payment. We conclude that the Act does not impose this limit on liability. But we also conclude that not every undisclosed violation of an express condition of payment automatically triggers liability. Whether a provision is labeled a condition of payment is relevant to but not dispositive of the materiality inquiry.

. . .

Nothing in the text of the False Claims Act supports Universal Health's proposed restriction. Section 3729(a)(1)(A) imposes liability on those who present "false or fraudulent claims" but does not limit such claims to misrepresentations about express conditions of payment . . . Nor does the common-law meaning of fraud tether liability to violating an express condition of payment. A statement that misleadingly omits critical facts is a misrepresentation irrespective of whether the other party has expressly signaled the importance of the qualifying information . . . The False Claims Act's materiality requirement also does not support Universal Health. Under the Act, the misrepresentation must be material to the other party's course of action . . . Nor does the Act's *scienter* requirement support Universal Health's position. A defendant can have "actual knowledge" that a condition is material without the Government expressly calling it a condition of payment. If the Government failed to specify that guns it orders must actually shoot, but the defendant knows that the Government routinely rescinds contracts if the guns do not shoot, the defendant has "actual knowledge." Likewise, because a reasonable person would realize the imperative of a functioning firearm, a defendant's failure to appreciate the materiality of that condition would amount to "deliberate ignorance" or "reckless disregard" of the "truth or falsity of the information" even if the Government did not spell this out.

. . .

Moreover, other parts of the False Claims Act allay Universal Health's concerns. "[I]nstead of adopting a circumscribed view of what it means for a claim to be false or fraudulent," concerns about fair notice and open-ended liability "can be effectively addressed through strict enforcement of the Act's materiality and *scienter* requirements" . . . Those requirements are rigorous.

. . .

As noted, a misrepresentation about compliance with a statutory, regulatory, or contractual requirement must be material to the Government's payment decision in order to be actionable under the False Claims Act. We now clarify how that materiality requirement should be enforced. Section 3729(b)(4) defines materiality using language that we have employed to define materiality in other federal fraud statutes: "[T]he term 'material' means having a natural tendency to influence, or be capable of influencing, the payment or receipt of money or property." . . . This materiality requirement descends from "common-law antecedents." . . . Indeed, "the common law could not have conceived of 'fraud' without proof of materiality." We need not decide whether §3729(a)(1)(A)'s materiality requirement is governed by §3729(b)(4) or derived directly from the common law. Under any understanding of the concept, materiality "look[s] to the effect on the likely or actual behavior of the recipient of the alleged misrepresentation."

. . .

The materiality standard is demanding . . . A misrepresentation cannot be deemed material merely because the Government designates compliance with a particular statutory, regulatory, or contractual requirement as a condition of payment. Nor is it sufficient for a finding of materiality that the Government would have the option to decline to pay if it knew of the defendant's noncompliance. Materiality, in addition, cannot be found where noncompliance is minor or insubstantial.

. . .

In sum, when evaluating materiality under the False Claims Act, the Government's decision to expressly identify a provision as a condition of payment is relevant, but not automatically dispositive. Likewise, proof of materiality can include, but is not necessarily limited to, evidence that the defendant knows that the Government consistently refuses to pay claims in the mine run of cases based on noncompliance with the particular statutory, regulatory, or contractual requirement. Conversely, if the Government pays a particular claim in full despite its actual knowledge that certain requirements were violated, that is very strong evidence that those requirements are not material. Or, if the Government regularly pays a particular type of claim in full despite actual knowledge that certain requirements were violated, and has signaled no change in position, that is strong evidence that the requirements are not material.

. . .

We emphasize, however, that the False Claims Act is not a means of imposing treble damages and other penalties for insignificant regulatory or contractual violations. This case centers on allegations of fraud, not medical malpractice. Respondents have alleged that Universal Health misrepresented its compliance with mental health facility requirements that are so central to the provision of mental health counseling that the Medicaid program would not have paid these claims had it known of these violations. Respondents may well have adequately pleaded a violation of §3729(a)(1)(A). But we leave it to the courts below to resolve this in the first instance.

The judgment of the Court of Appeals is vacated, and the case is remanded for further proceedings consistent with this opinion.

It is so ordered.

Vander Boegh v. Energysolutions, Inc.[861]

Gary Vander Boegh applied for a job with EnergySolutions. He alleges that the prospective employer did not hire him because he engaged in protected whistleblower activity at a prior job. The district court held that Vander Boegh lacked statutory standing as an applicant—not employee—and granted summary judgment in favor of EnergySolutions. Because we agree that Vander Boegh lacks statutory standing under the Energy Reorganization Act and False Claims Act, and we lack subject-matter jurisdiction over the remaining claims, we affirm.

. . .

In this case, we consider for the first time whether the term "employee" extends to applicants for employment under the ERA, FCA, or four federal environmental statutes—the SDWA, CWA, TSCA, or SWDA. It appears that no federal court of appeals has considered these questions, although at least one has assumed, without deciding, that applicants are employees under the ERA.[862]

. . .

Vander Boegh argues that "employee" is ambiguous, and asks this court to afford Chevron deference to the DOL's interpretation of the ERA.[863] He further asks us to extend that interpretation to the FCA and the four environmental statutes.

. . .

Vander Boegh also appeals the district court's ruling that he lacked statutory standing under the FCA. Applying the above plain meaning interpretation of "employee" to the FCA, we conclude that the term "employee" does not extend to applicants. Moreover, the FCA's legislative history and caselaw in other circuits reinforce our reading of the plain language.

As originally enacted, the FCA's anti-retaliation provision provided that "[a]ny employee who is discharged, demoted, suspended, threatened, harassed, or in any other manner discriminated against in the terms and conditions of his employment by his or her employer because of [a protected activity] shall be entitled to all relief necessary to make the employee whole."[864] Congress amended

---

[861] 772 F.3d 1056 (6th Cir. 2014).
[862] *See* Doyle v. Sec'y of Labor, 285 F.3d 243, 251 n. 13 (3d Cir.2002).
[863] *See* Samodurov v. Gen. Physics Corp., No. 89–ERA–20, 1993 WL 832030, at *3 (Dep't of Labor Nov. 16, 1993) (interpreting "employee" in the ERA to include applicants).
[864] 31 U.S.C. § 3730(h); False Claim Amendments Act, Pub.L. 99–562, 100 Stat. 3153 (1986) (emphasis added).

the FCA in 2009 to expand its scope to "[a]ny employee, contractor, or agent."[865] Although there is no binding precedent in our circuit, other courts have overwhelmingly concluded that the term "employee" in the FCA did not extend to persons outside the employer-employee relationship before the amendment.[866]

. . .

This body of caselaw and legislative history reinforces our conclusion that the FCA does not extend to non-employee applicants. Vander Boegh concedes that he was never an EnergySolutions employee, contractor, or agent. He simply argues that we should broadly construe the term "employee" because (1) the legislative history mentions "blacklisted" workers, and (2) this court has previously interpreted "employee" to include applicants under the Fair Labor Standards Act ("FLSA").[867]

. . .

Because the plain meaning of "employee" does not include applicants and the FCA's legislative history and caselaw from other courts reinforce that "employee" is limited to employment-like relationships, we agree with the district court that Vander Boegh lacks statutory standing under the FCA. Accordingly, EnergySolutions is also entitled to summary judgment in its favor on this claim.

. . .

For these reasons, we affirm the judgment of the district court.

---

[865] Fraud Enforcement and Recovery Act of 2009, Pub.L. 111–21, 123 Stat. 1617, 1624–25 (emphasis added).

[866] *See*, e.g., Mruz v. Caring, Inc., 991 F.Supp. 701, 708–09 (D.N.J.1998) (limiting "employee" to the "employment relationship" under the plain language); United States *ex rel.* Morgan v. Sci. Applications Int'l Co., 604 F.Supp.2d 245, 250 (D.D.C.2009) (observing that liability does not extend to non-employers); Palladino *ex rel.* U.S. v. VNA of S. New Jersey, Inc., 68 F.Supp.2d 455, 464–65 (D.N.J.1999) (same).

[867] *See* Dunlop v. Carriage Carpet Co., 548 F.2d 139, 144–47 (6th Cir.1977).

TABLE OF CASES

Abbott v. BP Exploration & Production, Inc. 27

Absher v. Momence Meadows Nursing Ctr., Inc. 36

Allison Engine Co. v. United States ex rel. Sanders 193, 257, 263, 284

Am. Textile Mfrs. Inst. 258, 264

Amphastar Pharmaceuticals Inc. v. Aventis Pharma SA 34, 82, 140

Ashcroft v. Iqbal 262

Bassett v. Nat'l Collegiate Athletic Ass'n 294

Bell Atlantic Corp., et al. v. Twombly 258

Bellevue v. Universal Health Services of Hartgrove, Inc. 35, 146

Beydoun v. Sessions 295

Bivins v. Wrap It Up, Inc. 213

Black Warrior Riverkeeper, Inc. v. Black Warrior Minerals, Inc. 248

Blum v. Stenson 298

Bly-Magee v. Cal. 311

Branson v. Nott 82, 143

Brown v. Daniels 294

Buckman Co. v. Plaintiffs' Legal Comm. 282

CBS Inc. v. PrimeTime 24 Joint Venture 243

Chattanooga Foundry v. Atlanta 279

Cheney v. Ricks 177

CNH Am. LLC v. Int'l Union, United Auto., Aerospace & Agr. Implement Workers of Am. (UAW) 295

Concha v. London 310

Cook County v. v. United States ex rel. Chandler 75, 243

Corsello v. Lincare, Inc. 48

Cotton v. United States 279

Coyne v. Amgen, Inc. 28

CRST Van Expedited Inc. v. E.E.O.C. 82
DiFiore v. CSL Behring, LLC 92, 150
Dingle v. Bioport Corp. 260
Dolan v. U.S. Postal Serv. 243
Doyle v. Secretary of Labor 94, 324
Dunlop v. Carriage Carpet Co. 325
Fakorede v. Mid-South Heart Center, P.C. 69, 154
Farrar v. Hobby 213
Fed. Recovery Servs., Inc. v. United States 216
Fogleman v. Aramco 266
Foglia v. Renal Ventures Mgmt., LLC 42
Fresenius Medical Care Holdings, Inc. v. United States 75
Friends of Earth, Inc. v. Laidlaw Environmental Services (TOC), Inc. 326
Goodman v. Sullivan 290
Grabcheski v. Am. Int'l Grp., Inc. 46
Graham Cty. Soil & Water Conservation Dist. v. United States ex rel. Wilson 220, 244
Guthrie v. Lady Jane Collieries, Inc. 290
Hagood v. Sonoma Cnty. Water Agency 142
Hamer v. Lentz 177, 178
Hamver v. Lentz 85
Harrington v. Texaco, Inc. 266
Harris v. Garner 243
Heath v. Indianapolis Fire Department 157
Hensley v. Eckerhart 84, 297
Hopper v. Solvay Pharm., Inc. 208
Illinois ex rel. Schad, Diamond & Shedden, P.C. v. My Pillow, Inc. 84
In re Nat. Gas Royalties .... passim
In re: Natural Gas Royalties Qui Tam Litigation 81

Islamic Ctr. of Nashville v. Tennessee *295*

Jones-McNamara v. Holzer Health Systems *220*

Kay v. Ehrler *85, 177*

Kellogg Brown & Root Servs., Inc. v. United States ex rel. Carter *204*

Koons Buick Pontiac GMC, Inc. v. Nigh *243*

Lawton ex rel. United States v. Takeda Pharm. Co. *193, 194, 285*

Leveski v. ITT Educational Services, Inc. *149*

Little v. Shell Exploration & Production Co. *217*

Long v. Satz *49*

Lujan v. Defenders of Wildlife *327*

McCarthy v. Dun & Bradstreet Corp. *224*

Medtronic, Inc. v. Lohr *35, 260, 272, 282*

Mendiondo v. Centinela Hosp. Med. Ctr. *219*

Merck & Co. v. Reynolds *246*

Minzer v. Keegan *155, 223*

Moore v. Illinois *279*

Moore v. Kayport Package Exp., Inc. *310*

Mruz v. Caring, Inc. *325*

Musick, Peeler & Garrett v. Employers Ins. of Wausau *328*

Newport v. Fact Concerts, Inc. *330*

O'Hara v. Nika Technologies, Inc. *92*

Palladino ex rel. U.S. v. VNA of S. New Jersey, Inc. *325*

Penn. Dep't of Corr. v. Yeskey *80, 314*

Race Tires Am., Inc. v. Hoosier Racing Tire Corp. *290*

Regan v. Wald *251*

Robinson v. Shell Oil Co. *244*

Rundus v. City of Dallas *266*

Rush v. Parham *290*

Samodurov v. Gen. Physics Corp. *94, 324*

Sanford v. MemberWorks, Inc. *310*

Simon v. Eastern Ky. Welfare Rights Organization *327*

Sinay v. Lamson & Sessions Co. *295*

Smith v. LHC Group, Inc. *95*

Smith v. Wade *330*

Steel Co. v. Citizens for a Better Environment *326, 328*

Stein v. Kaun *177*

Taniguchi v. Kan Pac. Saipan, Ltd. *265*

Texas Industries, Inc. v. Radcliff Materials, Inc. *330*

Thompson v. Gomez *298*

U.S. Duxbury v. Ortho Biotech Pro *287*

U.S. ex rel Doe v. DeGregorio *275*

U.S. ex rel. Drakeford v. Tuomey *199, 201, 275*

United States ex re. Vatan v. QTC Medical Services, Inc. *46*

United States ex rel Uhlig v. Fluor Corp. *91*

United States ex rel. Advocates for Basic Legal Equal., Inc. *35*

United States ex rel. Aflatooni v. Kitsap Physicians Services *4*

United States ex rel. Ambrosecchia v. Paddock Labs., LLC .... *passim*

United States ex rel. Armes v. Garman .... *passim*

United States ex rel. Atkins v. McInteer *208*

United States ex rel. Badr v. Triple Canopy, Inc. *26*

United States ex Rel. Bias v. Tangipahoa Parish School Bd. *90*

United States ex rel. Bodnar v. Secretary of Health & Human Servs. *290*

United States ex rel. Booker v. Pfizer *93*

United States ex rel. Bruno v. Schaeffer *197*

United States ex rel. Campie v. Gilead Sciences, Inc. *311*

United States ex rel. Carson v. Manor Care, Inc., et al. *37, 38, 202*

United States ex rel. Carter v. Halliburton Co. 184, 204

United States ex rel. Chase v. HPC Healthcare, Inc. .... *passim*

United States ex rel. Christiansen v. Everglades College, Inc. 83, 211

United States ex rel. Clausen v. Laboratory Corporation of America 207, 208, 209, 285

United States ex rel. Colquitt v. Abbott Laboratories 44, 214

United States ex rel. Cooper v. Blue Cross & Blue Shield of Fla., Inc. .... *passim*

United States ex rel. Crampie v. Gilead Sciences, Inc. 27, 28

United States ex rel. Crockett v. Complete Fitness Rehab. 95, 218

United States ex rel. D'Agostino v. ev3, Inc. 281, 282, 283

United States ex rel. Devlin v. California 142

United States ex rel. Eisenstein v. City of New York 246

United States ex rel. Fine v. Sandia Corp. 271, 272

United States ex rel. Foulds v. Texas Tech Univ. 328

United States ex rel. Fried v. West Indep. Sch. Dist. 217

United States ex rel. Ge v. Takeda Pharm. Co. 41, 194, 285

United States ex rel. Gear v. Emergency Med. Assocs. of Ill., Inc. 272

United States ex rel. Gilligan v. Medtronic, Inc. 272

United States ex rel. Grabcheski v. American International Group, Inc. 223

United States ex rel. Grubbs v. Kanneganti 44, 215, 286

United States ex rel. Gugenheim v. Meridian Senior Living, LLC, et al. 20

United States ex rel. Hafter v. Spectrum Emergency Care, Inc. 18, 225

United States ex rel. Hanlon v. Columbine Management Services, Inc. 230

United States ex rel. Hartpence v. Kinetic Concepts, Inc. 15, 233

United States ex rel. Hayes v. Allstate Insurance Co., et al. 37

United States ex rel. Heath v. AT&T, Inc. .... *passim*

United States ex rel. Hirt v. Walgreen Co. .... *passim*

United States ex rel. Hunt v. Cochise Consultancy, Inc. 87, 241

United States ex rel. Hyatt v. Northrop Corp. 252

United States ex rel. Ibanez v. Bristol-Myers Squibb Co. 42

United States ex rel. Karvelas v. Melrose-Wakefield Hosp. .... passim

United States ex rel. Kester v. Novartis Pharm. Corp. 271, 272

United States ex rel. King v. Solvay Pharmaceuticals, Inc. .... passim

United States ex rel. Lager v. CSL Behring, LLC, et al. 38, 269

United States ex rel. Lamers v. City of Green Bay 149

United States ex rel. Lockey v. City of Dallas 260

United States ex rel. Long v. GSDMIdea City, L.L.C. .... passim

United States ex rel. Long v. SCS Business & Technical Institute, Inc. 328

United States ex rel. Lutz v. Berkeley Heartlab, Inc. 274

United States ex rel. Marcus v. Hess .... passim

United States ex rel. Marlar v. BWXT Y-12, LLC 255, 294

United States ex rel. Mateski v. Raytheon Co. 142

United States ex rel. McDonough v. Symphony Diagnostic Servs., Inc. 295

United States ex rel. McGrath v. Microsemi Corp. 25, 26

United States ex rel. Milam v. Univ. of Tex. M.D. Anderson Cancer Ctr. 243, 249

United States ex rel. Misch v. Memorial Hospital of South Bend, et al. 13, 20

United States ex rel. Morgan v. Express Scripts, Inc. 273

United States ex rel. Morgan v. Sci. Applications Int'l Co. 325

United States ex rel. Nargol v. DePuy Orthopaedics, Inc. 45, 281

United States ex rel. Paulos v. Stryker Corp. 180

United States ex rel. Petratos v. Genentech, Inc., et al. 15

United States ex rel. Poteet v. Medtronic, Inc. .... passim

United States ex rel. Prather v. Brookdale Senior Living Cmtys., Inc. .... passim

United States ex rel. Presser v. Acacia Mental Health Clinic, LLC 310

United States ex rel. Rafizadeh v. Cont'l Common, Inc. 215

United States ex rel. Rost v. Pfizer, Inc. 285, 286

United States ex rel. Roycroft v. Geo Group, Inc., et al. 47, 293

United States ex rel. Ruckh v. Salus Rehabilitation, LLC, et al. 24

United States ex rel. Sanchez v. Lymphatx, Inc. 208, 210

United States ex rel. Sanders v. North American Bus Industries, Inc. 88

United States ex rel. Sant v. Biotronik, Inc. 83, 297, 298

United States ex rel. Schneider v. JPMorgan Chase Bank, Nat'l Ass'n 29

United States ex rel. Shea v. Verizon Commc'ns, Inc. 248

United States ex rel. Siewick v. Jamieson Science and Engineering, Inc. 90

United States ex rel. Sikkenga v. Regence Bluecross Blueshield of Utah 88, 247

United States ex rel. Taxpayers Against Fraud and Walsh v. General Electric Co. ...19, 84

United States ex rel. Troxler v. Warren Clinic, Inc. 15, 306

United States ex rel. Walker v. R&F Props. of Lake Cty., Inc. 208

United States ex rel. Weddington v. Scott & White Memorial Hospital 18

United States ex rel. Williams v. NEC Corp. 249

United States ex. rel Hanlon v. Columbine Management Services, Inc. 47

United States ex. rel. Takemoto v. Nationwide Mutual Insurance Company 48

United States v. Alabama 249

United States v. Alcan Elec. And Engineering, Inc. 34

United States v. Bornstein 75, 329

United States v. Cooper Corp. 329

United States v. First Choice Armor & Equip., Inc. 275

United States v. Johnson Controls, Inc. 82, 144

United States v. Lighthouse Disaster Relief 275

United States v. Mine Workers 329

United States v. United Healthcare Ins. Co. 311

United States v. Wallace 80, 316

Universal Health Services v. United States ex rel. Escobar .... passim

Valley Forge Christian College v. Americans United for Separation of Church and State, Inc. 327

Vander Boegh v. Energysolutions, Inc. 94, 324
Vermont Agency of Natural Resources v. Stevens 41, 326
Vimar Seguros y Reaseguros, S.A. v. M/V Sky Reefer 328
Welch v. Metro. Life Ins. Co. 297
Whitmore v. Arkansas 326
Will v. Michigan Dept. of State Police 329
Willard v. Basset 85, 177
Williams v. WMX Tech., Inc. 215
Wilson v. Omaha Indian Tribe 329

TABLE OF STATUTES

15 U.S.C. § 2607(e) *232*

21 U.S.C. § 321 et seq. *178*

21 U.S.C. § 360e(e) *129*

28 U.S.C. § 1920 .... *114, 115*

31 U.S.C. § 232(C) (1946) *4, 38*

31 U.S.C. § 3729 et seq. (1986) *4*

31 U.S.C. § 3729(a)(1)(B) *136*

31 U.S.C. § 3729(a)(4) (1986) *65*

31 U.S.C. § 3729(b)(3) (2010) *59, 65, 199*

31 U.S.C. § 3729(b)(4) *128*

31 U.S.C. § 3729-33 .... *130, 196*

31 U.S.C. § 3730(b)(2) (2010) *33, 216*

31 U.S.C. § 3730(b)(5) *168*

31 U.S.C. § 3730(b)(5) (2006) *201*

31 U.S.C. § 3730(d)(4) *114, 116*

31 U.S.C. § 3730(d)(4) (2010) *83*

31 U.S.C. § 3730(e)(4) (1986) *39, 223*

31 U.S.C. § 3730(e)(4)(A) (2009) *183, 201*

31 U.S.C. § 3730(e)(4)(A) (2010) *39, 181, 189, 190*

31 U.S.C. § 3730(e)(4)(B) (1994) *118*

31 U.S.C. § 3730(e)(4)(B) (2010) *39, 40, 192*

31 U.S.C. § 3730(h) (1986) *85, 91*

31 U.S.C. § 3730(h) (2010) *72, 122, 123, 232*

31 U.S.C. § 3730(h)(1) (2009) *85*

31 U.S.C. § 3731(b) (2009) *79, 162*

40 U.S.C. § 1315(c)(2) *234*

Reference	Page
42 U.S.C. § 1320a–7b	186
42 U.S.C. § 1320a-7b(b)	178
42 U.S.C. § 1396r–8(k)(2), (3), (6)	202
Act of Mar. 2, 1863, ch. 67, 12 Stat. 696 (1863)	3
Affordable Care Act of 2010	5, 65
Davis-Bacon Act	82
Debt Collection Improvement Act of 1996	15
False Claims Act	passim
Food, Drug and Cosmetic Act	202
Fraud Enforcement and Recovery Act of 2009	5, 65, 233
Health Information Technology for Economic and Clinical Health Act	30, 31, 228
Higher Education Act	25
Minn. Stat. Ann. § 256.969, subd. 3c(a) (2013)	62
Minnesota Statutes Annotated § 15C.01 et seq.	196
N.Y. State Fin. Law § 190(9)(b)	181
Program Fraud Civil Remedies Act	15
Pub.L. No. 111–148, tit. X, sec. 10104(j)(2), 124 Stat. 119, 901–02 (2010)	201
Toxic Substances Control Act	66, 232

TABLE OF REGULATIONS

Reference	Page
21 C.F.R. § 814.1(c)	126
21 C.F.R. § 814.46(a)	129
21 C.F.R. § 814.47(a)	129
21 C.F.R. § 814.82(a)	129
42 C.F.R. § 412.23(d)	198
42 C.F.R. § 415.110(a)(1)	130, 131
42 C.F.R. § 415.110(a)(1)(iii)	131
42 C.F.R. § 415.110(b)	131
42 C.F.R. § 415.110(b) (2015)	60

42 C.F.R. § 422.504(..*235*

42 C.F.R. §§ 414.46, 414.60 ....*130*

42 C.F.R. §§ 423.100, 447.512(b) (2015). *75, 144*

42 C.F.R. §§ 495.20 ....*229*

TABLE OF ADDITIONAL AUTHORITIES

Attenborough, F.L. (Ed.), The Laws of the Earliest Kings, *Cambridge University Press, Cambridge, UK (2015)* 3

Coke, Edward, Third Part of the Institutes of the Laws of England, Sixth Edition, *W. Rawlins, London, England (1680)* 3

Former Chief Executive of South Carolina Hospital Pays $1 Million and Agrees to Exclusion to Settle Claims Related to Illegal Payments to Referring Physicians, *USDOJ, September 7, 2016* 12

North American Health Care Inc. to Pay $28.5 Million to Settle Claims for Medically Unnecssary Rehabilitation Therapy Services, *USDOJ, September 19, 2016* 12

Remarks by Assistant Attorney General for the Criminal Division Leslie R. Caldwell at the Taxpayers Against Fraud Education Fund Conference, *Justice News, September 17, 2014, https://www.justice.gov/opa/speech/remarks-assistant-attorney-general-criminal-division-leslie-r-caldwell-taxpayers-against, viewed January 5, 2017* 99

S.Rep. No. 99-345, p. 24, 1986 U.S.C.C.A.N. 5266, 5289 (1986) 33

United States Settles False Claims Act Allegations Against Compound Pharmacy Owners For $7.75 Million 2016, USDOJ, September 14, 2016 12

Yates, Sally, Individual Accountability for Corporate Wrongdoing, *USDOJ, September 9, 2015, https://www.justice.gov/dag/file/769036/download viewed January 5, 2017* 105

INDEX

1986....3, 4, 17, 36, 37, 82, 89, 90, 115, 149, 166, 181, 224, 225, 278, 279, 333, 334, 335, 361, 363, 378, 379, 380, 384, 387

2009....4, 39, 40, 42, 49, 56, 87, 89, 90, 91, 94, 123, 151, 152, 153, 155, 172, 179, 183, 186, 190, 191, 199, 200, 202, 203, 207, 212, 214, 215, 218, 222, 228, 232, 246, 255, 275, 289, 291, 301, 312, 321, 325, 339, 343, 350, 357, 358, 361, 362, 365, 384, 385

2016 1

ACA 4, 5, 66, 67, 68

Accountability 107

actual knowledge....... *See* knowledge

Affordable Care Act........... *See* ACA

ACA 4, 37

agency 110

agent... 17, 89, 90, 91, 94, 189, 195, 198, 199, 201, 281, 361, 362, 374

amendment..3, 5, 12, 17, 19, 37, 38, 39, 53, 94, 194, 195, 196, 197, 199, 200, 213, 217, 219, 220, 288, 292, 326, 327, 331, 345, 361, 362

amicus 35

Anti-Kickback Statute................... 73

attorney 101, 102

Attorney General....xiv, 7, 9, 10, 14, 17, 36, 101, 105, 107, 111, 112, 115, 121, 251, 259, 269, 279, 304, 377, 379, 380, 381, 387

Attorneys' fees 84

avoid.. 1

billion 1, 102

bounty.. 3

Brand Memo...... xiv, 14, 15, 16, 121

causation.... 92, 93, 94, 95, 155, 156, 157, 158, 162, 186, 187, 374

Centers for Medicare & Medicaid Services

 CMS 5

civil..v, 101, 105, 107, 108, 109, 110, 111, 112, 113

Civil Division............................... 105

Civil War 2, 3, 35, 36, 45

claim...3, 4, 8, 45, 46, 246, 247, 349, 351, 352, 354, 355

claims 106, 111, 112

CMS ..... *See* Centers for Medicare & Medicaid Services

conceal 104

condition of payment 247, 349, 351, 353, 354

Congress.. ii, 3, 9, 17, 27, 35, 36, 37, 63, 88, 94, 116, 148, 149, 150, 189, 194, 199, 200, 269, 272, 273, 274, 275, 276, 278, 279, 280, 298, 304, 305, 306, 317, 336, 345, 351, 357, 359, 360, 361, 362, 363, 364, 365, 366, 367, 368, 369, 375, 376, 379, 380, 381

contract.... 19, 23, 27, 50, 58, 91, 94, 118, 132, 172, 200, 253, 267, 279, 333, 336, 338, 339, 340,

341, 342, 356, 358, 360, 369, 370, 371, 372

contractor. 4, 27, 60, 79, 89, 90, 91, 94, 117, 118, 126, 129, 175, 198, 199, 200, 201, 339, 345, 360, 361, 362

contractors

   conrtactor 4, 35, 45, 90, 355

cooperation credit 108, 109

costs 3

court 112

court of appeals 39, 53, 87, 170, 357, 369

criminal .. v, 101, 102, 104, 105, 107, 108, 110, 111, 112

Criminal Division 101, 102, 104, 105

culpable 107, 108, 110, 112

damages 3, 110, 355

demoted 89, 155, 162, 199, 218, 219, 361

Department 1, 101, 102, 104, 107, 108, 109, 110, 111, 112, 113

Department of Energy 94, 117, 300, 356

Department of Justice ... vii, 1, 7, 10, 11, 14, 16, 35, 55, 101, 102, 104, 107, 114, 117, 121, 122, 136, 202, 318

Department of Labor ... 94, 356, 360

discharged 89, 92, 94, 155, 162, 179, 182, 183, 185, 186, 187, 193, 199, 236, 340, 361, 363

disclose 109

discriminated 89, 155, 156, 162, 182, 199, 218, 361

doctor 103

doctors 1, 103

Donald J. Trump 9

drug 1

duties 103

employee .. 11, 27, 36, 48, 89, 91, 92, 94, 95, 96, 155, 156, 157, 161, 162, 164, 176, 177, 179, 180, 181, 182, 183, 184, 185, 186, 188, 199, 200, 201, 205, 206, 209, 218, 219, 237, 241, 243, 267, 273, 274, 316, 340, 341, 356, 357, 358, 359, 360, 361, 362, 363, 365, 369, 370, 371, 372, 376

   employees . 28, 52, 58, 89, 90, 93, 94, 111, 122, 132, 155, 161, 162, 164, 178, 182, 185, 186, 193, 198, 199, 221, 239, 240, 241, 243, 267, 282, 294, 296, 339, 350, 357, 362, 363, 370, 371, 373

employer 5, 26, 43, 89, 90, 91, 92, 93, 94, 95, 96, 133, 155, 156, 157, 172, 173, 174, 175, 176, 177, 179, 180, 181, 182, 183, 184, 185, 186, 199, 200, 205, 206, 212, 218, 219, 226, 242, 243, 258, 260, 266, 270, 273, 274, 328, 339, 356, 358, 359, 360, 361, 362, 363, 365, 371, 373

evidence 36, 104, 112, 246, 247, 354

expansion 89, 90, 91, 94, 200

extension 107

false certification 246, 349, 351

False Claims Act ...i, v, 1, 36, 45, 46, 87, 101, 102, 106, 109, 141, 246, 349, 350, 351, 353, 354, 355

FBI 35, 105

FCA v, xi, xiii, xiv, 1, 2, 3, 4, 5, 7, 8, 11, 13, 14, 15, 17, 18, 19, 20, 21, 23, 24, 25, 26, 27, 28, 29, 30, 35, 37, 38, 39, 40, 42, 43, 45, 46, 47, 48, 50, 51, 52, 54, 59, 63, 75, 77, 79, 80, 82, 83, 84, 87, 88, 89, 90, 91, 92, 93, 94, 95, 96, 114, 115, 116, 125, 135, 136, 144, 151, 154, 155, 156, 157, 158, 159, 165, 167, 168, 169, 171, 173, 174, 175, 184, 186, 188, 189, 192, 193, 194, 195, 196, 197, 198, 199, 201, 202, 203, 204, 205, 206, 207, 208, 209, 210, 221, 222, 223, 224, 231, 235, 236, 237, 238, 239, 240, 241, 242, 243, 244, 245, 246, 248, 249, 255, 256, 257, 258, 259, 260, 261, 266, 268, 269, 270, 271, 274, 275, 276, 277, 278, 279, 280, 281, 282, 283, 284, 285, 286, 287, 288, 289, 290, 293, 294, 298, 299, 300, 302, 303, 304, 307, 308, 311, 314, 328, 330, 331, 333, 338, 356, 357, 361, 362, 363, 373, 375, 376, 377, 378, 379, 380

federal .... v, 108, 113

Federal Rule..................................... 45

FERA .....4, *See* Fraud Enforcement and Recovery Act of 2009

Fifth Circuit... 19, 27, 49, 90, 91, 93, 94, 181

Final Rule... 5

Fourth Circuit 26, 88, 92

fraud... v, vi, vii, viii, 1, 2, 3, 4, 7, 15, 28, 29, 35, 38, 40, 41, 45, 46, 49, 50, 55, 59, 61, 63, 64, 65, 66, 75, 81, 87, 88, 89, 91, 92, 96, 101, 102, 103, 104, 105, 107, 113, 116, 123, 124, 126, 137, 142, 143, 144, 145, 146, 147, 151, 152, 166, 169, 172, 176, 177, 178, 180, 182, 184, 185, 186, 187, 191, 194, 195, 196, 203, 207, 208, 210, 211, 212, 213, 214, 215, 216, 224, 227, 229, 237, 238, 239, 240, 241, 242, 243, 244, 245, 251, 252, 253, 258, 259, 260, 261, 263, 264, 265, 266, 268, 269, 275, 277, 278, 281, 286, 288, 289, 290, 299, 300, 301, 302, 303, 304, 305, 307, 310, 311, 312, 313, 321, 323, 340, 342, 343, 352, 353, 354, 355, 380

Fraud Enforcement and Recovery Act of 2009 .... *FERA, FERA*

fraudulent............ 349, 351, 353, 354

fraud 2, 10, 27, 28, 39, 46, 47, 59, 62, 75, 91, 93, 95, 96, 124, 135, 144, 151, 172, 176, 177, 178, 180, 182, 184, 185, 186, 187, 193, 195, 203, 205, 206, 207, 208, 210, 214, 215, 216, 226, 230, 231, 236, 238, 239, 240, 244, 250, 253, 259, 263, 265, 266, 268, 281, 283, 284, 285, 286, 287, 288, 289, 290, 302, 305, 311, 313, 321, 322, 323, 324, 325, 342, 343, 348, 376

government.v, vi, viii, xiii, 1, 2, 3, 4, 7, 8, 11, 12, 13, 14, 15, 16, 18, 19, 23, 24, 25, 26, 27, 28, 29, 35, 36, 38, 43, 46, 47, 49, 50, 52, 56, 58, 59, 60, 62, 66, 75, 76, 77, 79, 80, 81, 82, 83, 84, 87, 89, 91, 95,

97, 101, 102, 104, 105, 110, 112, 114, 115, 116, 117, 118, 119, 120, 144, 145, 152, 153, 154, 161, 165, 166, 167, 169, 172, 175, 176, 177, 179, 180, 186, 195, 196, 200, 201, 202, 203, 204, 205, 206, 207, 208, 212, 214, 215, 216, 217, 221, 222, 223, 228, 229, 231, 233, 236, 237, 238, 239, 240, 241, 242, 243, 244, 247, 250, 251, 252, 255, 257, 258, 260, 263, 265, 266, 267, 268, 269, 270, 271, 273, 274, 275, 276, 277, 278, 279, 280, 281, 282, 283, 284, 285, 286, 287, 289, 290, 291, 292, 293, 294, 298, 299, 300, 301, 302, 303, 304, 305, 307, 308, 310, 311, 312, 313, 319, 322, 323, 326, 330, 334, 335, 338, 339, 340, 341, 343, 344, 345, 346, 347, 348, 374, 380

Granston Memo xiv, 12, 13, 16, 114

Hafter 18, 250, 251, 252, 253, 254

harassed 89, 155, 162, 186, 199, 361

healthcare .... v, 1, 4, 5, 247

Hess 35

HHS-OIG 105

hospitals

    hospital .... v, 1, 103

    identified 108, 111

implied certification 352

Individual 107

information 106, 109, 110

intent 107, 111

interpretation 351

Jeff Sessions 7, 9, 10

judgment 112

jurisdiction

    jurisdictional 17, 18, 36, 37, 38, 40, 42, 143, 144, 148, 149, 167, 189, 190, 209, 250, 300, 366, 367, 368, 373

jury 1, 92, 96, 102, 155, 157, 158, 162, 164, 177, 179, 180, 182, 185, 186, 204, 226, 309

know 104, 105, 106

knowingly 349

knowledge 3, 36, 37, 45, 107, 110, 246, 247, 353, 355

    actual knowledge; willful ignorance viii, 4, 23, 24, 25, 27, 28, 38, 41, 46, 47, 48, 60, 81, 88, 89, 92, 122, 129, 143, 144, 146, 147, 150, 152, 153, 154, 180, 185, 190, 191, 195, 196, 215, 216, 219, 221, 229, 230, 239, 240, 241, 243, 251, 252, 253, 254, 258, 260, 261, 264, 265, 271, 274, 275, 276, 280, 281, 283, 284, 285, 290, 304, 309, 318, 342, 343, 348, 370, 371, 372

Leslie R. Caldwell 101

    Caldwell .... xiv, xv, 7, 387

liability 108, 111

licensed .... ii, v, 103, 350

litigation 1, 5, 35, 108

    litigate .... vi, vii, viii, xiii, xiv, 1, 7, 12, 14, 18, 19, 20, 23, 29, 59, 76, 77, 79, 83, 84, 95, 96, 117, 118, 143, 146, 156, 169, 204, 223, 224, 225, 253, 270, 278,

299, 304, 328, 329, 332, 333, 334, 335, 336, 345, 348, 371, 375

long term care

LTC v

Marcus 35, 36

Marine Corps 90, 198, 199

materiality

material 24, 25, 26, 27, 29, 30, 31, 49, 110, 118, 120, 143, 145, 154, 159, 161, 204, 213, 214, 229, 246, 247, 248, 252, 258, 261, 266, 272, 279, 281, 283, 285, 309, 310, 313, 317, 318, 342, 343, 349, 352, 353, 354, 355

May 350

Medicaid v, 4, 8, 246, 247, 350, 352, 355

medically unnecessary 8

Medicare 4, 8, 102, 103

Medicare Fraud Strike Force 102

Michael D. Granston 11, 12, 114

million 103

minimum 109

motion to dismiss 351

Nashville Pharmacy Services, LLC 9

natural tendency 354

negotiation 109

North American Health Care, Inc. 8

obligations 353

off-label ... 48, 92, 93, 155, 202, 203, 204, 205, 206, 226, 228, 282, 283, 284, 287, 289, 290, 291, 294, 312, 313

original source 37

overpayment 4

particularity 18, 45, 46, 47, 49, 50, 51, 81, 96, 151, 159, 160, 167, 203, 214, 215, 216, 227, 228, 231, 237, 238, 240, 248, 249, 251, 263, 264, 265, 284, 290, 293, 310, 311, 313, 321, 323, 325, 342

penalties

penalty xiii, 2, 3, 7, 15, 29, 30, 31, 36, 37, 55, 59, 62, 75, 79, 83, 110, 123, 135, 136, 137, 138, 159, 222, 224, 235, 248, 269, 293, 305, 349, 355, 377, 378

percentage 1

physician v

policy .. 36, 83, 87, 94, 108, 111, 122, 132, 164, 183, 184, 193, 224, 225, 233, 236, 237, 244, 245, 275, 303, 304, 305, 333, 340, 353, 381

proceeding 37, 270, 364, 380

prosecution 3, 112

QMedRx 8

qui tam vii, xiii, 2, 3, 7, 12, 13, 16, 17, 18, 19, 20, 23, 24, 25, 27, 28, 30, 36, 37, 39, 40, 41, 42, 47, 48, 49, 52, 75, 77, 79, 81, 82, 83, 95, 96, 101, 102, 103, 104, 105, 114, 115, 116, 117, 118, 119, 142, 143, 144, 145, 151, 161, 162, 163, 164, 165, 167, 193, 194, 195, 196, 198, 202, 204, 207,

208, 209, 210, 211, 222, 223, 224, 225, 226, 228, 229, 235, 246, 250, 252, 253, 255, 258, 259, 261, 263, 265, 266, 269, 270, 271, 273, 274, 275, 276, 278, 280, 282, 298, 299, 300, 301, 303, 304, 311, 312, 315, 328, 332, 333, 334, 335, 336, 351, 373, 374, 375, 376, 377, 378, 379, 381

Rachel Brand 14

reasonable inquiry 5

reckless disregard .... *See* knowledge

recovery 1

regulations 1, 246, 247, 351

relator 2, 3, 18, 19, 20, 21, 25, 28, 29, 35, 37, 38, 41, 43, 46, 47, 48, 49, 50, 51, 52, 53, 75, 77, 79, 81, 82, 83, 84, 87, 88, 106, 115, 116, 117, 118, 120, 145, 152, 154, 167, 190, 195, 203, 204, 208, 211, 212, 215, 216, 218, 220, 228, 229, 236, 238, 239, 240, 243, 250, 252, 260, 261, 266, 270, 271, 272, 273, 274, 275, 276, 277, 278, 280, 281, 283, 284, 285, 286, 287, 288, 289, 300, 302, 308, 311, 318, 321, 322, 323, 324, 325, 326, 334, 374, 375, 378, 381

relators 105, 106

release 108, 111

relevant 108, 109, 111

retaliated

    retaliate, retaliation 3

retaliation xiv, 89, 90, 91, 92, 93, 94, 95, 96, 155, 156, 157, 158, 161, 162, 164, 174, 178, 180, 184, 186, 198, 199, 201, 202, 205, 206, 207, 209, 210, 211, 213, 218, 219, 231, 236, 237, 241, 242, 243, 244, 245, 259, 273, 339, 340, 341, 356, 360, 361, 362, 363, 364, 365, 367, 368

retention 4

reverse false claim 3

risk 1, 106

Rule 9(b) 45, 46

Sally Quillian Yates

    Yates 7

school 80, 90, 91, 198, 221, 334, 347

School Board. 90, 91, 198, 199, 200, 201

scienter 3, 353, 354

services ii

Sessions 9, 10, 11, 14, 326

settlement 1, 110, 111

    settlements 8

Seventh Circuit 40, 42, 91, 180, 301, 351, 365

specific intent 3

state .... v, 102

statute 1, 2, 3, 4, 36, 90, 111, 112

statute of limitations ... 3, 57, 59, 87, 88, 111, 112, 127, 266, 269, 271, 275, 276, 279, 280, 281

statutes 2, 87, 111, 354

submission. 5, 48, 49, 56, 58, 59, 60, 61, 62, 64, 66, 93, 125, 127, 128, 129, 132, 134, 135, 138, 205, 206, 213, 214, 215, 216, 222,

238, 240, 263, 264, 273, 285, 286, 287, 289, 290, 309, 311, 321, 325

summary judgment.... vii, 23, 27, 37, 81, 82, 83, 91, 93, 95, 143, 155, 156, 161, 162, 163, 167, 172, 173, 174, 175, 189, 202, 203, 204, 205, 226, 227, 229, 252, 254, 294, 295, 297, 339, 340, 356, 357, 361, 363, 365

Supreme Court...v, vi, vii, xiii, 1, 19, 23, 24, 25, 40, 46, 47, 75, 82, 88, 93, 148, 149, 155, 156, 157, 158, 162, 168, 181, 183, 184, 186, 223, 224, 225, 237, 246, 247, 273, 275, 278, 317, 318, 329, 337, 357, 358, 359, 360, 366

suspended 89, 155, 162, 199, 309, 361

Tax Cuts and Jobs Act.............. 5, 75

Tenth Circuit 52, 88, 181, 300

Third Circuit..................... 93, 94, 186

timely . 5, 76, 87, 125, 134, 194, 268, 269, 288, 323, 357, 364

Toumey Healthcare 8

Trevor N. McFadden 10

trial ... v, vii, 8, 18, 19, 20, 24, 37, 38, 39, 40, 43, 50, 80, 81, 82, 83, 84, 85, 87, 92, 94, 95, 96, 102, 120, 177, 206, 221, 222, 223, 225, 295, 332, 335, 337, 372

United States ex rel. Hafter v. Spectrum Emergency Care, Inc....................... 18

United States ex rel. Taxpayers Against Fraud and Walsh v. General Electric Co.... 19

United States ex rel. Weddington v. Scott & White Memorial Hospital........ 18

United States Supreme Court

    Supreme Court v

    USSC, Supreme Court 35

Universal Health Services

    Escobar.................... 246, 349, 350

unlicensed.............. 91, 246, 339, 350

Walsh ... 19, 332, 333, 334, 335, 336, 337

Weddington 18, 19

whistleblower.. v, viii, 1, 2, 3, 5, 7, 9, 12, 18, 20, 21, 35, 36, 43, 172, 173, 174, 175, 199, 243, 258, 332, 339, 356

whistleblowers .. v, xiii, 2, 3, 4, 7, 11, 13, 15, 16, 17, 20, 35, 62, 83, 89, 161, 210, 224

    whistleblower........3, 4, 36, 37, 45

willful ignorance........ *See* knowledge

wrongdoing1, 7, 107, 108, 110, 112, 387

Yates 107

NOTES